Black
Language
Reader

Black Language Reader

Robert H. Bentley
University of Michigan–Flint

Samuel D. Crawford
Creighton University

Scott, Foresman and Company
Glenview, Illinois   Brighton, England

Acknowledgments

Jean Malmstrom, "Dialects—Updated." Reprinted with permission of the *Florida FL Reporter* from the special anthology issue entitled *Linguistic-Cultural Differences and American Education*, Vol. 7, No. 1, Spring/Summer 1969, pp. 47–48, 168; Alfred C. Aarons, Barbara Y. Gordon, and William A. Stewart, Eds. "The Language of the City" by Raven I. McDavid, Jr. from *Midcontinent American Studies Journal* (Spring 1969), pp. 47–59. Reprinted by permission of American Studies, The Linguistic Atlas of the Middle and South Atlantic States, and the American Council of Learned Societies. "West African Pidgin-English—An Overview: Phonology-Morphology" by Gilbert D. Schneider. Reprinted by permission from the *Journal of English Linguistics*, 1 (March 1967), 49–56. William A. Stewart, "Sociolinguistic Factors in the History of American Negro Dialects." Reprinted with permission of the *Florida FL Reporter* from Vol. 5, No. 2, Spring 1967, pp. 11, 22, 24, 26, 30; Alfred C. Aarons, Ed. William A. Stewart, "Continuity and Change in American Negro Dialects." Reprinted with permission of the *Florida FL Reporter* from Vol. 6, No. 1, Spring 1968, pp. 3–4, 14–16, 18; Alfred E. Aarons, Ed. "The English Language Is My Enemy" by Ossie Davis. Reprinted from the *American Teacher*, publication of the American Federation of Teachers, AFL-CIO, April 1967. "The Language of the Ghetto Child" by Joan C. Baratz. Reprinted with permission, from the January 1969 issue of *The Center Magazine*, a publication of the Center for the Study of Democratic Institutions in Santa Barbara, California. J. L. Dillard, "Negro Children's Dialect in the Inner City," Reprinted with permission of the *Florida FL Reporter* from Vol. 5, No. 3, Fall 1967, pp. 7–8, 10; Alfred C. Aarons, Ed. "Interrelatedness of Certain Deviant Grammatical Structures in Negro Nonstandard Dialects" by Riley B. Smith. Reprinted by permission from the Journal of English Linguistics, 3 (March 1969), 82–88. "Language Characteristics: Blacks" by William Labov from *Reading for the Disadvantaged*, edited by Thomas D. Horn, © 1970, by Harcourt Brace Jovanovich, Inc. and reprinted with their permission. Portions of this article are adapted from "Some Sources of Reading Problems for Negro Speakers of Non-Standard English" by William Labov in *New Directions in Elementary English*, edited by A. Frazier. Copyright © 1967 by the National Council of Teachers of English. Thomas Kochman, "Social Factors in the Consideration of Teaching Standard English." Reprinted with permission of the *Florida FL Reporter* from the special anthology issue entitled *Linguistic-Cultural Differences and American Education*, Vol. 7, No. 1, Spring/Summer 1969, pp. 87–88, 157; Alfred C. Aarons, Barbara Y. Gordon, and William A. Stewart, Eds. "Social Backgrounds: Blacks" by Kenneth R. Johnson from *Reading for the*

PREFACE

Several years ago, the co-editors of this book began team-teaching a course in "nonstandard" dialects, with special emphasis on Black English. At the time, the course was a relative novelty in higher education. It was given the mouth-filling title "Dialectology and Developmental Reading for Disadvantaged Youth." It began as an experiment: we would teach in-service teachers in primarily black schools about Black English, about the realities of life in an urban ghetto, and about some of the more successful approaches to teaching reading in ghetto schools.

Today the importance of this subject matter is widely understood, and courses are more readily available. We have been asked regularly to speak to education classes—both methods and reading—as well as classes in sociology, linguistics, and even philosophy; we have been told by many teachers that they would like to include dialect as a topic in their courses and that they wished some appropriate book was available. To that end we have compiled *Black Language Reader*, which grew out of the course we taught.

We have identified as our primary audience the teachers of America, and the teachers-of-teachers as well. While we hope that the articles gathered herein will be of interest to many, it is the teacher and the prospective teacher we hope to reach. Therefore, we have tried to select, generally, articles which can be read by people who are not trained in linguistics. This book is not intended to be a purely linguistic textbook; rather it is an attempt to make known to a wider audience some of the implications of linguistic findings.

Some basic assumptions guided our selection of the articles, and the aims of the book should be clearer if we spell them out for the reader's consideration. We are assuming that some of the massive failure to educate "nontraditional" students is, in part, a failure to understand that "culturally different" is not the same as "culturally deprived," and that "linguistically different" is not the same as "linguistically deprived."

We have tried to show, therefore, that Black English is a legitimate dialect of English which reflects a rich cultural tradition in America. We believe that a teacher who is attempting to impart reading/writing skills to students needs to understand not only those students, but also the culture they come from and the language capabilities they bring with them into the classroom.

At the conclusion of our course, we asked the in-service teachers to write some papers for us, and in Part Four of this book, we present what five of the teachers had to say about the problems of teaching in the ghetto and about implementing the subject matter of our course into their day-to-day teaching. We include their remarks to suggest that a class (or unit) in dialects need not be just the abstract theory to which many of our students object. The subject matter can be translated into useful classroom practices.

We wish to thank our wives, Nada and Naomi, for their patience with us, and for their understanding and encouragement as we troupe trouped off to night classes, to speaking engagements, to planning sessions, to conventions, and to observe classes. We thank our students, both undergraduates and in-service teachers, for their help and encouragement in preparing this book—their idealism and dedication has inspired us.

We thank our teachers and colleagues for their advice and criticism; Nancy Godlewski and Richard Welna of Scott, Foresman for their patient help and their belief in the importance of the book; and the authors who gave us permission to use their words to convey our message—we hope we have not distorted their intentions. Finally, we wish to acknowledge the contribution of the late Father Clement J. Schneider, S. J., Academic Vice-President of Creighton University, who helped us get started, and who believed in our work.

R. H. B.
S. D. C.

CONTENTS

INTRODUCTION

I say it with no anger; I say it with very careful forethought. The language you and I have been speaking to this man in the past hasn't reached him. And you can never really get your point across to a person until you learn how to communicate with him. If he speaks French, you can't speak German. You have to know what language he speaks and then speak to him in that language.

Malcolm X
December 20, 1964[1]

In America, we have not done a very good job of communicating with each other. This is a book about the medium by which we do most of our communicating: it is a book about language. It is also a book about black people in America. What is increasingly called "the black experience" in America is reflected in the language of black people. *Black Language Reader* is a collection of essays which explore the profound differences between the white, so-called "standard English" and the various varieties of Afro-American speech.

The subject of "nonstandard" dialects in America is a controversial one. Parents want their children to speak "correct" English so that they may "get ahead" in life—and who can blame them? Teachers, like most other humans, wish to be successful in their work—and who can blame them? We are stepping into troubled waters in the hope that we can help increase understanding by explaining the language skills of speakers of minority dialects.

There are few subjects as controversial as black dialect. Long hours are spent at scholarly meetings debating whether there is any

---

[1] Malcolm X, *Malcolm X Speaks* (New York: Grove Press, 1966), pp. 106-107.

such thing as black speech. Such debates usually generate more heat than light, and, in the meantime, young black children of the lower socioeconomic class continue to be deprived of the necessary language-oriented skills. The facts are quite clear: large numbers of black children (and speakers of other "minority" dialects) are not being taught to read and write well. If they lack reading and writing skills, virtually all other educational doors are closed to them.

In the selections that follow, we have tried to represent more than one point of view—but it is a basic premise of the book that there is a definable phenomenon called by some "Black English." It is spoken widely in urban ghettos, it is surprisingly uniform across the nation, and many of the people who speak it are not being taught to read and write well.

There are several positions taken on the subject of black dialect. One such position is that black speech patterns are simply the same as Southern white speech patterns; some claim that blacks have "large lips and lazy tongues" and are unable to pronounce words properly, and that a lack of education and/or innate ability account for the grammatical differences. Many reject the subject entirely, apparently because they wish to emphasize the similarities between the races, not the differences. Finally, there are those who think the problem is nothing more complicated than "good, correct English" versus "incorrect English." These people mostly wish everyone would quit talking while the teachers of America get back to teaching good old-fashioned "correct English."

BLACK SPEECH AND WHITE SOUTHERN SPEECH

It is impossible to deny the relationship between black dialects and Southern dialects generally. We hope to present enough evidence in the book to show that there are too many *differences* between dialects for them to be the same.

Certainly, if one were to consider only the lexicon of black dialect, the differences between it and Southern speech are readily apparent. White people generally do not know the meanings of such terms as "shuckin' and jivin'," "playing the dozens," "capping a rap," or "copping a plea." Words such as "doothless," "blood," and "process" contain special meanings of which most whites are unaware.

Those who take the position that black speech is basically transplanted Southern regional dialects have much evidence to support their position. There are some differences that have been accounted for in other ways, suggesting African origins of the dialect—which, in turn, suggests an interesting "who influenced whom?" argument.[2] While this matter may not be settled yet, one explanation *may* be rejected.

LARGE LIPS

Perhaps the most odious, and basically racist, explanation of Black English is the large-lips/lazy-tongue/innate inability explanation—in all its varieties. Some black people have even accepted this explanation and believe that it accounts for pronunciation of, for example, "both" as "bof," or "asked" as "axed."

The theory is patent nonsense. Notice that when our late president, John F. Kennedy, pronounced "Cuba" as "Cubir" and "barn" as "bahhn," nobody accused him of having "large lips and a lazy tongue"! In both cases, the explanation is the same: *dialect.* Dialect will be discussed in more detail below under the heading "Dialect vs. Correct English." Suffice it to say that there is no inherent inferiority, either biologically or intellectually, which can convincingly account for Black English. There are far too many blacks who speak standard regional dialects—who don't "sound black"—to make this theory work.

DIALECT VS. "CORRECT" ENGLISH

For many people, including some educators, there is no such thing as "black dialect" or virtually any other kind of dialect. The problem is simply one of good English versus bad English, correct versus incorrect, educated versus uneducated. Those who take this position have to ignore a large body of linguistic evidence that has accumulated over the years—evidence which proves the problem is far more complex than "right-versus-wrong." Since the views of the "correct English" advocates are widely held and readily accessible (in most newspapers, for example), we will concentrate instead on the linguistic position and consider the pedagogical implications later under the heading "Implications for Education."

Linguistics is a relatively recent intruder upon the educational scene, although the study of language as a phenomenon is very ancient. In the United States, linguistics is usually classified as a social

[2] This argument is discussed at length in J. L. Dillard's *Black English* (New York: Random House, 1972).

science, and more explicitly, as a branch of anthropology. Within recent years, the science has been applied eclectically and "linguistics courses" at the college level may deal with computers, reading instruction, the histories of languages, or English grammar—to name but a few areas.

Like any discipline, linguistics has certain assumptions, arrived at inductively, which guide inquiry. Some of these assumptions are relevant to a discussion of Black English.

The first such assumption might be tagged "linguistic equality" of languages and dialects. What we mean by this is that the study of languages, thousands of them, has revealed no such thing as a language that is inherently better or worse than any other. Each and every language is sufficient to communicate the needs of its speakers.

Every language has a limited number of sounds, and rules for combining them into meaningful units. Each language has syntactic rules or "grammar," and a theoretically infinite lexicon, or word list. What might seem then to be a "primitive" language—say one with a small lexicon—will still be completely adequate to communicate the thoughts of its various speakers. A small lexicon might reflect a culture that is technologically unsophisticated, but as new concepts and artifacts are introduced, the language will find words to describe them.

The point of the preceding two paragraphs is that the linguist looks at language in much the same way as a marine biologist looks at a specimen: he looks at it as objectively as he can. If a linguist discovers that a large number of speakers pronounce *creek* to rhyme with *freak*, while an equally large number rhyme it with *brick*, then he can only report that fact. To ask him which pronunciation is "correct" makes very little sense; one might as well ask the marine biologist if West Coast clams are more "correct" than East Coast clams. (See Figures 1 and 2.)

It is this very objectivity that has caused outsiders to label linguistics a "permissive" discipline. The average person has been taught to believe in absolute standards of "correctness," and when an expert on language refuses to tell him what is correct, he is often upset.

Such standards of right and wrong exist in the society at large, but not necessarily within linguistics. We will return to this point also under the heading of "Implications for Education."

A second assumption, similar to the first, of linguistics is that all languages (excluding perhaps very small ones) have dialects. It is relatively easy to give a superficial definition of *dialect:* significant, systematic differences within a language constitute dialects. If two speakers sound very much the same, they are probably speaking the same dialect; if they sound very different from each other, but are able to understand each other, then they are speaking different dia-

Figure 1. Mosaic view of language. Dialects, social and/or regional, seen as substandard variations on the fringe of a recognized "standard."

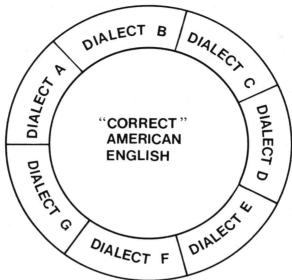

Figure 2. Language seen as the sum total of all its dialects. No one dialect seen as any better or worse than any other.

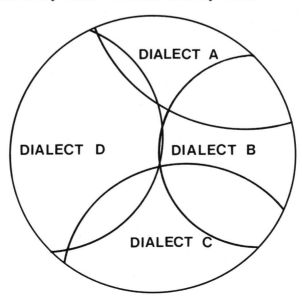

lects; if they can't understand one another, then they are speaking different languages. Dialects, then, are mutually intelligible but with marked differences.

Regional or geographic dialects are fairly widely understood by the general populace; everyone is aware that the person from England speaks differently from the person from Chicago, and we all know about southern "accents." What is less widely understood is that dialects also pattern *socially*. If the reader is familiar with Shaw's *Pygmalion*, or the popularized movie version, *My Fair Lady*, he will recall that the heroine spoke Cockney, a socially unacceptable lower-class dialect, and had to learn "the Queen's English" or "BBC-Standard" to move up socially.

And now the picture begins to cloud a bit. We have regional dialects—and lines are not easy to draw—and dialects which are socially stratified within a given area. Some people refer loosely to a "Southern dialect" as if it were a single, identifiable thing, but the person from Alabama doesn't sound like the person from Texas, and within the city of, say, Austin, we find dialects which pattern along socioeconomic and educational lines. "Wheels within wheels."

Dialects exist because language is always changing. When the first settlers arrived in America from England, they brought with them a variety of English. Over the years, the language changed, just as the language that stayed in England changed. Because of the isolation created by a big ocean, the changes were in different directions and differing dialects are the result. Left alone, in a thousand years or so the two dialects would have become different languages. Latin, for example, did not "die," it *became* French, Spanish, Italian, etc. These Romance languages were once mutually intelligible dialects of Latin. *Dialect* explains why Mexican Spanish is different from Spanish in Spain; why Australian English is different from American English; and finally, we hope to show that it also explains why Black English is different from "white" English. Finally, most linguists assert that whatever dialect a person speaks (called "performance"), his basic "competence" to speak is demonstrable.

Dialects are natural and a fact of language. The linguist does not choose among them—one is not "better" than another. Dialects may be separated from one another by oceans, mountains, political divisions, or the part of town one lives in. Usually, especially in an "educated" country, one dialect or another becomes the prestige dialect. That dialect is usually the one spoken by those who are considered educated and powerful. For a while in America, the prestige dialect was that of the New England area, and pronunciations in early dictionaries were based upon that area. Now we have a kind of widespread "standard" spoken by educated people. There are actually many regional educated "standards," but it is, in general, possible to define American "standard" dialect as that variety spoken by many network news broadcasters.

Any person who has done some traveling, or who has simply kept his ears open, will be aware that a large number of people in this country do not sound anything like network news broadcasters when they speak. This is natural; it is also the cause of many of our educational problems. Those who believe that the "standard" dialect of English is the only "correct" version of the language attempt to force speakers of differing dialects to learn the "correct" version. They instill inferiority complexes in speakers of "bad" and "incorrect" English, and they discriminate against those who do not acquire "correct" English. In the meantime, those who speak these "nonstandard" or "substandard" dialects are not being taught the important skills—reading and writing—which they need to compete successfully in our society.

BLACK ENGLISH

We should make it clear from the beginning of our discussion of black dialect that we do *not* contend that all blacks and only blacks speak "Black English." No one speaks a language or a dialect *because* of his color. There are many, many black people in the United States who do not speak the dialect we are calling Black English. But there are poor white people, those living in black communities, for example, whose speech closely resembles Black English. What we have in the urban North in this country is large numbers of black people living together in communities, virtually isolated socially and economically from mainstream society. Many of these people, generally the very poorest, speak a version of English which differs systematically from standard English. The articles that follow describe the differences rather thoroughly, so that a description here would be redundant.

Insofar as language reflects culture, however, it is possible to point out that Black English reflects the experience of a people forced to invent their own lexicon. It is a "fact" of language that a given interest group will develop a specialized vocabulary. Various professions, for example, coin words and change the meaning of existing words for their own purposes. Professional groups, to cite but one example, almost always possess what is popularly termed a "jargon." One of the authors once heard a professor of education talking about "fortunate and unfortunate deviates." When asked what he meant, the professor smiled and replied "smart kids and dumb kids." Sometimes these "jargons" come into being because of a legitimate need for specialized vocabulary to cover special concepts, artifacts, and processes. Much jargon, however, seems to fulfill psychological needs: it has the effect of keeping outsiders out, and of reinforcing a sense of community among insiders. Teen-agers will generally have a number of terms which they are reluctant to share with adults; a case in point involves the semantic change that took place in the '40s and '50s with the word *queer*. To older speakers, the word was synonymous with *odd*. No doubt many a teacher and parent wondered at the smirks and giggles the word elicited from youngsters for whom the word meant *homosexual*.

Jargon or *slang* is difficult to describe for posterity: by the time it gets recorded, new words have replaced those recorded. If it is the desire of the speakers to keep outsiders out, then the process is accelerated. Readers of the following discussion of black lexicon should bear in mind that terms do come and go, and currency in one area of the country does not mean universal currency; also, there are extreme differences in terms used by older and younger blacks, just as there are among whites. The discussion, therefore, should be taken as an example of black lexicon, not as a definitive study.

Perhaps one of the least-understood features of black culture by "mainstream" society is the value which is placed upon verbal ability. On the street, a good *rap* is a highly prized commodity. *Rap* is a word which has been borrowed into general slang, as have many other black terms. To most people, to "rap" means to talk—but in most black dialects the meaning is more specialized: it may mean idle conversation, but often it means a serious discussion. If a black leader spends the evening "rapping with the brothers," he generally means he attended a strategy session discussing important community problems. Sometimes a "rap" is an out-and-out performance. This performance would consist of retelling the events of some significant activity, complete with all the conversation, motions, and gestures—plus a running commentary on these events.[3]

A young black woman of our acquaintance had the opportunity to hear, and later meet, some very popular black entertainers. For the occasion she bought a new dress, went to a concert, and, after going backstage in pursuit of an autograph, was invited to the airport to see the entertainers off on their flight to their next stop. She told us the story a few days later, and kept us enthralled as she described in detail her trip to the clothing shop, the concert itself, and her confrontation with the entertainers. The words themselves became almost secondary as she moved about, gesturing and telling of her emotions, their reactions, and her reactions to their reactions.

[3] For a more detailed discussion, see Thomas Kochman's "'Rapping' in the Black Ghetto," *Transaction*, 6 (February 1969).

This love of verbal ability starts early in black culture. Young blacks entertain themselves by "sounding" on those around them. A "sound" (probe?) is an insult thrown—it is also a challenge to participate in an insult game. The game is often centered around the opponent's mother, and this is widely known as "playing the dozens."

To be "doothless" is to be really down-and-out. Possible etymology: "without even a duffle bag." To "run it down" is to explain it thoroughly, and, of course, "The Man" is the white society in general, often a policeman in particular. The reader will find other terms defined elsewhere—our purpose here is to show that a black lexicon indeed exists, and that the average white does not know its contents, and indeed may not even be aware of its existence.

IMPLICATIONS FOR EDUCATION

The findings of linguistics have importance and implications for teachers, and especially "inner-city" teachers, but these findings have not yet permeated education courses. One such finding is the linguistic *competence* of normal speakers of a language, thoroughly articulated in the work of the linguist Noam Chomsky. While the argument is quite technical in detail, it can be summarized rather easily: a normal human being knows most of the "rules" of his language by the age of six.

By "knowing the rules," we mean roughly that a six-year-old child (who may be still having difficulty tying his shoes) has somehow learned to speak and understand his language. The almost miraculous rapidity of this acquisition has led many linguists to hypothesize that the rules must be in some form innate in the human mind. In any event, it is quite clear that while a child's *performance* will change over his lifetime as he learns new words and concepts and more intricate syntactical patterns, his basic *competence* to speak and understand the language is established well before he encounters his first "English" or "Language Arts" teacher—who is hired to teach him a language he already knows.

If understood more widely, this competence/performance distinction should have a profound effect upon pedagogy; nevertheless, theories of "verbal deprivation" abound and provide the assumption behind many reading and writing programs in "inner-city" schools.[4]

[4] A powerful and thorough counter argument to "verbal deprivation" assumptions is William Labov's "The Logic of Non-Standard English." In Georgetown Monograph Series on Languages and Linguistics, No. 22, James Alatis, ed., (1969), and reprinted widely elsewhere.

Further, the inability to perceive children generally (and speakers of "nonstandard" dialects particularly) as linguistically competent is translated into teaching practices which we contend are damaging and counter productive. A teacher may be able to accept a child while rejecting his language, but is the child capable of making that distinction—or does he simply feel rejected? If the teacher views the student as "deprived," in some way "wounded," or less than a whole human being, the stance presented to the student is entirely different from the attitudes projected by a teacher who sees the student as linguistically competent to speak and understand his dialect of the language.

If the reader doubts the depth of the attitudinal problem on the part of teachers, he is urged to consult the literature of teaching the "disadvantaged" (the label says it all) and look at the "medical metaphors": the student may be sent to a reading or writing *clinic* where his *problem* is *diagnosed*, and *treatment prescribed.* Some linguists and educators (the authors among them) now think that the massive failure to teach reading and writing skills to "inner-city" children is not a failure in method at all, but a failure to restructure the linguistic attitudes of teachers.[5]

At this point, an alert reader will perceive the dilemma in which a linguistically-aware teacher of minority students finds himself: if he follows the path where the argument here leads him, he will accept the language of his students and go from there. An outsider, however, might observe that the teacher following this course of action is racist. His argument is that standard English is necessary to survive and compete in modern America; the student who is not taught it will be doomed to spend the rest of his life in the ghetto.

On the other hand, if a teacher (also linguistically aware) opts for bidialectical teaching, that is, teaching standard English as a second dialect, he may also be accused of racism: he is forcing the black child to learn *two* dialects of English while his white, middle-class counterpart gets by with one. He is forcing the child to reject the very language of his own culture. (Here the reader is especially directed to the work of linguist James Sledd, included in the book.)

And the teacher is caught in the middle: racist if he/she teaches that the language brought to the classroom is sufficient for survival in mainstream America, and racist if he/she teaches standard English. What is the teacher to do if he/she finds that, in teaching speakers of "nonstandard" dialects, any action is wrong or "racist"?

[5] This subject is discussed at some length in "Remediation, Deprivation, and Social Dialects—Who Is Deprived of What?" by Robert H. Bentley and Patrick M. Hartwell, a speech to the 1972 NCTE Convention, scheduled, at the time of printing, to be available on tape from the National Council of Teachers of English.

To answer this question, another fundamental finding of linguistics obtains: spoken language is different from written representations of it. This distinction has not been made often enough in professional literature on teaching reading and writing skills: learning to *speak* a second dialect is different from learning to *read* and *write* standard English.

It is our opinion that the crucial problem is the teaching of reading and writing skills to speakers of socially nonstandard dialects. If we put our emphasis upon teaching these skills, rather than upon half-baked attempts to teach "correct" speech, we might stand a reasonable chance of succeeding.

ABOUT THE ARTICLES

There are at least four statements that need be made to explain the articles we have selected for the book. First, the reader will notice that the terms "Negro" and "Black" are interspersed throughout the text. Many of the articles were written before the term "Negro" became almost a symbol of a state of consciousness now being rejected by many. We trust that readers will be sensitive to writers who are attempting to use the politest term in their vocabularies.

Second, there is a wide range of level within the articles: i.e., some are relatively easy reading for the nonspecialist, but some require considerable linguistic sophistication. This is intentional: we attempted to give depth to the book, hoping it might be of use in more than one area. We are aware that not all of the articles are of interest to all readers, and make no apologies for the range.

Third, there is a considerable difference in the orientation of the articles. Linguistics is an exciting (and fragmented) discipline: some of the articles reflect a "structural" (or "descriptive") orientation, and some a "transformational-generative" orientation. We do not have the space or inclination to go into this topic here, but wish simply to acknowledge that views differ. We think, however, that the important "message" about the naturalness of dialects is relatively constant in the articles.

Fourth, we have included a section entitled "And the Others" which superficially considers the problems of other linguistic minorities: American Indians, Spanish-speaking Americans (and rural white dialects!). We do not have the space to develop these important considerations—they would require entire books—but merely wish to remind the reader that the problem is not limited to speakers of Black English. We do feel that the general attitudes toward language presented in this book are transferable to speakers of other dialects and languages.

In conclusion, the articles that follow are intended to give the reader some insight into the structure of "Black English"; more importantly, we hope that these articles will move the reader to consider the important educational and human issues involved.

PART ONE

WHAT IS A DIALECT?

Jean Malmstrom

DIALECTS—UPDATED*

Each human being is as individual in speech as in fingerprints. Each person has his own idiolect, his own individual dialect. In physics laboratories, sound spectrographs make sound spectrograms— visible pictures of speech. These pictures show the infinite variations. Actually we cannot repeat a single sound identically even once. Although our naked ears cannot hear the tiny variations, the sound spectrograph senses and records them.

However, these differences are too small to be significant. Idiolects group into dialects. *Dialect* means a variety of language spoken by a distinct group of people in a definite place. A dialect varies in pronunciation, vocabulary, and grammar from other varieties of the same language. People united by dialect form a *speech community*. The members of a speech community share interests, values, ambitions, and communication.

For example, terms like *pattern practice*, *tape course*, *FLES program*, and *target language* are in-group dialect uniting language teachers into a professional speech community. Families are speech communities, too. Their members share "family sayings," incomprehensible to outsiders. Backyard barbecuers, water skiers, and photographers constitute three other speech communities. They use certain words not understood by those who do not share these hobbies.

*This article is an updated version of "Dialects," which first appeared in the Winter 1966-67 Issue of the *Florida FL Reporter*.

Clearly, everyone speaks more than one dialect. Language teachers may be water skiers; barbecuers may be photography buffs.

Dialects arise because languages change differently in different parts of the world, even though originally they came from the same parent language. Throughout history men have migrated from their homes for economic, political, social, and religious reasons. When they migrated, they took their language with them. Always the transported languages have changed, and in different ways. Edward Sapir, the great anthropological linguist of the 1920's, compared the situation to two men starting on a journey. Each man agrees to depend on his own resources while traveling in the same general direction.

For a considerable time the two men, both as yet unwearied, will keep pretty well together. In the course of time, however, the varying degrees of physical strength, resourcefulness, ability to orient oneself, and many other factors, will begin to manifest themselves. The actual course traveled by each in reference to the other and to the course originally planned will diverge more and more, while the absolute distance between the two will also tend to become greater and greater.[1]

In this comparison, the two men are two dialects of the same language. After they have left home and "diverge more and more," they become mutually unintelligible. Then they are two separate languages.

Often the line between a dialect and a language is hard to draw. A dialect is enough like another form of speech to be understandable to speakers of the latter. Thus American English and British English are dialects of the same language. Great Russian and White Russian are dialects of the same language. In fact, languages are collections of dialects, and any one of these dialects may eventually become an independent language.

In ordinary conversation, *dialect* often means "a corrupt form of a language." In the light of history, this view puts the cart before the horse. For instance, in the fifteenth century many dialects of English were flourishing in England. The dialect of London won over the other dialects and became the standard for speakers of English because London was the commercial, political, and cultural center of England in late medieval times. Non-Londoners continued to speak their local dialects, which often preserved older forms lost in the standard language. These local dialects did not have the social prestige of the London dialect even though they were as old as it was, if not older.

---

[1] Language and Environment." In *Selected Writings of Edward Sapir in Language, Culture, and Personality*, David G. Mandelbaum, ed. (Berkeley and Los Angeles: University of California Press, 1949) pp. 102-103.

The German language in Germany, Austria, and Switzerland developed in much the same way. The dialects spoken are all quite different from the High German used in literature, in church, on the stage, and for cultural activity in general. However, these folk dialects go back unbrokenly to the Old High German of early medieval times. The German taught in schools is comparatively new and is the result of one of the Upper Saxon dialects being chosen as standard German. Luther's Bible helped considerably to spread this one dialect as the recognized standard.

More or less the same pattern has occurred in the other national languages of Europe and many other parts of the world. For one reason or another, one of the many local dialects became the approved form of speech within the linguistic community. This approved dialect then became the symbol of culture, and consequently it spread at the expense of the other local dialects.

In the United States, contrariwise, no one dialect of American English became the recognized national standard. In the nineteenth century some people valued a "Harvard accent," the New England dialect of Boston and Cambridge, seats of learning, literature, and wealth. Today such treasures are not concentrated in one place, and no regional dialect predominates as "correct." Consequently, the dialect situation is complex and interesting.

Regional dialects are studied by linguistic geographers, trained to investigate geographic speech communities. Having selected a region that is unified in some way—historically, politically, religiously, sociologically—and using a questionnaire to elicit information about pronunciation, vocabulary, and grammar, linguistic geographers interview selected "informants" of both sexes, young and old, well and poorly educated, urban and rural, from representative parts of the region. Finally, they publish their findings on maps or in tables of figures. Thus today we have the famous linguistic atlases of Georg Wenker in Germany, Jules Gilliéron in France, Jaberg and Jud in Italy, and Hans Kurath in New England. These great linguistic atlases are storehouses of information about geographic dialects.

In the United States, linguistic geographers have discovered three main dialect areas—Northern, Midland, Southern—stretching from east to west across the continent. These dialect areas are clearest on the Atlantic Coast, where they reflect the original patterns of settlement. The farther west we go, the more the dialect areas blend and fuse, mirroring the westward migrations of our people. The three dialect areas are defined by consistent differences in pronunciation, vocabulary, and grammar. H. L. Mencken summarizes the situation thus:

The differences in pronunciation between American dialects seldom impede free communication, for a man who converts *pass* to *pahs* or drops the final *r* in *father* is still usually able to palaver readily with one who gives *pass* the *a* of *Dan* and wrings the last gurgle out of his *r*'s. The differences in vocabulary are sometimes more puzzling, but they are not very numerous, and a stranger quickly picks them up. A newcomer to Maryland soon abandons *faucet*, or *tap*, or whatever it was that prevailed in his native wilds, and turns to the local *spigot*. In the same way an immigrant to the Deep South is rapidly fluent in the use of *you-all*, *yonder*, and *to carry* in the sense of to convey. Even the differences in intonation are much less marked between any two parts of the United States than they are between any two parts of England, or than between England and this country as a whole. The railroad, the automobile, the mail-order catalogue, the movie, and above all, radio and television have promoted uniformity in even the most remote backwaters.[2]

In addition to geographic information about dialects in the United States, linguistic geographers uncovered some sociological relationships between education and dialect. Within each region they regularly interviewed college graduates, high-school graduates, and adults with less than a high-school education. Within each region they found the English of each group distinctive.

However, the procedures of linguistic geographers in our country obscured many linguistic facts of prime sociological importance. Though they took geography and education into consideration, linguistic geographers ignored many other social variables, such as race, racial isolation, social class, economic level, occupation, contextual style, group loyalties and values, mobility of population, and urbanization. Moreover, they paid much less attention to grammar than to vocabulary and pronunciation, and so they often missed important connections of words and sounds with grammar. Thus, by design or accident, their syntactic conclusions are often incomplete and unreliable.

Specifically, their language samples were not representative of the populations they studied. No children were included, even though children's speech is highly informative linguistically, especially before they learn to switch dialects to match different situations, as teenagers regularly do. Moreover, the linguistic geographers preferred to interview elderly adults, considering them the most representative informants within any region. This policy discounts the extreme mobility of our population. Furthermore, Negroes were not adequately represented in the regional surveys. For example, in the Middle and Southern Atlantic States, fewer than two percent of the informants were black, and they were characteristically from the lower working class and so spoke Nonstandard language. The records of the interviews with blacks were not analyzed separately from those with

[2] *The American Language*, abridged by Raven I. McDavid, Jr. (New York: Alfred A. Knopf, 1963), p. 450.

whites. Indeed, they could not be usefully analyzed separately because such a small collection of data could provide only anecdotal, not statistical, information.[3]

Most importantly of all, the linguistic geographers underemphasized our cities. The United States is highly urbanized, and each city is socially stratified in complex ways. The most accurate indicator of social class is one's use of language, but the linguistic features of cities do not yield to broad geographic analysis. As sociologist Glenna Ruth Pickford pointed out in 1956, "The cities remain anomalies of linguistic geography."[4] For example, the speech of New York City does not fit into the dialect of its surrounding region; it reveals no strictly geographical pattern of speech.[5] In Texas, the speech of Dallas differs extensively from that of East Texas around it.[6]

Today, linguists and sociologists are working together to develop new techniques of reliable sampling and valid interviewing in order to illuminate the complex sociolinguistic stratification of large cities like New York, Washington, Chicago, and Detroit. Social classes are determined by regular patterns of linguistic variation. Dialects range from *acrolect* to *basilect*, to use William A. Stewart's terms for describing the topmost (*acro-* "apex" plus *-lect* as in *dialect*) social dialect in Washington, D.C., to the bottom (*basi-* "bottom") social dialect. A city person speaks several social dialects as he mingles with other city people.

Although acrolect differs also in sounds and words from basilect, grammatical differences between them create the real blocks to communication. For instance, Stewart explains:

. . . basilect does not normally inflect the verb in any way to show the differences between the simple present and the preterite, e.g., *I see it*, which can mean either "I see it" or "I saw it." On the other hand, basilect has, in addition to a simple perfect construction, e.g., *I seen it* "I have seen it," a completive perfect which has no equivalent in acrolect, e.g., *I been seen it* (with primary stress on *been*) "I have seen it (already some time ago)."[7]

[3] E. Bagby Atwood comments on the need for a larger Negro sample to permit insightful analysis of their syntax. *Verb Forms of the Eastern United States* (Ann Arbor: University of Michigan Press, 1953), p. 44.

[4] "American Linguistic Geography: A Sociological Survey," *Word*, Vol. 12 (1956), p. 225.

[5] Allan F. Hubbell, *The Pronunciation of English in New York City* (New York: King's Crown Press, 1950), p. 11.

[6] Mary M. Galvan and Rudolph C. Troike, "The East Texas Dialect Project: A Pattern for Education," *The Florida FL Reporter*, Vol. 7, No. 1 (Spring/Summer 1969), 31.

[7] "Urban Negro Speech: Sociolinguistic Factors Affecting English Teaching." In *Social Dialects and Language Learning*, Roger W. Shuy, ed. (Champaign: National Council of Teachers of English, 1964), pp. 15-16.

That the simple present and the preterite both exist as grammatical categories in basilect, however, is clear from the fact that the two are negated differently: *I don't see it* "I don't see it," but *I ain't see it* "I didn't see it." Furthermore, a few basilect speakers do inflect the un-negated simple present with *-s*, e.g., *I sees it* "I see it" beside *I see it* "I saw it."[8]

In New York City William Labov discovered similar social stratification marked by dialects. Patterns are regular; the linguistic norms defining social strata are clear; each person speaks several social dialects. In addition, Labov found that New Yorkers recognize the social meanings of dialect differences in the speech of their fellow New Yorkers. For instance, Standard English speakers in New York City rarely omit the *r* in words like *guard* and *horse*, and they practically never say *ting* or *tin* fcr "thing" or "thin," or *den* and *de* for "then" and "the." New Yorkers of all classes are quick to hear markers like these in the speech of other New Yorkers and to recognize the social meaning of these dialectal signals.

In addition, Labov made the important discovery that younger Negroes, Puerto Ricans, and lower-class whites avoid the prestige forms of New York City speech and increasingly use Nonstandard forms of Southern Negro speech. He comments:

. . . this is due to the influx of Negroes raised in the South, but it also reflects a reversal of the value system held by the older generation, and a rebellion against the middle class norms.[9]

The Detroit Dialect Study reveals further evidence of "peer-group pressure" on teen-agers to reject adult norms. Here is a conversation between a sixteen-year-old Negro boy and an interviewer.

Interviewer: What did he have to do to get in the group?
Informant: He gotta hang around with us more—come to visit; he have to talk cool, you don't understand.
Interviewer: How do you talk cool?
Informant: Talk hip, man!—you know. Like you don't talk like you supposed to. If you a square you can get out.[10]

---

[8] *Ibid.*, footnote 13.

[9] "A Proposed Study of Negro and Puerto Rican Speech in New York City." In *Project Literacy Reports* (Ithaca, New York: Cornell University, 1964), p. 15. For a complete report of Labov's work see his Columbia University dissertation, "The Social Stratification of English in New York City" (1964), published by the Center for Applied Linguistics, Washington, D.C.

[10] Quoted in Walter A. Wolfram, *A Sociolinguistic Description of Detroit Negro Speech* (Washington, D.C., Center for Applied Linguistics, 1969), p. 123.

At a different social level—for example, among black college students who speak only Standard English—this group loyalty manifests itself by ethnic slang and black intonation patterns superimposed on Standard English grammatical patterns.

Comparing Labov's research in New York with the Detroit Dialect Study, the Chicago Study—"Communication Barriers to the Culturally Deprived"—and the Urban Language Study of the District of Columbia reveals remarkable likenesses in the Nonstandard English spoken by blacks in these widely separated cities.[11] Three frequent patterns are the "zero copula," "the zero possessive," and "undifferentiated pronouns." The zero copula means the omission of *BE* in certain sentence patterns where Standard English requires it. Examples are *He old* for "He is old," *Dey runnin'* for "They are running," *She a teacher* for "She is a teacher." The zero possessive means the omission of the possessive suffix as in *My fahver frien'* for "My father's friend." Undifferentiated pronouns appear when the same forms are used indiscriminately for subject and object. That is, where Standard English has "He knows us," Negro Nonstandard has *Him know we*, *Him know us*, and *He know us*. Moreover, possessive and subject forms show undifferentiated use also, varying with Standard use: *He fahver* or *His fahver* for Standard "His father"; *We house* or *Our house* for Standard "Our house."[12]

On the other hand, black Nonstandard differs systematically from white Nonstandard English. For example, in Appalachia, white children who are Nonstandard speakers use both *He's workin'* and *He's a-workin'*, whereas black children who are Nonstandard speakers say both *He workin'* and *He be workin'*. Standard English has only "He is ("He's") working"; both Nonstandard varieties make a distinction that is lacking in Standard English. *He's workin'* and *He workin'* both mean that the person is doing a specific task close by. *He's a-workin'* and *He be workin'* mean either that the person has a steady job or that he is away working somewhere.[13]

Another example concerns double and multiple negatives. Such negatives are frequent in both black and white Nonstandard: *He didn't do nothin'*, *We ain't never had no trouble*. But in Detroit certain Nonstandard negatives occur only in Negro Nonstandard:

[11] Marvin D. Loflin, "A Note on the Deep Structure of Nonstandard English in Washington, D.C.," *Glossa*, Vol. 1 (1967), 26, footnote 3; J. L. Dillard, "Nonstandard Negro Dialects—Convergence or Divergence?" *The Florida FL Reporter*, Vol. 6, No. 2 (1968), 9-10, 12.

[12] These examples are cited in William A. Stewart's "Continuity and Change in American Negro Dialects," *The Florida FL Reporter*, Vol. 6, No. 1 (Spring 1968), 3.

[13] William A. Stewart, *Language and Communication Problems in Southern Appalachia* (Washington, D.C.: Center for Applied Linguistics, 1967), pp. 26-29.

Nobody didn't do it, Didn't nobody do it, and *It wasn't no girls couldn't go with us.*[14]

How can we explain both the consistent patterns of black Nonstandard recurring in widely separated parts of the country and also the systematic contrasts between black and white Nonstandard dialects? Some linguists see answers in history.[15] Recent studies of Afro-American dialects suggest that the deep grammar of Negro Nonstandard reflects a creole predecessor developing from an ancient pidgin language. Pidgin languages evolve to meet a communication emergency. When two groups of people speaking different languages are forced to talk together, they invent a pidgin language to communicate with each other. The pidgin is not the native language of either group. It is a mixed language with a simplified version of the grammar of one language into which is inserted the vocabulary of the other language. Pidgin English may have originated on the West African coast where traders mixed slaves from various tribes, each speaking a different African language. Later generations of Negroes in the United States spoke this pidgin language as their creole mother tongue, their native and only language. The deep structure of the creole is still retained in modern Nonstandard Negro speech and is reflected especially in its verb system, even though its vocabulary is mostly English. Linguistic geographers discovered this English vocabulary since they were more interested in words than in syntax. Yet it is in syntax, not words, that the real relationships appear.

One full-fledged type of creole English still exists today. This is Gullah, the language spoken by Negroes in the Carolina Sea Islands. Gullah was not analyzed by the linguistic geographers, who regarded it as a problem completely separate from the English language of the United States.[16] There is some evidence that Gullah, or a transition dialect between it and Negro Nonstandard English, is still spoken in

---

[14] Wolfram, p. 164.

[15] William A. Stewart, *Non-Standard Speech and the Teaching of English* (Washington, D.C.: Center for Applied Linguistics, 1964); "Urban Negro Speech: Sociolinguistic Factors Affecting English Teaching," *op. cit.;* "Sociolinguistic Factors in the History of American Negro Dialects," *The Florida FL Reporter,* Vol. 5, No. 2 (Spring 1967), 11, 22, 24, 26; "Continuity and Change in American Negro Dialects," *op. cit.* J. L. Dillard, "Negro Children's Dialect in the Inner City," *The Florida FL Reporter,* Vol. 5, No. 3 (Fall 1967), 7-8, 10; "Non-Standard Negro Dialects—Convergence or Divergence?" *op. cit.,* 9-10, 12. Beryl Loftman Bailey, "Toward a New Perspective in Negro English Dialectology," *American Speech,* Vol. 40 (October 1965), 171-177; "Some Aspects of the Impact of Linguistics on Language Teaching in Disadvantaged Communities," *Elementary English,* Vol. 45 (May 1968), 570-577.

[16] A detailed study of Gullah is presented in Lorenzo Turner's *Africanisms in the Gullah Dialect* (Chicago: University of Chicago Press, 1949).

Charleston, S.C.[17] Here is a set of sentences contrasting Standard English, white Nonstandard, black Nonstandard, and Gullah.

STANDARD ENGLISH—We were eating—and drinking, too.
WHITE NONSTANDARD—We was eatin'—an' drinkin', too.
BLACK NONSTANDARD—We was eatin'—an' we drinkin', too.
GULLAH—We bin duh nyam—en' we duh drink, too.[18]

The four examples pair off syntactically, the white Nonstandard matching Standard English in omitting both the subject pronoun and the auxiliary in the *and* clause. The black Nonstandard and the Gullah repeat the subject pronoun and omit the auxiliary. The word *nyam*, meaning "to eat," is an instance of a Gullah word entirely different from either Standard or Nonstandard English.

Some linguists believe that Negro Nonstandard is a relexification of Gullah.[19] This means that it leaves the Gullah syntax intact but grafts the more traditional English grammatical markers on to what are essentially creole grammatical categories. In the above sentences, for example, *bin duh nyam* is relexified to *was eatin'*. That is to say, not only has the Gullah verb *nyam* been replaced by the English-derived *eat*, but also the past marker *bin* has been replaced by *was*, and the pre-verbal *duh* by the verbal suffix *-in'*, all of these changes producing the Nonstandard *was eatin'*. Relexification explains many of the syntactic relationships between black speech and the underlying creole. As Beryl Loftman Bailey says, ". . . Southern Negro 'dialect' differs from other Southern speech because its deep structure is different, having its origins as it undoubtedly does in some Proto-creole grammatical structure."[20]

During the last century creole markers have all but disappeared from adult Negro speech. However, young children retain these markers, since children characteristically learn more from their peers than from their parents, especially in black society. As black children mature, they give up this "baby talk" or "small-boy talk" as no longer appropriate to their age. This process is called "age-grading."[21]

[17] Dillard, "Non-Standard Negro Dialects: Convergence or Divergence?" *op. cit.*, p. 12.

[18] Stewart, "Continuity and Change in American Negro Dialects," *op. cit.*, p. 16.

[19] William A. Stewart, "Creole Languages in the Carribean." In *Study of the Role of Second Languages in Asia, Africa, and Latin America*, Frank A. Rice, ed. (Washington, D.C.: Center for Applied Linguistics, 1962), pp. 34-52; Bailey, "Toward a New Perspective in Negro English Dialectology," *op. cit.*, p. 172; Dillard, "Non-Standard Negro Dialects: Convergence or Divergence?" *op. cit.*, p. 9.

[20] *Ibid.*

[21] Dillard, "Negro Children's Dialect in the Inner City," *op. cit.*, p. 8; Stewart, "Continuity and Change in American Negro Dialects," *op. cit.*, pp. 4, 14.

It can help educators judge which features of Nonstandard speech need classroom attention and which will automatically eliminate themselves as the child grows into adolescence and adulthood.

The complex urban dialect situation challenges teachers to absorb sociolinguistic findings into their theory of instruction. In teaching English to speakers of foreign languages, we practice sentence patterns, we use language laboratories to improve pronunciation and comprehension, and we steep students in the culture of our country. These are techniques of modern foreign language teaching. They are based on a contrastive analysis of Standard English and the student's native language. The speaker of Nonstandard English in a modern metropolis is not a speaker of a foreign language. Although his speech is different from the language of the classroom, it is closer to the Standard English of his own city than to any other language. He finds himself in a "quasi-foreign language" situation, as Stewart has said. His teacher needs foreign language techniques to accomplish more than random and piecemeal "correction" that sounds arbitrary to the Nonstandard speaker. No one has told him that "English" in the classroom means Standard English. He is rightly convinced that he too speaks English. He knows that his English is his passport into his most intimate, important groups. Thus a contrastive analysis of the vertical dialect spectrum is much needed. Teachers must know enough about Nonstandard English to make illuminating contrasts with Standard English if they are to pacify the rebels and persuade them to add Standard English to their native dialects.

Raven I. McDavid, Jr.

THE LANGUAGE
OF THE CITY

1

In a sense, to speak of the language of the city is a contradiction in terms. There is no one voice for the city, any more than there is a single type of urban personality. Nor, to be sure, is there much reason to speak of *the* city; each city has its own set of characteristics—as anyone will recognize who has changed jobs or residence from one community to another. Chicago is not Cleveland; Greenville, South

Carolina, is not Gary—nor is it Greenville, Texas. The function of a
city is determined by its location and its history; location and history
and function in turn determine what ethnic, religious and social
groups make up the population—and the relationships between these
groups are responsible for the varieties of language to be found in a
city, the amount of prestige assigned each variety and the kind and
degree of difference among them.[1] In a small midwestern town in the
belt of Yankee settlements the only overt social markers in language
may be relatively slight differences in grammar; in a comparable city
in the South there will be significant and more striking differences in
pronunciation and grammar. In an older city, particularly one with a
relatively stable population, the differences are likely to be well established by tradition and recognized by all groups; in a newer city,
or one with a great deal of recent immigration, the differences may
not be so well agreed upon, and the new arrivals, or their children,
may even reject the traditional standards of the community as represented by the old élite families.[2]

Those who have studied the rise of cities are in fair agreement
that with increasing importance and better transportation, a city will
grow in size and complexity and attract special groups to handle
manufacturing, wholesale and retail trade, service industries and the
proliferation of government services, including public education.
Moreover, as cities grow in size and complexity, they become increasingly dependent on this outside world. Not only is this true of food—
an American city may get some of its milk supply from five hundred
miles away—but of other commodities as well. Chicago's steel mills
and electrical system are both dependent on soft coal mined far
downstate. Likewise, no city out of its own resources can fill all the
jobs created as the economy expands; it must lure workers from elsewhere—from smaller communities in its own region, from other regions of the nation and from other nations. As the groups are brought
together in the relatively impersonal urban scene, those of similar
background will tend to live in the same neighborhood—whether by
choice or by design. But at work—and in going to and from work—
each person will come in contact with representatives of all kinds of
regional, ethnic and social groups. In the course of a day he will hear
all kinds of accents and evaluate their speakers, often most cruelly, in
the light of his past experiences. This has been true of urban communities of the last five thousand years, but the more rapid urbaniza-

[1] See Lee Pederson, *The Pronunciation of English in Chicago: Consonants and
Vowels, Publication of the American Dialect Society*, 44 (1965), and William M.
Austin and Raven I. McDavid, Jr., eds., *Communication Barriers to the Cultur-
ally Deprived*, Cooperative Research Project 2107 (Chicago, 1966).

[2] For a dramatic change in attitudes toward certain features, see William Labov,
The Social Stratification of English in New York City (Washington, D.C., 1966).

tion of the United States and the development of faster means of transportation have recently juxtaposed more cultural groups, of more diverse background than ever before—with greater shock at difficulties in the way they communicate.

Speech, we must remember, never takes place without other behavior. The speakers stand in a physical relationship to each other, and in no two societies is this exactly the same. Edward Hall[3] and others have calculated that in the United States two men communicate most effectively when they stand about two feet apart; we become uncomfortable when another man comes closer to us—but Latin Americans cannot relax if they are more than a foot apart, and Arabs like to be close enough to smell each other's breaths. We may feel there's something wrong but not notice it specifically unless we are trained to observe it. In 1967, to my surprise, I felt vastly more at home in Helsinki than I had been in Bucharest or even in Prague, though my Swedish is subminimal and my Finnish nonexistent; then I realized that Finns just don't like to crowd each other, even in department stores or when lining up for a trolley at rush hours. When I commented on this to Tauno Mustanoja, Professor of English at the University of Helsinki, he was surprised that I had noticed this so soon, and went on to say that this difference in comfortable space was one of the most noticeable differences the Finnish soldiers had found between themselves and their temporary German allies. Perhaps the reason that the Southern poor whites are the most difficult group to cope with in Northern cities is that they don't like to think of themselves as a group or get into organized crowds but prefer to go their ways as individuals.

In speaking we do not confine ourselves to the vocal tract but accompany ourselves with all kinds of body movements.[4] Sometimes the accompaniment is more significant than the overt words, as when we say "yes" but shake our heads. We often think that there is something sinister about the way the other person uses body movements in communication: to the American white Protestant, Italians and Levantines seem to gesticulate wildly, while Orientals are impassive. Still, despite my six generations of Upcountry South Carolina ancestry, some of my Northern friends have commented on my "Jewish" gestures; one of my childhood friends observed, perhaps more accurately, that some hand movements we both use are found nowhere else in America.

And even in our speech, the language itself is only a part. We frequently make up our minds about a person or a group on the

[3] *The Silent Language* (New York, 1959); *The Hidden Dimension* (New York, 1965).

[4] Ray Birdwhistell, *An Introduction to Kinesics* (Louisville, Kentucky, 1954).

strength of the accompanying orchestration of speech—loudness, tempo, rhythm, rasp, nasality and the like—before we hear clearly a single sentence they have uttered.[5] Those who speak a different language from our own—especially if their language is one we have learned painfully and imperfectly—always seem to talk fast; those who belong to groups we do not normally associate with always talk loud and with a pitch level unpleasantly high or unpleasantly low. The salient quality of hillbilly music is the strong accompanying nasality. Even occupations seem to induce peculiar vocal orchestrations. It is inconceivable that a Southern politician could campaign successfully in the back precincts without at least a simulation of a Bourbon baritone or without the throaty prolongation of what he thinks are his most important syllables, or that a Marine topkick could induce the proper *esprit de corps* in recruits without his rasp, or that a kindergarten teacher could convey the mystique of the public schools without the Miss Frances wheedle.

With these differences existing in the behavior accompanying the use of language, it is no wonder that we find a wide range of differences in the way people use the English language. The Middle Western American—even though he is only a statistical abstraction—thinks the Englishman has a wider pitch range and a greater variety of speech tunes. The Southerner is likely to consider the speech of the Middle Westerner as monotonous, because it has a narrower range of pitch and stress than he is accustomed to. The Middle Westerner, in turn, thinks the Southerner has a "lazy drawl," though the actual tempo of Southern speech may be more rapid than his own, because the stressed syllables of Southern speech are relatively more heavily stressed and more prolonged. In compensation, the Southerner—like the Englishman—weakens and shortens the weak-stressed syllables, with accompanying neutralization of their vowels, so that *borrow* and *Wednesday* become /bár / and /wénzdiy/, with the final vowels of *sofa* and *happy* respectively; the Middle Westerner labels this as "slurring." But turning the coin again, the Middle Westerner often pronounces the final syllables of *borrow* and *Wednesday* with the full vowels of *day* and *go* respectively; the Southerner is likely to consider such pronunciations as affectation, if not the over-precise articulation of foreigners.

We often notice that people in other groups have different pronunciations of vowels than our own. Differences in the pronunciations of consonants are less common. Nevertheless we do notice the "peculiar" sounds made by many New Yorkers (and by some speakers in

---

[5] Robert E. Pittenger, Charles F. Hockett, and John J. Danehy, *The First Five Minutes* (Ithaca, New York, 1960); William M. Austin, "Some Social Aspects of Paralanguage," *Canadian Journal of Linguistics*, XI (1965-66), 31-39.

other cities) when they pronounce /t, d, n, s, z, r, l/ with the tip of the tongue against their teeth instead of against the gums, which is the usual American fashion. It is quite evident that most Southerners have a different kind of /r/ and /l/ from what Chicagoans use in *borrow* and *Billy*. In the Upcountry of South Carolina we used to laugh at the peculiar vowels the Charlestonians had in *date* and *boat*; in recent years I have learned to tolerate the Northerner's amusement at my vowel in *all*, or the fact that the Northerner may interpret the Upcountry pronunciation of *oil* as his own pronunciation of *all*.[6] Americans from the Mississippi Valley have often commented about the very high vowels found along the Atlantic seaboard, from New York to Baltimore, in such words as *bad* and *dog*. And what seems to have become a standard Southern pronunciation (though it is not my own), the use of a long vowel instead of a diphthong in *nice white rice* (as well as in *high rise*, where I do have it), has never ceased to bewilder unsophisticated Northerners, even to the barbarous assumption that Southerners confused *right* and *rat*.

But even more disturbing to us are the contrasts that our fellow speakers of English make where we don't make them and don't make where we do. I was twenty-five before I was aware that an educated person might not make a distinction between *do* and *due*, between *hoarse* and *horse*, between *merry* and *marry* and *Mary*.[7] I recall that even as a child I was irritated when a poet rhymed *hill* with the preposition *till*; I pronounce *hill* with the vowel of *hit*, but *till* with a vowel halfway between that of *hit* and that of *put*. Later I found myself a source of delight to my fellow linguists and of distress to my students because the vowel I have in *till* also occurs, in my speech, in such words as *dinner, sister, milk, mirror, scissors, ribbon, pillow*, to mention only a few; for me these words contrast with *sinner, system, silk, spirit, schism, ribbing, billow*, all of which have the vowel of *hit*. None of my Chicago-born students have such a contrast. Few of my students have my three-way contrast between *have, salve, halve*, or *had, sad, bad*.[8] No true-born Englishman has my contrast between

---

[6] One cannot be reminded too often that "confusions" among *speakers* of a given dialect are usually confusions in the perception of *listeners* accustomed to other dialects. The Southerner makes a clear distinction between *all* and *oil*; the Middle Westerner is not accustomed to perceiving the kind of difference that the Southerner makes.

[7] All these differences are characteristic of the South and South Midland areas, from the Potomac and Kanawha south. Older speakers in the areas of early New England settlement distinguished *horse* (with the vowel of *law*) and *hoarse* (with the vowel of *low*), *merry* (with the vowel of *met*) and *marry* (with the vowel of *mat*) and *Mary* (with the vowel of *mate*), but these differences have disappeared as the Yankees moved west into upstate New York and the Great Lakes region.

[8] I have a short vowel in *have* and *had*, a higher and longer vowel in *salve* and *sad*, an upgliding diphthong in *halve* and *bad*.

wails and *whales;* no Charlestonian makes a distinction between the night *air* and the ring in her *ear*. Despite decades of ridicule, some educated New Yorkers of the older generation still pronounce alike a *curl* of hair and a *coil* of rope. I was well over thirty when I learned that Pittsburghers and Bostonians did not distinguish *cot* and *caught*, *tot* and *taught*, *collar* and *caller*. It was my wife who apprised me that this homonymy was also found in Minneapolis, and later I found it in most of Canada and in parts of the Rocky Mountain area.[9] But even today some European observers, who know only British Received Pronunciation, refuse to believe that such homonymy can exist. Nevertheless, even if I have close to the maximum number of contrasts found among speakers of English, there are some which I lack; I do not have the peculiar "New England short *o*" of *coat*, *road* and *home*, which I have recorded in some of the smaller communities of Northern Illinois.

Needless to say, we do not always agree on which vowel or consonant we will use, even when we share the whole repertoire. North of Peoria one is likely to find *greasy* with /-s-/, further south with /-z-/; a person familiar with both pronunciations is likely to consider one more repulsive than the other—depending on which is his pronunciation at home. In metropolitan Chicago the natives of smaller suburban communities are likely to pronounce *fog*, *hog*, *Chicago* with the vowel of *father;* in the city itself these words normally have the vowel of *law*. The words with derivatives of Middle English long $\bar{o}$ have a wide variety of pronunciations today. My own pattern is unlikely to be duplicated by anyone native to the Chicago area:

/uw/	/u/	/ə/
the vowel of *do*	the vowel of *foot*	the vowel of *cut*
root	*coop*	*gums*
roof	*Cooper*	
food	*hoop*	
spoon	*soot*	
moon		
soon		

With *broom*, *room* and *hoof*, I may have either the vowel of *do* or that of *foot*. Many Pennsylvanians rhyme *food* with *good;* many highly educated Southerners rhyme *soot* with *cut*. *Roof* with the

---

[9] In some areas this vowel is unrounded, like the vowel Americans who distinguish these pairs usually have in *father;* in others it is rounded, like the usual vowel in *law*. The significance is that in these areas there is no contrast between such paris as *cot* and *caught*.

vowel of *foot* is widespread in the area of New England settlement and some of the areas settled from Pennsylvania; *coop* with the vowel of *do* is almost universal north of the Kanawha River; *root* rhyming with *foot* is characteristic of Yankee settlements. President Ruthven of the University of Michigan, an Iowan of Yankee descent, always said *gums* with the vowel of *do;* a former president of the American Academy of Physicians, a native of the belt of Yankee settlement in northern Illinois, consistently says *soon* with the vowel of *foot.*

We even show differences in our grammar. No one in South Carolina, however uneducated, would say *hadn't ought,* which is still current in educated Northern speech, nor would we say *sick to the stomach,* which in the North is almost universal. But many educated Southerners—and I include myself—find a place in conversation for *might could, used to could* and *used to didn't.* I have heard the basketball announcer for the Chicago *Tribune* become almost schizoid as he hesitated between *dived* and *dove* (with the vowel of *go*), and there seems to be no regional or social distinction between *kneeled* and *knelt.* Even *ain't*—a four-letter word still taboo in writing despite *Ulysses, Lady Chatterly* and Norman Mailer[10]—may be found in educated conversation, especially among the first families of Charleston. When we realize this, we can take calmly the diversity of names for the grass strip between sidewalk and street, the earthworm, the dragon fly or cottage cheese; the debate among New Englanders as to whether a doughnut should be made with yeast; or the fact that the New Orleans *poor boy* sandwich may be a *hoagy* as in Philadelphia, a *submarine* as in Boston, a *grinder* as in upstate New York or a *hero* as in New York City. Only in recent years have people outside learned that *clout* is our local Chicago name for political influence, a *Chinaman* is a dispenser of such influence, a *prairie* is a vacant lot and a *gangway* is a passage, usually covered, between two apartment buildings. I would not be surprised if these terms were unfamiliar to many who have grown up as close to the city as the DuPage Valley.

2

Yet if we are sometimes bewildered by the differences in American English, we should be comforted to learn that by European standards these differences are very small. We can notice, in fact, that not only are differences along the Atlantic seaboard fewer and less sharp than one finds in the much shorter distance between Cumberland and Kent, but that differences diminish as we go west. We owe

---

[10] In a review of Morton Bloomfield and Leonard Newmark, *A Linguistic Introduction to the History of English,* James H. Sledd observes sardonically that "the agonizing deappraisals of *Webster's Third New International* show that any red-blooded American would prefer incest to *ain't.*" *Language,* XL (1964), 473.

our relative uniformity of speech to several forces. First, the speakers of the more extreme varieties of British local speech were not the ones who migrated; most of the early settlers had already migrated, in Britain, from village to towns, especially to seaport towns. There was dialect mixture in all of the early settlements—a situation re-peated in the westward movement—so that what survived in each area was a compromise. There has always been a tradition of geographical mobility, epitomized in various ways by Daniel Boone, Sam Houston and Steinbeck's Joads. There has been an equal tradition of social mobility; except for Taft and the Roosevelts, no president of the United States since 1890 has come from an old family of social pres-tige and inherited wealth. There has been a tradition of industrializa-tion—of substituting better tools and more intricate machinery, wherever possible, for human hands and muscle. The Yankee farmer was the son of a townsman—uninhibited by traditional English ways of farming but determined to make a good living. The curved Ameri-can ax-handle made it easier to clear the forests; the computer and scanner promise to make it easier to collect citations for dictio-naries—though no technological development can eliminate the need for judgment. There has been a tradition of urbanization—of cities arising in response to opportunities for trade and providing in turn greater opportunities for industry and the arts alike; if we are aware of the open spaces of colonial America and the rugged strength of the frontiersman, we should be equally aware that in 1775 Philadel-phia and Boston were the second and third most important cities under the British crown and that they provided the sophisticated citi-zen with most of the cultural advantages of his British counterpart. And finally, there has been a tradition of general education, beginning when the Northwest Ordinance provided that public schools be financed from the public lands, and proceeding through coeducation and the great state universities first established on a large scale in the Middle West but now found everywhere. All of these forces have combined—and are still combining—to replace local and even regional terms with commercial terms of national use, to eradicate the most noticeable non standard grammatical features and even to reduce the differences between the pronunciation of one region and that of an-other.

Yet though these forces have reduced some of the regional differences in American English, they have not eliminated them. If cottage cheese is now a commercial product, so that only the older people are likely to remember *Dutch cheese*, *smearcase* or *clabber* cheese, the regional designations for the large complicated sandwich are becoming established, and the designations for the grass strip near the street seem to be fairly stable, and indeed often peculiarly local, as *tree belt* in Springfield, Massachusetts, *tree lawn* in Cleveland, and

devil strip in Akron. Many of these differences are due to the nature
of the original population: *pail* and *swill* were spread westward by
New Englanders and York Staters, *bucket* and *slop* by Pennsylvanians
and Southerners, in the same way that East Anglians brought to eastern New England the "broad *a*" and the loss of /-r/ in *barn*. Where
Germans have settled, one may say *got awake;* in communities settled
heavily by Scandinavians, one *cooks coffee.*

The routes of communication often stay the same, though the
mode of transportation has changed; relatively few of these routes—
the Mississippi is a notable exception—cross the major dialect boundaries. Even the monstrous expenditures for highways have not
reduced the isolation of some of the more striking relic areas: the
Maine coast, the eastern shore of Chesapeake Bay, the Outer Banks
of North Carolina and parts of the Kentucky mountains are still off
the beaten track; even in Illinois the tongue of land between the
Illinois and the Mississippi has become accessible to metropolitan
St. Louis only in the last few years. Since our system of public education is highly decentralized (in most ways, a source of strength,
since it allows one community to learn from the successes or failures
of another), the differences in taxable wealth make it possible for
expenditures per pupil to be much less in Mississippi than in Illinois,
even though Mississippi spends a far greater proportion of her tax
revenues on education, so that libraries are far smaller and the best-
trained teachers are tempted to go elsewhere; as a result, regional
nonstandard grammatical forms in Mississippi prove strikingly resistant to the influence of the classroom.

Because the nation is too large for any single center to establish
its speech as a model of excellence—even if we had not had a number
of stubbornly autonomous regional centers of culture from the beginning—we can expect to have a number of regional varieties of cultivated speech, unlike the situation in France or Spain or England. If
some of the colonial centers no longer have the prestige they once
had—Newport, Charleston and Savannah have certainly ceased to
exert much influence on their neighbors—new centers have come into
existence, such as Chicago and St. Louis, Atlanta and Nashville,
Houston and Denver, Salt Lake City and San Francisco. It is certain
that the differences among educated speech—always less than those
among uneducated varieties—will become even less with the passing
of time. But some differences will remain. And as corporations emulate the traditional policy of the army and the older policy of the
Methodist Church, in shifting their executives around as they rise in
the hierarchy,[11] we can be sure that any respectable suburban classroom will contain children speaking several varieties of cultivated
American English. It behooves the teacher to recognize that in the
long run one such variety is as good as another, and to make the di-

versity a source of both more interesting instruction at present and greater cultural understanding in the future.

3

Social differences arise essentially in the same way as regional ones, through close association with those who speak one variety of the language, and remote association—or none—with those who speak other varieties. Standard or cultivated speech is such because it is used by those people who make the important decisions in the speech community. There is nothing sacred about any particular variety; what was once unacceptable becomes acceptable if its speakers rise to positions of economic and social prestige, and it may change under the influence of other speakers who come into the prestige group. After the Norman Conquest, Winchester yielded to London as the cultural center of the south of England, and by the end of the four-teenth century—despite some brilliant writers in the North—London English was so dominant that even a Yorkshireman like Wyclif had to use it in his writings. But London English did not remain static; under the influence of the rich wool merchants and others from the north of England, it replaced the -th of the present indicative third singular with -s; it replaced be as an indicative plural with are; it established she as the feminine nominative third person pronoun, and they and their and them as pronouns of the third person plural. And as we are well aware, every long vowel and diphthong of fourteenth-century London English has changed in pronunciation, and some have fallen together, as the verb see /se:/ and the noun sea /sæ:/ have both be-come /siy/. For a more recent example we can take the rise in status of the Southern monophthongal /ay/ in nice white rice: as a boy I was taught that this was substandard, but it is now widely heard from educated Southerners.[12]

Social differences in language have always been with us, but in the contemporary American scene there are three forces which make for a different kind of situation from that which prevailed in older societies, more rural than ours. In such older societies, the social in-tervals in the speech of one community in a given country were likely

[11] For example, in early 1965 in Baton Rouge I met the husband of one of my former students, a personnel scout for the Humble division of Jersey Standard, attached to the Baton Rouge office. Later that year he was transferred to Houston; in September, 1967, he was shifted to New York and to suburban living in New Canaan, Connecticut.

[12] This vowel, as in right nice, is characteristic of the upper Piedmont and moun-tain regions of the South. As the inhabitants of those regions acquire education and money, their speech acquires prestige; since they constitute the overwhelm-ing majority of white Southerners, it is to be expected that their accents will pre-vail, like their votes, in the South of the future.

to be about the same as those elsewhere. Migration was likely to be in terms of individuals, or at most of separate families, and the aspiring— or at least their children—had a fair chance of breaking into the group of standard speakers in their new home. Finally, there was no hard- and-fast segregation between wealthy and poor neighborhoods. To take myself once more as an example, though my parents lived half a block from the richest street in town, we were the same distance from one of the Negro enclaves and not too far from immigrant and less affluent local whites. We all played together even though we didn't all go to school together; we were familiar with most of the local varieties of English and took their existence as a matter of course, assuming that the difference would grow less as more people became educated, and meanwhile delighting in the tunes and figures of speech each group of speakers used. For the most part we not only had the same sound system but—except for such shibboleths as *nice white rice*—the same pronunciations of the vowels and consonants; the differences were in distribution of sounds, in vocabulary and in grammar.

But in metropolitan areas there is now a different kind of situa- tion. Some of this began long ago when—after the rise of the steam- boat—immigrants from overseas, brought in to tend heavy industry, settled in ethnic neighborhoods under the watchful eye of their clergy and political leaders; with affluence, many of them left the old neighborhoods and entered into the dominant culture. Their con- sciousness was perhaps aggravated by the rampant xenophobia of World War I,[13] but the language tended to disappear. When German— a language used in urban and rural communities on all social levels— could be stigmatized, it is small wonder that the Slavic groups, usually peasants and often illiterate, should give up their language.

During my five-year stretch at Western Reserve, though at least half of my Cleveland students were of East European descent, less than one percent admitted knowing the languages of the countries from which their parents and grandparents had come. Culturally they have been deracinated. Immigrants from other parts of the United States, however, had usually followed the traditional pattern of indi- vidual movement, settling in a neighborhood according to their eco- nomic situation and mingling with those who were already there. Among Negroes[14] who were born in Chicago before 1900 there is essentially the same range of variation as there is among their white contemporaries.

---

[13] In 1917 the Texas legislature abolished the teaching of German in all state institutions because (among other reasons) Eduard Prokosch, head of the Ger- man Department in the state university, had referred to English as a Low German dialect.

But the situation changed when it became convenient to encourage heavy migration of unskilled labor from other parts—mostly rural areas—of the United States. This became noticeable during World War I, when the migration from Europe was cut off; but even before then some companies had found it expedient to introduce Negroes and Southern whites as strikebreakers, to counter the influence of the unions among the recent arrivals from Europe. Like the immigrants from Europe, these new groups—and after them the Puerto Ricans and Mexicans—tended to come in blocks and settle in patterns like the old ethnic neighborhoods, but lacking their structured community life. (Mexicans and Puerto Ricans have had such a community structure, and in this way strikingly differed from Negroes and rural whites.) The economic threat these groups posed to those who had arrived just before them—those from Southern and Eastern Europe—provoked hostility and fear, which was especially directed toward the more visible Negro: the bitterness between Negro and Hunky is an old story, which Rap Brown did not have to invent.[15] The demands for labor during World War II and the later mechanization of Southern agriculture accelerated the northward movement, and the Negro and poor white neighborhoods continued to spread—most noticeably the former. Nevertheless, although the newspapers have ignored the fact, Metropolitan Cleveland contains 200,000 Southern poor whites, most of them disadvantaged.

The very economic forces that led the poor Southerners north contributed to their problems after they arrived, except during times of unusually full employment, as in World War II. The South until very recently has been a region of unskilled labor;[16] the trend in all industry has been to upgrade the skills of labor and to transfer the unskilled work to machinery. With this trend increasing at the same time that migration from the South increased, employment opportunities for the unskilled tailed off, and with them the chance to participate in the well-advised affluence of the community. Moreover, the Southern tradition of unskilled labor was paralleled by a regional

[14] The designation *Negro* is now rejected by many of the self-designated leaders, who prefer *Black*, however, for other members of the group, *Black* is still an offensive label. For various designations of ethnic groups in America, and the record of their acceptance or rejection, see H. L. Mencken, *The American Language* (one-volume abridged edition, New York, 1963), 367-389. As George Schuyler, the distinguished columnist for the Pittsburgh *Courier*, once said, it seems rather trivial to raise points of protocol about designations while those designated lack the right to participate fully in American society.

[15] Nor did he invent the pronunciation of *hunky* as *honky*, with the vowel of *law*; the analogous pronunciation of *hungry* is widely used in the rural South, without racial distinction.

[16] See Marshall R. Colbert, "Southern Economic Development: Some Research Accomplishments and Gaps," *Perspectives on the South*, Edgar T. Thompson, ed. (Durham, N.C., 1967), 17-32.

inferiority in the educational system, especially in the schools available to the groups from which the northward migration was drawn. Thus the new arrivals from the South were at an added disadvantage where reading and mathematical skills were required. And in the South, finally, there has always been a wider difference between educated and uneducated speech than one finds in other regions. So what we have seen in the urban slums (especially in the North and West) is the establishment locally of strongly divergent varieties of nonstandard English, with a larger proportion of nonstandard grammatical forms than one finds in uneducated Northern English, and with strikingly different features of pronunciation. And as the children of uneducated Mississippians and Alabamians grow up hearing at play such varieties of uneducated speech, they tend to perpetuate these varieties even when by chance they go to school alongside sizeable numbers of speakers of Northern types of English. In short we are now witnessing the establishment in our Northern cities of nonstandard varieties of English that diverge sharply from the local standard.

Last, we are getting into a pattern of one-class neighborhoods, where we seldom know people of different social strata from our own. We have indicated the rise of such neighborhoods through negative forces—the inability of the poor to buy or rent alongside other groups. But such neighborhoods have also arisen from the ability and desire of the affluent to flock with their kind. The automobile, which (among its other deleterious social effects) isolates the individual traveler from all but his own kind, has accelerated the trend, and so have the corporations, through an insistence that executives live in a style and community befitting their income and status. So there has been an increasing flight from the city, and new bedroom suburbs spring up, with their inmates insulated not only from the city but from all those below or above a narrow economic range. In the ninety-odd major suburbs in northeastern Illinois, a survey about ten years ago worked out a clear pecking order from Kenilworth down to Robbins; as their income grows, there is a clearly defined drift of young executives from Mount Prospect to Barrington; and the turnover of property in Park Forest is nationally notorious.[17] Under these circumstances, not only are some of the more effective models of standard English removed from the city, but those who grow up using these models have no chance to hear at close range what other varieties of English are like and are confirmed in linguistic myths and sociological stereotypes of superiority and inferiority.

[17] For information on the local migrations of the upward-mobile in Metropolitan Chicago, I am indebted to Lee Pederson.

4

I shall not conclude by trying to instigate a crusade. In too many aspects of American life—in education no less than in foreign affairs—we have sounded too many trumpets to hasty action without looking into the possible consequences. But I think we can rationally conclude that the problems of dialect differences are highly complex, and that where—as is apparent with some groups in our cities—these differences interfere with participation in the benefits our society has to offer, we must somehow contrive to bridge these differences. But we must not try to bulldoze out of the way the habitual idiom of the home and neighborhood; whatever we do, for the short term, must be done by adding without taking away, by full appreciation of the fact that all dialects are acquired in the same way, that each is a part of the speaker's personality and that each is capable of expressing a wide range of experience. In the intermediate range, the success of any program of commingling widely diverse neighborhoods in a school will depend on how well the teachers understand the nature of dialects and impart this understanding to their students—particularly to those who up to now have had economic and social advantages. In the long run the solution will come as more communities are opened to a greater variety of ethnic groups and social classes; it is apparently working in such a racially diverse middle-class neighborhood as Hyde Park in Chicago. The new developments in the outer suburbs, such as those which the Weston atomic reactor has already inaugurated in northern Illinois, are certain to bring to many communities a greater amount of population diversity than they now have. To produce stability, to reduce tensions rather than aggravate them, it is important that teachers and pupils, school board members and the public at large, realize the nature of diversity in language behavior, that aspect of behavior most closely identified with the human condition.

PART TWO

THE ORIGINS:
ENGLISH IN AFRICA AND EARLY AMERICA

Gilbert D. Schneider

WEST AFRICAN PIDGIN-ENGLISH—AN OVERVIEW: PHONOLOGY-MORPHOLOGY

This paper is the result of many years of interest in Pidgin-English of the African West Coast.[1] My first field notes are dated February 14, 1947 and include idiomatic expressions and proverbs collected on a journey from Victoria to Bamenda in the West Cameroon (the Southern Cameroons in 1947).

An historical statement of development, a contrastive Standard-English—Pidgin-English study, or a relational comparison with other pidgins and creoles, would be possible, and should be of great interest and value to linguists. These topics, however, are beyond the scope of this presentation.

INTRODUCTION

Pidgin-English, hereafter abbreviated P-E, is the most common name given to a lingua franca spoken throughout West Africa from Sierra Leone to the Gabon. It is a medium of communication for

---

[1] Historical sources also call the lingua franca: Broken-English, Coast-English, Kitchen-English, Bastard-English, to name only a few commonly used terms.

African peoples who have no first language in common, for white men of various ethnic backgrounds, and for the West African working man, trader, and transient peoples.

P-E is not a mere simplification of English, but a separate and describable language. Its vocabulary is predominantly English-based, but these lexical forms have changed their meaning to fit into the value and world view of the African people. At the present time P-E is not learned as a first language in a number of polyglot communities in urban and plantation areas of the West Cameroon and Fernando Po. Here it is used by children of African parents who have only P-E in common.

The P-E speech-community of West Africa, which shares many characteristics including grammatical structure and vocabulary, is neither continuous nor homogenous. However, though each speaker's usage has some variants, all dialects of P-E are mutually intelligible to speakers who constantly use it in their everyday pursuits.

THE SOUNDS OF P-E (PHONOLOGY)

Our purpose in this section will be to note the shared sound features of speakers with differing first language backgrounds.[2] A fact worth recording is that long-time speakers of P-E recognize a "common core" and this fact affords a frame of reference for dealing with the extremes of anglicization and patterned differences between the many African dialects. It is this broad P-E which will concern us now.

The twenty consonants arranged below make-up the consonant inventory of broad P-E spoken in the Cameroon area.[3]

	Labial	*Dental*	*Palatal*	*Post-palatal*
Voiced stops	b	d	j	g
Voiceless stops	p	t	ch	k
Voiceless spirants	f	s	sh	h
Nasals	m	n	ny	ng
Liquids	w	r	y	l

[2] The author wishes to state that any speaker of P-E, introducing distinctive features not found in the consonant and vowel inventories is either anglicizing or assimilating.

[3] Dr. William Stewart and Dr. Lloyd Swift made several suggestions for paralleling these sets of P-E consonants. The Cameroon area is perhaps the most active P-E community on the East Coast today (1966).

Seven vowels make up the vowel inventory of broad P-E.[4]

	Front	Central	Back
High	i		u
Mid	ey		ow
	e		o
Low		a	

The twenty consonant and seven vowel inventories represent the primary sound system of P-E. A secondary system of features, however, is necessary to interpret the meaningful phenomena of transition between successive consonant and vowel sounds, to distinguish successive syllables from each other by the level of tone on a given syllable, and to signal the direction of terminals at the end of a sound sequence. This system includes three terminal markers, two of tone, and one which we shall call open transition.

Of interest to the readers of this journal will be a few examples of the phonotactic differences between English and P-E.[5]

Initially   1. /str-/ E > P-E/tr-/

Examples: 'stranger' > /trénja/, 'straight' > /tréyt/

2. /sp-, st-, sk-, sl-, sm-, sn-/ E > P-E/si-p-,

si-t-, si-k-, si-l-, si-m-, si-n-/

Examples: 'spear' > /sipía/, 'stick' > /sitík/,

'sleep' > /silíp/, 'small' > /simól/,

'snake' > /sinék/, 'school' > /sikúl/

Finally   1. /-mp, -nt, -n'k/ E > P-E /-m, -n, -ng/[6]

Examples: 'camp' > /kám/, 'plant' > /plán/, 'bank' > /báng/

2. /-b, -d, -g, -v, -z/ E > P-E/-p, -t, -k, -f, -s/

---

[4] The vowel symbols /ey/ and /ow/ are not to be interpreted as diphthongs or glides in closed or open syllables. The decision to utilize these symbols is a practical one making it possible to type P-E on most English typewriters. [ɛ] = /e/ and [ɔ] = /o/.

[5] Low tone will not be marked. High tone will be marked /´/.

[6] /-ng/ represents the post-palatal nasal in final position, namely / /. For convenience the cluster of post-velar nasal plus post-velar voiced stop /ngg/ is written /n'g/, and the cluster of post-velar nasal plus post-velar voiceless stop /ngk/ is written /n'k/.

Examples: 'rub' > /róp/, 'bad' > /bát/, 'dog' > /dók/,

'twelve' > /twéf/, 'nose' > /nóws/

Replacements 1. / l/ E > P-E /u/

Examples: 'table' > /tébu/, 'bundle' > /bóndu/,

'bottle' > /bótu/, 'bicycle' > /básku/,

'chisel' > /chísu/, 'apple' > /ápu/

2. / r/ E > P-E /a/

Examples: 'rubber' > /róba/, 'order' > /óda/,

'better' > /béta/, 'conquer' > /kón'ka/,

'father' > /fáda/, 'danger' > /dénja/

WORD FORMATION IN P-E (MORPHOLOGY)

A striking feature of P-E, compared with English from which it drew most of its lexical forms, is that the inflectional system is very limited. Grammatical information is signalled by tone, reduplication, word composition, and the syntactic system. P-E has none of the bound forms of English.

Free contentives (content words as opposed to function words) in P-E can be reduplicated and compounded. They also enter into complex forms which differ from compound forms in that the compound is made up of free forms, while the complex contains at least one bound form.

Only a few examples will be given to illustrate the complex forms in P-E.

			Free form			*Bound form*		
1.	/sidóng/	'sit'	/dóng/	<	'down'	/si-/	<	'sit'
2.	/tanóp/	'stand'	/óp/	<	'up'	/tan-/	<	'stand'
3.	/trowéy/	'throw'	/wéy/	<	'away'	/tro-/	<	'throw'
4.	/fulóp/	'full'	/óp/	<	'up'	/ful-/	<	'full'
5.	/dokfáwu/	'duck'	/fáwu	<	'fowl'	/dok-/	<	'duck'
6.	/shipgówt/	'sheep'	/gówt/	<	'goat'	/ship-/	<	'sheep'
7.	/fáyawut/	'firewood'	/fáya/	<	'fire'	/-wut/	<	'wood'

Reduplication

Reduplication or reiteration is a productive morphological process in the formation of P-E contentives. This is to be expected for
the working vocabulary contains reduplicated forms which are indi-
visible.[7] The following examples will illustrate this point.

1. /fufú/ 'food made of corn, yam, cassava or other staple,' 2. /potapótá/ 'mud|
plaster, muck, marshy place,' 3. /biabíá/ 'hair, pelt,' 4. /bakabáká/ 'tiny silver
fish,' 5. /kwékwé/ 'tiny, insignificant,' 6. /kwíkwík/ 'quickly,' 7. /kwátákwátá/
'completely.'

Reduplication of the noun form makes for plurality. Examples
are:

1. /písís-písis/ 'rags, cloth remnants, pieces,' 2. /bá-bá/ 'bars,' 3. /dók-dók/
'dogs,' 4. /sansán-sansán/ 'sands (of different kinds),' 5. /het-pán-het-pán/
'head-pans' (used by the laborers in construction work).

Reduplication of the verb makes for repetition and sometime
continuity of action. Examples are:

1. /tok-tók/ 'talk constantly,' 2. /tif-tíf/ 'steal continually,' 3. /ron-rón/ 'run
continually or repeatedly,' 4. /tai-fés-tai-fés/ 'frown or scowl continually.'

Reduplication of the adjective marks intensification.[8] Examples:

1. /fán-fán/ 'very fine or very good,' 2. /bík-bík/ 'very big,' 3. /fós-fós/ 'very
first,' 4. /sháp-sháp/ 'very early.'

Reduplication of the adverb marks intensification. Examples:

1. /tróng-tróng/ 'strongly,' 2. /sófli-sófli/ 'slowly, cautiously,' 3. /wán-wán/
'singly,' 4. /kwátákwátá-kwátákwátá/ ' completely.'

---

[7] Reduplication or reiteration is common to all languages of West Africa. Many
reduplicated forms enter idiophonic and onomatopoeic fields foreign to the
Standard English speaker.

[8] The feature of intensification need not stop with a reduplicated form. The
author has heard such examples as: /fán-fán-fán/, and /shwít-shwít-shwít-shwít/.
This phenomenon becomes common as one encounters the assimilated African
language idiolects of P-E.

Word Compounding

The following characteristics mark the P-E compounds.

1. The meaning of a P-E compound is different from the sum of the meanings of the individual parts.
2. P-E compounds are not subject to the rules which bind its individual parts.
3. P-E compounds possess the status of free forms. When reduplicated the compounds mark plurality in nouns, intensity in adjectives and adverbs, repetition and continuity of action in verbs.
4. Many P-E compounds follow definite tone patterns which help in their identification. We can illustrate only a few common patterns.

P-E compounds functioning as nouns

The *Verb + Noun* compound has a low-high tone pattern. This compound contrasts with the order *verb* plus *noun* in syntactic constructions where the tone is high-high. Examples are:

1. /tif-mán/ 'thief' < /tíf/ 'thieve' + /mán/ 'man'
2. /was-rúm/ 'washroom' < /wás/ 'wash' + /rúm/ 'room'
3. /tai-hét/ 'kerchief' < /tái/ 'tie' + /hét/ 'head'
4. /browk-mérish/ 'a fish, nylon head scarf, or any object coveted by a woman' < /brówk/ 'break' + /mérish/ 'marriage'

The *Adjective + Noun compound* has a high-low tone pattern. This compound contrasts with the order *adjective* plus *noun* in the noun phrase where the tone is high-high. Reduplication of this compound marks plurality. Examples:

1. /bík-man/ 'elder, respected person' < /bík/ 'big' + /mán/ 'man'
2. /simól-boi/ 'novice, apprentice' < /simól/ 'small' + /bói/ 'boy'
3. /lóng-wan/ 'tapeworm' < /lóng/ 'long' + /wán/ 'one'
4. /shót-boi/ 'Short Boy' (a personal name) < /shót/ 'short' + /bói/ 'boy'

P-E compounds functioning as verbs

The Verb + Noun compound has a low-high tone pattern. The resulting compound is intransitive. Reduplication marks repetition or continuity of action.

1. /tai-fés/ 'frown, scowl' < /tái/ 'tie' + /fés/ 'face'
2. /mas-fút/ 'walk' < /más/ 'mash' (to step) + /fút/ 'foot'
3. /nak-móf/ 'discuss' < /nák/ 'knock' + /móf/ 'mouth'
4. /was-hán/ 'withdraw' < /wás/ 'wash' + /hán/ 'hand'

P-E compounds functioning as nouns, adjectives, verbs or adverbs

The Adjective + Noun compound has a low-high tone pattern. Reduplication is possible as adjective and adverb. As a noun or verb, however, it expresses a property, quality, or some relation which is considered from the characteristics which take an object. It is not reduplicated when it functions as a noun or a verb. Examples are:

1. /trong-hét/ 'stubborn' AJ, 'stubborness' N, 'be stubborn' V, 'stubbornly' AD < /trong/ 'strong' + /het/ 'head.'
2. /bik-ái/ 'greedy' AJ, 'greediness' N, 'be greedy' V, 'greedily' AD < /bik/ 'big' + /ai/ 'eye.'
3. /blak-hát/ 'wicked' AJ, 'wickedness' N, 'be wicked' V, 'wickedly' AD < /blak/ 'black' + /hat/ 'heart.'
4. /hai-sikín/ 'proud' AJ, 'pride' N, 'be proud' V, 'proudly' AD < /hai/ 'high' + /sikin/ 'skin' (meaning 'body' in P-E).

Names in P-E

P-E speakers take great pleasure in giving new names to people, trucks, canoes, places, and new products. Morphologically these formations all enter into an open class of proper nouns. Only a few examples can be given on this fascinating subject. *Personal names:* sénspás-kíng/ Wiser than King, /trokí/ Turtle, /tú-fo-péni/ Two for a Penny, /lóng-bói/ Tall Fellow, /belí-káu/ Belly Cow. *Truck names:* /gót-déy/ God is, /moní-hát/ Money Comes Hard, /nów-wóri/ Don't Worry, /mán-nów-rés/ Man Doesn't Rest, /léfam-fo-gót/ Leave it to God. *New products:* /mán-pás-mán/ Banocide (for filariasis), /ém-n-bí/ Sulfa (from Mayer and Baker—the makers), /tú-tén/ Shoes (good shoes), etc.

A P-E Text

The following text has been taken from *Conversations at Hospital* prepared by G. D. and M. M. Schneider in 1963. They first appeared in *First and Second Steps in Wes-Kos*, a pedagogical manual developed for the Peace Corps Training Program, Cameroon II at Ohio University, July-August, 1963.

CONVERSATION—kontri tok

A middle-aged woman with a deep ulcer

Helen: gut moni mami.
          Good morning, madame.

          huskan komplen yu get-am?
          What's your complaint?

Mami: na kot fo fut, ma.
          An ulcer on my leg, miss.

          yu wan luk-am?
          Would you like to see it?

Helen: muf lif, we yu koba-am dey.
          Remove the leaf you covered it with.

          a gow was-am.
          I will clean it.

Mami: i di peyn mi plenti.
          It gives me severe pain.

          wat-wata don bigin komot.
          Pus is beginning to drain from it.

Helen: dis kot don bik.
          This ulcer is very large.

          ha yu tey long sow?
          Why didn't you come sooner?

Mami: na sowsow fam di meyk mi.
          I had so much gardening to do.

          pikin krai now gut.
          It would be a shame for the children to suffer from hunger

Helen: ow-mami!
          Oh, my dear woman!

          som-tam, hospitu gow howl yu.
          We may need to keep you here at the hospital.

dis kot don gow fa.
:   This ulcer is in an advanced stage.

dokta mos luk-am.
:   The doctor will have to check it.

Mami: ha a gow du ma?
:   What can I do?

moni now dey, pikin gow sofa.
:   I have no money. My children will suffer.

Helen: na yu meyk-am mami.
:   You allowed it to happen, madame.

man we i bon i biabia na i gow hia i simel.
:   If you create trouble you must suffer the consequences.

Mami: wa-a-a. tudey na tudey fo mi-ow.
:   Oh, my! This is my unlucky day.

William A. Stewart

SOCIOLINGUISTIC FACTORS IN THE HISTORY OF AMERICAN NEGRO DIALECTS

Within the last few years, the increased national commitment to bettering the lot of socially and economically underprivileged groups of Americans—the so-called "disadvantaged"—has caused educators to consider ways in which the schools may involve themselves in this task. Of the many possibilities, certainly one of the most obvious is to deal with the chronic language problems associated with many of the disadvantaged. Yet, although there is a general awareness that certain of the disadvantaged do have language problems, there is at the same time a lack of agreement as to what these problems entail, and therefore what to do about them. Some investigators (often educational psychologists) have maintained that the disadvantaged characteristically do not use verbal communication to the extent that members of the middle class do, and are thus impoverished in "communicative skills." To alleviate this situation, they have recommended programs aimed at encouraging the use of verbal communication of a variety of kinds by disadvantaged pupils. A few investigators have theorized that members of disadvantaged groups may even engage less in abstract thinking than do middle-class persons. For this there have been suggested programs designed to teach more perception and conceptualization on the part of the disadvantaged pupils.

On the other hand, linguists have tended to emphasize one other type of language problem which some disadvantaged groups often have, and for which evidence is quite accessible—being encountered every day in the nation's classrooms. This is the purely structural conflict between on the one hand the patterns of a nonstandard dialect which an individual may have learned at home or in peer-group interaction, and on the other hand the equivalent patterns of standard English—the language of modern technology and of the middle class. This is one kind of problem which many of the nation's schools ought to be ready and willing to cope with. One indication of the readiness of the schools is the fact that traditional English teachers are rapidly abandoning the older "sloppy speech" and "lazy tongue" views of nonstandard speech in favor of a realization that it usually represents the speaker's use of some language system which, though it may differ from standard English in form and sometimes even in function, is nevertheless logical, coherent, and (in its own way) grammatical. Another indication of the readiness of schools to cope with the problem of dialect differences is the growth of a cadre of specialists in the teaching of English to speakers of other languages. With them, there has come into being a set of new techniques for teaching English to persons coming from a different language background.

Just as they are ready, America's schools certainly ought to be willing to deal with dialect-based problems, since there are a number of ways in which, by themselves, they can render a nonstandard speaker dysfunctional in exchanges with standard English-speaking members of the middle class. One way is for minor pronunciation differences between a nonstandard and standard English—each one perhaps trivial by itself—to pile up in an utterance to such an extent that the nonstandard version becomes unintelligible to a middle-class listener, even though in grammar and vocabulary it may be quite similar to its standard equivalent. Thus, a nonstandard version of "I don't know where they live" might, in one dialect, become cryptic to the standard-speaking listener, merely because of its being pronounced something like *Ah 'own know wey 'ey lib.* Or, a standard-English speaker may misunderstand a nonstandard utterance, even though he thinks he has deciphered it correctly, because it contains nonstandard grammatical constructions which are unknown to him. For example, a middle-class listener may take a nonstandard sentence *Dey ain't like dat* to mean "they aren't like that," when it really means "They didn't like that." The standard-English speaker is simply unaware that *ain't* is this particular dialect's way of negating verbs in the past tense, as he is unaware that the usual equivalent in the same dialect of "They aren't like that" would be either *Dey not like dat* or *Dey don't be like dat* (the two variants indicating a difference in meaning which is not easily expressed in standard English). Of course, similar breakdowns in intelligibility may also occur in the other direction, when the nonstandard speaker tries to understand standard English. Finally, even when he does succeed in making himself understood by his middle-class listeners, the nonstandard speaker may still fall victim to the difference in social prestige between his dialect and standard English. In other words, although middle-class persons may understand what he is saying, they may still consider him uncouth for saying it the way he does.

Professionally able though the schools may now be to embark on programs which would deal effectively with this kind of problem, the likelihood of their actually doing so in the near future is certainly not increased by the unwillingness of many educators and even some applied linguists to approach the problem in any but the most general terms. For, unfortunately, the technical know-how necessary to teach standard English to speakers of nonstandard dialects is simply not embodied in an awareness of the problem at the level of "Some children should probably be taught standard English as a second dialect" —no matter how true such statements may be. The necessary know-how will begin to be adequate when and only when applied linguists can give, and educators will take seriously, details of the type "The verb system of such-and-such a nonstandard dialect operates in such-and-such a way, and the verb system of standard English operates in such-and-such a way, so that structural interference is most likely to occur at points *a*, *b*, and *c*. Therefore, the following lessons and drills in the standard English verb system is what children who speak this nonstandard dialect will need."[1]

One reason why there is little remedial English now being taught based upon a systematic comparison of the differences between nonstandard dialects and standard English is that information about one of the pedagogically most important features of nonstandard dialects —their grammatical systems—is still largely lacking. This lack is due in

[1] See William A. Stewart, ed., *Non-Standard Speech and the Teaching of English* (Washington, D.C.: Center for Applied Linguistics, 1964).

great part to the fact that American dialect studies have traditionally emphasized differences in pronunciation and vocabulary, at the expense of information on systematic grammatical differences.

Now that linguists have begun to fill this information gap, however, they are finding their observations on language variation among the disadvantaged received with uneasiness and even hostility by many teachers, administrators, and community leaders. The reason for this is undoubtedly that the accurate description of dialect variation in American communities—particularly in urban centers—is turning out to show a disturbing correlation between language behavior on the one hand and socio-economic and ethnic stratification on the other.[2] The correlation is particularly controversial insofar as it involves the speech of large numbers of American Negroes, since at the present time Negro leadership (and this includes most Negro educators) is probably more achievement-oriented than any other. Because of this orientation, Negro elites tend not to welcome any evidence of uniform or stable behavioral differences between members of their own group (even lower-class ones) and those of the white-dominated middle class. Yet the fact is that Negroes account for most of the most pedagogically problematic nonstandard dialect speakers in the larger cities, and also include within their group speakers of the most radically nonstandard dialects of natively spoken English in the entire country.[3] Furthermore, because de facto segregation in housing has caused nonstandard-dialect-speaking Negroes to predominate in many schools and because these Negroes appear in many cases to have different kinds of problems with standard English than nonstandard-dialect-speaking whites have (even in the same area), the sweeping, for political purposes, of Negro dialect descriptions under the white-oriented geographic dialect rug would probably be more detrimental to disadvantaged Negro children than it would be advantageous to Negro elites.[4]

[2] The American Dream notwithstanding, it is well known to social scientists that American society is stratified into a number of social classes and ethnic groups, and that each of these exhibits a "characteristic" configuration of customs, attitudes, roles, lifeways and, as it turns out, speech patterns. The literature on social and ethnic stratification is extensive, but good introductions are Egon Ernest Bergel, Social Stratification (New York: McGraw-Hill Book Co., 1962), and Tamotsu Shibutani and Kian M. Kwan, Ethnic Stratification (New York: The Macmillan Co., 1965). For an exhaustively documented study of the correlation between language variation and social class, ethnicity, and age in an American metropolis, see William Labov, The Social Stratification of English in New York City (Washington, D.C.: The Center of Applied Linguistics, 1966).

[3] These two facts may not be entirely unrelated. For a graphic indication of the relatively more nonstandard grammatical norms of Negro children over white children in a single city, see Figure 18 (page 53) in Walter Loban, Problems in Oral English: Kindergarten Through Grade Nine (Champaign, Ill.: National Council of Teachers of English, 1966).

On the other hand, linguists should realize that the fears and anxieties of Negro leaders about public discussion of ethnically correlated behavioral differences may have some foundation. It is possible, for example, that quite objective and innocently made statements about dialect differences between whites and Negroes might be interpreted by white racists as evidence of Negro cultural backwardness or mental inferiority, or even seized upon by black racists as evidence of some sort of mythical Negro "soul." Linguists should not censor their data, but they should make sure that their statements about Negro-white differences are not divorced from an awareness of the historical, social, and linguistic reasons why such differences may have come into existence and been maintained. Perhaps it would serve that end to point out here some of the sociolinguistic factors involved in the evolution of American Negro dialects, factors which explain why certain kinds of American Negro dialects are both different from the nonstandard dialects of American whites, and more radically deviant from standard English.

Although the linguistic history of the Negro in the United States can be reconstructed from the numerous literary attestations of the English of New World Negroes over the last two and a half centuries, and by comparing these with the English of Negroes in the United States, the Caribbean, and West Africa today, this has never been done for the English teaching profession. In presenting a historical sketch of this type, I realize that both the facts presented and my interpretations of them may embarrass or even infuriate those who would like to whitewash American Negro dialects by claiming that they do not exist—that (in spite of all sorts of observable evidence to the contrary) they are nothing but Southern white dialects, derived directly from Great Britain. I will simply make no apologies to those who regard human behavior as legitimate only if observed in the white man, since I feel that this constitutes a negation of the cultural and ethnic plurality which is one of America's greatest heritages. On the other hand, I do regret that such a historical survey, although linguistically interesting, may at times conjure up out of the past memories of the Negro-as-slave to haunt the aspirations of the Negro-as-equal.

Of those Africans who fell victim to the Atlantic slave trade and were brought to the New World, many found it necessary to learn some kind of English. With very few exceptions, the form of English which they acquired was a pidginized one, and this kind of English

---

[4] For a discussion of Negro dialect in one urban community, see William A. Stewart, "Urban Negro Speech: Sociolinguistic Factors Affecting English Teaching" in Roger W. Shuy, editor, *Social Dialects and Language Learning* (Champaign, Ill.: National Council of Teachers of English, 1965). The nonstandard dialect patterns cited earlier in the present article are also Negro dialect.

became so well established as the principal medium of communication between Negro slaves in the British colonies that it was passed on as a creole language to succeeding generations of the New World Negroes, for whom it was their native tongue.[5] Some idea of what New World Negro English may have been like in its early stages can be obtained from a well-known example of the speech of a fourteen-year-old Negro lad given by Daniel DeFoe in *The Family Instructor* (London, 1715). It is significant that the Negro, Toby, speaks a pidginized kind of English to his boy master, even though he states that he was born in the New World.

A sample of his speech is:[6]

Toby:	Me be born at Barbadoes.
Boy:	Who lives there, Toby?
Toby:	There lives white mans, white womans, negree mans, negree womans, just so as live here.
Boy:	What and not know God?
Toby:	Yes, the white mans say God prayers,—no much know God.
Boy:	And what do the black mans do?
Toby:	They much work, much work,—no say God prayers, not at all.
Boy:	What work do they do, Toby?
Toby:	Makee the sugar, makee the ginger,—much great work, weary work, all day, all night.

[5] In referring to types of languages, linguists use the terms *pidgin* and *creole* in a technical sense which has none of the derogatory or racial connotations of popular uses of these terms. When a linguist says that a variety of language is pidginized, he merely means that it has a markedly simplified grammatical structure compared with the "normal" (i.e., unpidginized) source-language. This simplification may be one way in which speakers of different languages can make a new language easier to learn and use—particularly if they have neither the opportunity nor the motivation to learn to speak it the way its primary users do. In addition, some of the unique characteristics of a pidgin language may be due, not to simplification, but to influences on it from the native languages of its users. What is important to realize, however, is that pidginized languages do have grammatical structure and regularity, even though their specific patterns may be different from those of the related unpidginized source-language of higher prestige. Thus, the fact that the sentence *Dem no get-am* in present-day West African Pidgin English is obviously different from its standard English equivalent "They don't have it" does not necessarily indicate that the Pidgin English speaker "talks without grammar." In producing such a sentence, he is unconsciously obeying the grammatical rules of West African Pidgin English, and these determine that *Dem no get-am* is the "right" construction, as opposed to such ungrammatical or "wrong" combinations as *No dem get-am, No get dem-am, Get-am dem no,* etc. If a pidgin finally becomes the native language of a speech community (and thereby becomes by definition a creole language), it may expand in grammatical complexity to the level of "normal" or unpidginized languages. Of course, the resulting creole language may still exhibit structural differences from the original source-language, because the creole has gone through a pidginized stage. For more details, see Robert A. Hall, Jr., *Pidgin and Creole Languages* (Ithaca, N. Y.: Cornell U. Press, 1966).

[6] The same citation is given in a fuller form, along with a number of other attestations of early New World Negro speech, in George Philip Krapp, *The English Language in America* (New York: The Century Co., 1925), Vol. I, pp. 255-265. Other attestations are cited in Tremaine McDowell, "Notes on Negro Dialect in the American Novel to 1821," *American Speech* V (1930), pp. 291-296.

Even though the boy master's English is slightly nonstandard (e.g., *black mans*), it is still quite different from the speech of the Negro.

An idea of how widespread a pidginized form of English had become among the Negro population of the New World by the end of the seventeenth century can be gathered from the fact that it had even become the language of the coastal plantations in the Dutch colony of Surinam (i.e., Dutch Guiana), in South America. In an early description of that colony, the chapter on the Negro ends with a sample conversation in the local Negro English dialect. The dialogue includes such sentences as *Me bella well* "I am very well," *You wantee siddown pinkininne?* "Do you want to sit down for a bit?" and *You wantee go walka longa me?* "Do you want to take a walk with me?"[7] In these sentences, the use of the enclitic vowel in *wantee* recalls the same in DeFoe's example *makee*. Also, the speaker, like Toby, uses *me* as a subject pronoun. In the first Surinam sentence, we see an early example of a construction without any equivalent of the standard English verb "to be." Toby also would probably have said *Me weary*, since the *be* in his first sentence was in all likelihood a past-tense marker (as it is in present-day West African pidgin English)—the sentence therefore meaning "I was born in Barbadoes." In the last Surinam sentence, a reflex of English *along* is used with the meaning of standard English "with." It may or may not be accidental that in the Gullah dialect, spoken by the Negroes along the South Carolina coastal plain, the same phenomenon occurs, e.g., *Enty you wantuh walk long me?* "Do you want to take a walk with me?" Some Gullah speakers even still use *me* as a subject pronoun, e.g., *Me kyaan bruk-um* "I can't break it," and enclitic final vowels seem to have survived in such Gullah forms as *yerry*, *yeddy* "to hear."

Early examples of Negro dialect as spoken in the American colonies show it to be strikingly similar to that given by DeFoe for the West Indies and by Herlein for Surinam. In John Leacock's play, *The Fall of British Tyranny* (Philadelphia, 1776), part of the conversation between a certain "Kidnapper" and Cudjo, one of a group of Virginia Negroes, goes as follows:[8]

Kidnapper: . . . what part did you come from?
Cudjo: Disse brack man, disse one, disse one, disse one, come from

---

[7] J. D. Herlein, *Beschryvinge van de volksplantinge Zuriname* (Leeuwarden, 1718), pp. 121-123. Herlein gives the Negro English dialogues in Dutch orthography. I have retranscribed these sentences in the kind of spelling which his English contemporaries would have used in order to show better the relationship between the Surinam dialect and the other examples. In the Dutch spelling, these sentences appear as *My belle wel. Jou wantje sie don pinkinine?*, and *Jo wantje gaeu wakke lange mie?*

[8] This citation also occurs in Krapp, and with others in Richard Walser, "Negro Dialect in Eighteenth-Century American Drama," *American Speech XXX* (1955), pp. 269-276.

	Hamton, disse one, disse one, come from Nawfok, me come from Nawfok too.
Kidnapper:	Very well, what was your master's name?
Cudjo:	Me massa name Cunney Tomsee.
Kidnapper:	Colonel Thompson—eigh?
Cudjo:	Eas, massa, Cunney Tomsee.
Kidnapper:	Well then I'll make you a major—and what's your name?
Cudjo:	Me massa cawra me Cudjo.

Again, the enclitic vowels (e.g., *disse*) and the subject pronoun *me* are prominent features of the Negro dialect. In the sentence *Me massa name Cunney Tomsee* "My master's name is Colonel Thompson," both the verb "to be" and the standard English possessive suffix *-s* are absent. Incidentally, Cudjo's construction is strikingly similar to sentences like *My sister name Mary* which are used by many American Negroes today.

One possible explanation why this kind of pidginized English was so widespread in the New World, with widely separated varieties resembling each other in so many ways, is that it did not originate in the New World as isolated and accidentally similar instances of random pidginization, but rather originated as a *lingua franca* in the trade centers and slave factories on the West African coast.[9] It is likely that at least some Africans already knew this pidgin English when they came to the New World, and that the common colonial policy of mixing slaves of various tribal origins forced its rapid adoption as a plantation *lingua franca.*

In the course of the eighteenth century, some significant changes took place in the New World Negro population, and these had their effect on language behavior. For one thing, the number of Negroes born in the New World came to exceed the number of those brought over from Africa. In the process, pidgin English became the creole mother-tongue of the new generations, and in some areas it has remained so to the present day.[10]

In the British colonies, the creole English of the uneducated Negroes and the English dialects of both the educated and uneducated white were close enough to each other (at least in vocabulary) to allow the speakers of each to communicate, although they were still different enough so that the whites could consider creole English to be "broken" or "corrupt" English and evidence, so many thought, of the mental limitations of the Negro. But in Surinam, where the

[9] See, for example, Basil Davidson, *Black Mother; The Years of the African Slave Trade* (Boston: Little, Brown and Co., 1961), particularly p. 218.

[10] In the West Indies, creole English is usually called *patois*, while in Surinam it is called *Taki-Taki.* In the United States, the only fairly "pure" creole English left today is Gullah, spoken along the coast of South Carolina.

European settlers spoke Dutch, creole English was regarded more objectively. In fact, no less than two language courses specifically designed to teach creole English to Dutch immigrants were published before the close of the eighteenth century.[11]

Another change which took place in the New World Negro population primarily during the course of the eighteenth century was the social cleavage of the New World-born generations into underprivileged field hands (a continuation of the older, almost universal lot of the Negro slave) and privileged domestic servant. The difference in privilege usually meant, not freedom instead of bondage, but rather freedom from degrading kinds of labor, access to the "big house" with its comforts and "civilization," and proximity to the prestigious "quality" whites, with the opportunity to imitate their behavior (including their speech) and to wear their clothes. In some cases, privilege included the chance to get an education and, in a very few, access to wealth and freedom. In both the British colonies and the United States, Negroes belonging to the privileged group were soon able to acquire a more standard variety of English than the creole of the field hands, and those who managed to get a decent education became speakers of fully standard and often elegant English. This seems to have become the usual situation by the early 1800s, and remained so through the Civil War. In Caroline Gilman's *Recollections of a Southern Matron* (New York, 1838), the difference between field-hand creole (in this case, Gullah) and domestic servant dialect is evident in a comparison of the gardener's "He tief one sheep—he run away las week, cause de overseer gwine for flog him" with Dina's "'Scuse me, missis, I is gitting hard o' hearing, and yes is more politer dan no" (page 254). A more striking contrast between the speech of educated and uneducated Negroes occurs in a novel written in the 1850s by an American Negro who had traveled extensively through the slave states. In Chapter XVII, part of the exchange between Henry, an educated Negro traveler, and an old "aunty" goes as follows:[12]

> "Who was that old man who ran behind your master's horse?"
> "Dat Nathan, my husban'."
> "Do they treat him well, aunty?"
> "No, chile, wus an' any dog, da beat 'im foh little an nothin'."
> "Is uncle Nathan religious?"

[11] These were Pieter van Dijk, *Nieuwe en nooit bevoorens geziende onderwijzinge in het Bastert Engels, of Neeger Engels* (Amsterdam, undated, but probably 1780), and G. C. Weygandt, *Gemeenzame leerwijze om het Basterd of Neger-Engelsch op een gemakkelijke wijze te leeren verstaan en sprecken* (Paramaribo, 1798).

[12] Martin R. Delany, *Blake; or the Huts of America*, published serially in *The Anglo-African Magazine* (1859). The quotation is from Vol. I, No. 6 (June 1859), p. 163.

"Yes, chile, ole man an' I's been sahvin' God dis many day, fo yeh baun! Wen any on 'em in de house git sick, den da sen foh "uncle Nathan" come pray foh dem; "uncle Nathan" mighty good den!"

After the Civil War, with the abolition of slavery, the breakdown of the plantation system, and the steady increase in education for poor as well as affluent Negroes, the older field-hand creole English began to lose many of its creole characteristics, and take on more and more of the features of the local white dialects and of the written language. Yet, this process has not been just one way. For if it is true that the speech of American Negroes has been strongly influenced by the speech of whites with whom they came into contact, it is probably also true that the speech of many whites has been influenced in some ways by the speech of Negroes.[13]

Over the last two centuries, the proportion of American Negroes who speak a perfectly standard variety of English has risen from a small group of privileged house slaves and free Negroes to persons numbering in the hundreds of thousands, and perhaps even millions. Yet there is still a sizeable number of American Negroes—undoubtedly larger than the number of standard-speaking Negroes—whose speech may be radically nonstandard. The nonstandard features in the speech of such persons may be due in part to the influence of the nonstandard dialects of whites with whom they or their ancestors have come in contact, but they also may be due to the survival of creolisms from the older Negro field-hand speech of the plantations. To insure their social mobility in modern American society, these nonstandard speakers must undoubtedly be given a command of standard English; that point was made in the early part of this paper. In studying nonstandard Negro dialects and teaching standard English in terms of them, however, both the applied linguist and the language teacher must come to appreciate the fact that even if certain nonstandard Negro dialect patterns do not resemble the dialect usage of American whites, or even those of the speakers of remote British dialects, they may nevertheless be as old as African and European settlement in the New World, and therefore quite widespread and well established. On various occasions, I have pointed out that many speakers of nonstandard American Negro dialects make a grammatical and semantic distinction by means of be, illustrated by such constructions as he busy "He is busy (momentarily)" or he workin' "he is working (right now)" as opposed to he be busy "he is (habitually) busy" or he be workin' "he is working (steadily)," which the gram-

---

[13] See Raven I. McDavid, Jr., and Virginia Glenn McDavid, "The Relationship of the Speech of American Negroes to the Speech of Whites," *American Speech* XXVI (1951), pp. 3-17.

mar of standard English is unable to make.[14] Even this distinction goes back well over a century. One observer in the 1830s noted a request by a slave for a permanent supply of soap as "(If) Missis only give we, we be so so clean forever," while *be* is absent in a subsequent report of someone's temporary illness with "She jist sick for a little while."[15]

Once educators who are concerned with the language problems of the disadvantaged come to realize that nonstandard Negro dialects represent a historical tradition of this type, it is to be hoped that they will become less embarrassed by evidence that these dialects are very much alike throughout the country while different in many ways from the nonstandard dialects of whites, less frustrated by failure to turn nonstandard Negro dialect speakers into standard English speakers overnight, less impatient with the stubborn survival of Negro dialect features in the speech of even educated persons, and less zealous in proclaiming what is "right" and what is "wrong." If this happens, then applied linguists and educators will be able to communicate with the nonstandard-speaking Negro child. The problem will then be well on its way toward a solution.

[14] See, for example, *The Florida FL Reporter*, Vol. 4, No. 2 (Winter 1965-1966), p. 25.

[15] Frances Anne Kemble, *Journal of a Residence on a Georgian Plantation in 1838-1839* (New York, 1862). The first quotation is from page 52, and the second is from page 118.

William A. Stewart

CONTINUITY AND CHANGE IN AMERICAN NEGRO DIALECTS

In a previous article on the history of American Negro dialects[1] I cited examples of the kind of literary and comparative evidence which exists for determining earlier stages of these dialects, and which practically forces the conclusion that the linguistic assimilation of the Afro-American population to the speech patterns of English-

[1] William A. Stewart, "Sociolinguistic Factors in the History of American Negro Dialects" *The Florida FL Reporter*, Vol. 5, No. 2 (Spring 1967). [See p. 45 in this book.]

speaking American whites was neither as rapid nor as complete as some scholars have supposed.[2] Of the Negro slaves who constituted the field labor force on North American plantations up to the mid-nineteenth century, even many who were born in the New World spoke a variety of English which was in fact a true creole language—differing markedly in grammatical structure from those English dialects which were brought directly from Great Britain, as well as from New World modifications of these in the mouths of descendants of the original white colonists.[3] And, although this creole English subsequently underwent modification in the direction of the more prestigious British-derived dialects, the merging process was neither instantaneous nor uniform. Indeed, the nonstandard speech of present-day American Negroes still seems to exhibit structural traces of a creole predecessor, and this is probably a reason why it is in some ways more deviant from standard English than is the nonstandard speech of even the most uneducated American whites.

For the teacher, this means that such "Negro" patterns as the "zero copula,"[4] the "zero possessive,"[5] or "undifferentiated pro-

[2] E.g., "The Negroes born in this country invariably used, according to these records, good English." Allen Walker Read, "The Speech of Negroes in Colonial America," *The Journal of Negro History*, Vol. 24, No. 3 (the quote is from page 258). The records which Read refers to are for the most part runaway slave advertisements published before the American Revolution. Of course, the evidence which they supply on slave speech is indirect (i.e., they give impressions of the particular slave's competence in English, but no examples of that English), since the information was merely intended to help identify the runaway. If these indirect records say what Read interprets them as saying, then they are certainly at variance with what direct evidence (quotations in slave dialect) is available from the same period. Furthermore, the far larger number of attestations of slave speech during the nineteenth century which show widespread use of nonstandard dialect, together with a similar situation observable today, would mean that American Negro speech generally became less standard after that first generation of American-born slaves. Needless to say, such a process would be difficult to explain either structurally or historically. The trouble with Read's conclusion seems to be that, in interpreting such advertisements, he did not consider the possibility that in the parlance of slave owners a term like "good English" might have meant something very different when applied to Negroes than it would have if applied to whites. Indications that this was probably the case seem to exist in the advertisements quoted on pp. 252-253.

[3] The Gullah (or Geechee) dialect, spoken by many Negroes along the South Atlantic coast, appears to be a fairly direct descendant of the older kind of plantation creole.

[4] The term "zero copula" refers to the absence of an explicit predicating verb in certain dialect constructions, where standard English has such a verb (usually in the present tense). Compare nonstandard Negro dialect *He old, Dey runnin'*, and *She a teacher* with standard English "He is old," "They are running," and "She is a teacher."

[5] The term "zero possessive" refers to the absence of an explicit suffix in noun-noun constructions, where standard English has such a suffix. Compare nonstandard Negro dialect *My fahver frien'* with standard English "My father's friend."

nouns"[6] should not be ascribed to greater carelessness, laziness, or stupidity on the part of Negroes, but rather should be treated as what they really are—language patterns which have been in existence for generations and which their present users have acquired, from parent and peer, through a perfectly normal kind of language-learning process.[7]

Since the main purpose of the earlier article was to document the use of creole English by native-born American Negroes during the colonial and ante-bellum periods, almost nothing was said about the course of Negro dialects since Emancipation. But, as anyone can see who compares written samples of Negro dialect from around the Civil War with Negro dialect today, there have been changes. And, equally interesting, one can also see that there are still many similarities between the two. An overview of the interacting processes of continuity and change in American Negro dialects as they relate to one important aspect of language variation—grammatical structure—will help educators to put the classroom language problems of today's disadvantaged Negro children into a clearer perspective.

One of the more important changes which have occurred in American Negro dialects during the past century has been the almost complete decreolization of both their functional and lexical vocabulary. Although this process actually began long before the Civil War (particularly in areas with a low proportion of Negroes to whites), the breakdown of the plantation system apparently accelerated it considerably, even in the coastal areas of South Carolina and Georgia. In the process, overt creolisms which were so common in early attes-

[6]The term "undifferentiated pronoun" refers to the use of the same pronoun form for both subject and object, and sometimes for possession as well. The pronominal form used may be derived from either the standard English object form, or the subject form. Compare such nonstandard forms as *Him know we*, *Him know us*, (beside *He know us*) with the standard English "He knows us" to which they are equivalent. Or compare *He fahver* (beside *His fahver*) and *We house* (beside *Our house*) with standard English "His father" and "Our house."

[7]If the term "Negro dialect" is understood to refer to nonstandard varieties of American English whose more unique (i.e., nonwhite and non-British) structural features are simply due to the historical influence of an earlier plantation creole, then it should be clear that such a term does not imply any direct genetic determination of speech patterns, in spite of its ethnic reference. The "Negro" in "Negro dialect" is merely a recognition of the fact that the creole predecessor for such structural features was itself the result of African migration to and acculturation in Anglo-Saxon America, and that those present-day dialects which show the greatest influence from such a creole are precisely those which are used by the descendants of the Negro field hands who originally spoke it. In addition, the speech of American Negroes is often characterized by special kinds of syllable and breath dynamics, as well as unique uses of pitch, stress and volume. But even these language habits are always socially learned and transmitted ones, although it is difficult to tell whether they represent survivals of African speech habits, creole speech habits, or are more recent innovations. That they are not the product of any special Negro vocal physiology should be obvious from the fact that some whites can mimic such features quite well, while there are some Negroes in whose speech the same features are not normally present.

tations of slave speech, such as *been* for marking past action (with no basic distinction between preterite and perfect), undifferentiated pronouns for subject and object (e.g., *me*, *him*, and *dem* also as subject pronouns and *we* also as an object pronoun), a single subject pronoun form (usually *him* or *he*) for masculine, feminine and neuter in the third person singular, *-um* (or *-am*) as a general third person (all genders and numbers) object suffix, *no* as a verbal negator, and *for* as an infinitive marker became quite rare in even the more nonstandard speech of Negroes born after Emancipation.[8]

However, the speed and thoroughness with which the plantation fieldhand dialects were thus made more "proper" varied both according to the region and according to the social characteristics of the speakers themselves. Because people learn most of their language forms from others, the change took place more rapidly and completely in areas where speakers (white or Negro) of more-or-less standard varieties of English were present in numbers than it did in areas with a high concentration of field laborers. On the other hand, because children generally are more affected by the language usage of other children than by that of grownups, and because lower-class child peer groups tend to remain rather isolated from the stylistic innovations of adult discourse, the change took place more slowly and less thoroughly in the speech of young children than it did in that of adolescents and adults.

The result of this uneven "correction" of the older plantation dialects was that, while they seemed to have died out by the end of the nineteenth century (particularly outside the South Atlantic

---

[8] Judging from the literary treatment of Negro dialect, these features were characteristic of the nonstandard speech of even New England Negroes up to the close of the eighteenth century. Within the first decades of the nineteenth century, however, the northern limit of their common occurrence in adult speech appears to have receded to the Delaware region, and to somewhere in the Carolinas by the middle of the same century. Of course, most of these creolisms still occur in Gullah—at least sporadically. And it is likely that the *for to* infinitives of some Deep South Negro dialects are the result of incomplete decreolization (the adding of noncreole *to*, without giving up the creole *for*), rather than the borrowing of a white nonstandard dialect pattern, as some might suppose. In the first place, such white dialects (Appalachia, Georgia, etc.) usually have a contrast between *to* and *for to*, e.g., *I come to see it* (i.e., "It dawned on me") vs. *I come for to see it* ("I came in order to see it"), while many Negro dialects in which *for to* occurs do not make such a distinction. In the second place, there is piecemeal evidence of the addition of *to* after *for* along the South Atlantic coast, where the change has been relatively recent. For example, in *Drums and Shadows: Survival Studies Among the Georgia Coastal Negroes* (Athens, Ga.: 1940, p. 144) a team of the Georgia Writers' Project interviewed an old lady (then approximately one hundred years old) who, speaking of an African-born slave whom she knew in her youth, recalled "I membuh he say 'Lemme cook sumpm fuh nyam.' He mean sumpm fuh to eat." Notice also the decreolization of the Gullah and Caribbean Creole English verb *nyam* "to eat." In some areas, the changeover was not so complete, cf. a literary reflection of a Gullah Negro's alternation between the same two verbs in Ambrose E. Gonzales, *The Captain: Stories of the Black Border* (Columbia, S.C.: The State Co., 1924, p. 149), "You hab mout' fuh nyam da' haa'd hoecake you juntlemun gi' you fuh eat."

coastal area and the Mississippi Basin), juvenile versions of them actually continued to survive in many Negro speech communities as "baby talk" or "small-boy talk."[9] That is, the older nonstandard (and sometimes even creole-like) dialect features remained in use principally by younger children in Negro speech-communities—being learned from other young children, to be given up later in life when "small-boy talk" was no longer appropriate to a more mature status.[10] And even though the adult dialects which these child dialects were ontogenetically given up for were also structurally nonstandard and identifiably Negro in most cases, they were still more standard— enough, at least, so that conspicuous retentions of child-dialect forms in the speech of an adult could sometimes result in the accusation that he or she was "talking like a child" or simply "talking bad."[11]

[9] The impression that the rustic and creole features of the older plantation dialects died out entirely during this period is easy to get, considering that the speech of children hardly appears at all in the records of folklorists or dialectologists, or even in the fictional use of dialect, since the main concern of the social scientist and the novelist alike has been the adult. Evidence that the older dialects have in fact survived in the speech of children is only now coming to light through recent studies of present-day Negro speech communities. See William A. Stewart "Urban Negro Speech: Sociolinguistic Factors Affecting English Teaching" in Roger W. Shuy, editor, *Social Dialects and Language Learning* (Champaign, Ill.: National Council of Teachers of English, 1965), particularly pp. 16-18, and J. L. Dillard, "Negro Children's Dialect in the Inner City" *The Florida FL Reporter*, Vol. 5, No. 3 (Fall 1967). It would seem that the preservation of a more conservative dialect by young children in communities where the older language forms are being encroached upon by imported ones is not limited to Negro communities. During a recent sociolinguistic survey of the Appalachian region, I found full-fledged mountain dialect still being used by pre-school-age white children in communities where it had been abandoned by all but the oldest adults.

[10] Like Dillard, I feel that this constitutes the most plausible explanation of the sporadic but not infrequent occurrence in the speech of lower-class Negro children of such "mistakes" as *been* as a general past-time marker (e.g., *He been hit me*), pronominal forms which are undifferentiated for case or gender (e.g., *Me gonna try* and *He out playin'*—the latter said in reference to a girl), etc., since these same features were quite normal in older forms of Negro dialect (and still are in Gullah) and since there is, after all, an uninterrupted chain of language transmission from those earlier speakers to Negro children of the present day. Because some of the features are similar (at least superficially) to ones which are characteristic at certain stages of language development in virtually all English-speaking children, most specialists have attributed the Negro child patterns to development causes. However, since the Negro patterns are sometimes used by children who are well beyond the developmental stage (which normally ends at age 3.6 or 4 for whites), this would imply that Negroes develop linguistically more slowly than do whites. And, since there are even Negro octogenarians who use these forms, one would be forced to the absurd conclusion that some Negroes must not have completed the developmental process at all.

[11] In Washington, D.C., I know of an adolescent Negro who for some reason had retained many child-dialect features in his speech. His peers characterized his speech by saying that "He talk just like a small boy." And in her *Folk-Lore of the Sea Islands, South Carolina* (Cambridge, Mass.: American Folklore Society, 1923), Elsie Clews Parson gives a Negro folk-tale (No. 148, The Girl Who Learned to Talk Proper) in which the speech of a young lady who was said to "talk very bad" is marked by the use of creole pronominal forms (e.g., "Me ain' col', suh!"). It is interesting that the conclusion of this tale also shows popular recognition of the effect of out-migration on speech habits, since the same girl finally did "learn to talk proper" when an outsider married her and "kyarried her to his country."

Interestingly enough, the use of an older, more conservative form of Negro dialect as child speech was not always limited to Negroes. In the Old South, many upper-class whites went through a similar linguistic metamorphosis from the nonstandard dialect of their Negro playmates to the relatively standard English of their adult station in life. As John Bennett described the situation for the Charlestonian aristocracy of his day:

It is true that, up to the age of four, approximately, the children of the best families, even in town, are apt to speak an almost unmodified *Gullah*, caught from brown playmates and country bred nurses; but at that age the refinement of cultivation begins, and "the flowers o' the forest are a' weed awa!"[12]

It was undoubtedly in this manner that such white Southern writers as Joel C. Harris and Ambrose E. Gonzales first acquired their knowledge of the Negro dialects which they immortalized in print.[13]

Today, genteel Southern whites no longer learn nonstandard Negro dialects as children, since the social conditions which once prompted them to do so have now become part of history. In their pre-school childhood, however, many Negroes still learn and use such dialects, and although they may modify these in later life, few ever attain anything like the elegant standard English which was the famil-

[12] John Bennett, "Gullah: A Negro Patois" *The South Atlantic Quarterly*, Vol. 7 (Oct. 1908) and Vol. 8 (Jan. 1909), quote from Vol. 7, p. 339. This same process had evidently been going on for at least a century and a half before Bennett's time. It was noted during the first half of the eighteenth century by G. L. Campbell, a British traveler to the American colonies. "One Thing they are very faulty in, with regard to their Children," he wrote of the white planters in the July 1746 number of *The London Magazine*, "which is, that when young, they suffer them too much to prowl amongst the young Negroes, which insensibly causes them to imbibe their Manners and broken Speech." Quoted in Allen Walker Read, "British Recognition of American Speech in the Eighteenth Century," *Dialect Notes*, Vol. 6, Part 6 (July 1933), p. 329. Since even the most aristocratic British children undoubtedly picked up nonstandard English or Scottish dialects from children of the servant class, it must have been the "broken" (i.e., creolized) character of colonial Negro speech which Campbell found so disagreeable in the North American situation.

[13] Elsewhere ("Urban Negro Speech . . .," *loc. cit.*, p. 13, fn. 7), I have taken Ambrose E. Gonzales to task for his racistic explanation of some of the structural characteristics of the Gullah dialect. At the same time, one can see how he would come to such a point of view, since he was obviously unaware of pidginization as a linguistic phenomenon, and therefore unable to account scientifically for its operation in the speech of the Gullah Negroes. In addition, a genetic explanation of language differences fitted quite comfortably into the rhetoric of the caste-cloven society of which Gonzales was so much a product. This theoretical weakness notwithstanding, Gonzales' literary rendition of Gullah was superb. Considering the accuracy of his dialect phonology and syntax, and the ease with which he handled subtle dialect differences and even individual switching behavior, he can certainly qualify as America's greatest dialect writer. For a similar opinion of Gonzales, see Ann Sullivan Haskell *The Representation of Gullah-influenced Dialect in Twentieth Century South Carolina Prose: 1922-1930* (University of Pennsylvania Ph.D. Dissertation, 1964), pp. 238-241.

ial and social heritage of the older white aristocrats. Yet, when they enter the standard English milieu of the school, Negro children from this kind of language background are expected to compete linguistically with children (usually white) who have known and used standard English all their lives. Of course, a few of these Negro children do succeed, not because of good teaching, but because of their own exceptional abilities. But a far greater proportion of these children—the average ones, as well as the few who are truly below average—fail conspicuously. And, because there is obviously some sort of ethnic correlation between pupil success and failure in newly integrated school situations, the embarrassed educational establishment and the frustrated public enter into a crisis relationship. Some whites charge (privately, at least) that the schools are being given the impossible task of teaching unteachable Negroes. And some Negroes charge (not so privately) that white educators are involved in a conspiracy to deliberately keep Negro children from learning. Parents protest blindly, and school administrators run helter-skelter, holding councils of despair with colleagues who understand the problem no better.

A basic reason why so many Negro children fail in school is not that they are unteachable, but that they are not being taught efficiently or fairly. And this fact may have little or nothing to do with a white conspiracy against integrated schools. Rather, it may be the result of a far less deliberate yet equally devastating insensitivity of the educational process to the social and cultural characteristics of the school population. This is probably nowhere more striking than in the area of language since, as speakers largely of nonstandard dialects which are among the most deviant from standard English now being used in America, many Negro children are burdened at every turn with achievement barriers in the form of extra (and uncompensated for) language learning requirements. For example, all children are expected to learn how to read in school. But, for many Negro pupils, the problem is made more difficult by the fact that they are unfamiliar, not only with the sound-spelling-meaning correspondences of many of the words, but even with the grammatical patterns which these words make up in their reading lessons. Consequently, the reading achievement of these children becomes dependent upon their own success in deciphering standard English sentence structure. And the same type of problem is reflected in other subject areas in the schools. The irony, here, is that the traditional educational system is itself creating much of the pedagogical disadvantagement of its linguistically different pupils by requiring them to accomplish, on their own, as much again as middle-class pupils from a standard English background are expected to accomplish with expert help.

In many ways, the plight of the Negro child who enters school speaking a nonstandard dialect is similar to that of a foreign-language-speaking child entering an American school. And, while it can be argued that no Negro dialect is as different from standard English as is, say, Spanish, this does not necessarily mean that the linguistically different Negro's task is that much easier. For, while the boundaries between a full-fledged foreign language and English are usually clear cut (the Spanish-speaking child, for example, will usually know at any given point whether Spanish or English is being used, and so will the teacher), the many similarities between any Negro dialect and standard English makes it difficult to tell exactly where one leaves off and the other begins.[14] Thus, even the linguistic similarities between a nonstandard dialect and standard English can be pedagogically and psychologically disadvantageous, since they can camouflage functional differences between the two linguistic systems. Furthermore, while a wealth of linguistic knowledge and pedagogical knowhow is currently brought to bear on the language problems of the child who speaks a foreign language such as Spanish, no similar competences have yet been developed to help the child who speaks a nonstandard dialect, although his needs are just as great—and his numbers greater. Considering his educational prospects as they stand at present, the linguistically different Negro child might well say "I look down de road an' de road so lonesome."

Although English teachers, speech therapists, and other language-oriented educators are now dedicating themselves more than ever to the task of helping disadvantaged children—and especially disadvantaged Negro children—acquire proficiency in standard English, very few of these dedicated professionals have demonstrated any real understanding of the language characteristics of the communities from which these children come. For their part, teachers of English to Spanish-speaking Mexican, Puerto Rican or Cuban children know that an understanding of the structure of Spanish will give insights into the problem which such children have with English, and these teachers would be shocked by any suggestion that a comparative approach to the language of the school and the language of the child is unnecessary. In contrast, teachers of English to disadvantaged Negro children have generally remained aloof from the serious study of nonstandard Negro dialect.

This lack of interest on the part of many English teachers in the nonstandard language of Negro children is in large part the product of a normative view of language which has long been the mainstay of

[14] Because the structural relationships which hold between the two "dialects" in such a case are in part like those between completely foreign languages and in part like those between two style levels of a single language, I have coined the term "quasi-foreign language situation" to describe it. See my "Foreign Language Teaching Methods in Quasi-Foreign Language Situations" in William A. Stewart, editor, *Non-Standard Speech and the Teaching of English* (Washington, D.C.: Center for Applied Linguistics, 1964).

traditional teacher training. Either overtly or by implication, the
teacher-to-be is taught that the kind of usage which is indicated in
grammar books, dictionaries and style manuals (and which is presum--
ably followed by educated speakers and writers) represents a maximum of structural neatness, communicative efficiency, esthetic taste
and logical clarity. Once this normative view has been inculcated in
the prospective teacher (and it must be admitted that popular beliefs
about "correct" and "incorrect" language practically guarantee this)
then the teacher will quite naturally regard departures from the norms
of standard English as departures from structure, clarity, taste, and
even logic itself.[15]

Of course, there have always been exceptional teachers who
have seen that chronic deviations from standard English usage on the
part of their pupils may indicate simply their normal use of some
other variety of English, with its own structure and logic. William
Francis Allen was an early example of a teacher who not only discovered this, but came to realize that even apparent "ignorance" in
coping with logical or experiential problems could sometimes be
traced to mere difficulty with the language in which the problems
were posed. He recorded the following incident, which occurred
while he was teaching Gullah Negro children on Port Royal Island,
South Carolina, during the Civil War.

I asked a group of boys one day the color of the sky. Nobody could tell me.
Presently the father of one of them came by, and I told him their ignorance,
repeating my question with the same result as before. He grinned: "Tom, how
sky stan'?" "Blue," promptly shouted Tom.[16]

But in attempting to teach standard English to children who
speak a nonstandard dialect, even those teachers who understand that
there is a language conflict involved, and who would accordingly like
to borrow techniques from foreign-language teaching methodology,
are likely to find their efforts hampered by too limited a knowledge
of the structural characteristics of whatever nonstandard dialect the
children speak. For, in all too many cases, the best pedagogical grasp
of the structural features of a particular nonstandard dialect will consist of little more than a list of certain "folk" pronunciations and an
awareness of the use of such grammatical shibboleths as *ain't* and the

[15] Linguistic and cultural relativists will be pleased to learn that the dialect tables
have been turned on the normativists at least once. In his essay, John Bennett
(*op. cit.*, Vol. 7, p. 340) reports that Gullah-speaking Negroes passed judgment
on visiting Yankees with "Dey use dem mout' so funny!"

[16] William Francis Allen, Charles Pickard Ware, and Lucy McKim Garrison, *Slave
Songs of the United States* (New York: 1867), p. xxvii. What the father of the
boy knew was that, in Gullah, observable characteristics are usually indicated by
means of the verb *stan'* (or *'tan'*) which can be translated roughly as "look,"
"seem," or "appear."

double negative. Unfortunately, this kind of superficial knowledge of the structural details of the speech of disadvantaged children will not only prevent the teacher or therapist from understanding the reasons for many of these children's "mistakes" in standard English, but it is also likely to lead to an inadvertent lumping together of children who speak different dialects (and therefore who have different kinds of problems with standard English) under a generalized remedial English approach which would not take these differences into account. In the likely event that both Negroes and whites make up the disadvantaged student population of a school system, this egalitarian approach to their language problems may prove almost irresistible in the face of a particularly unsophisticated kind of social liberalism, currently in vogue among educators, which regards it as a manifestation of racism to entertain even the most well qualified hypothesis that differences in ethnicity (such as being "white" or "Negro" in America) might possibly correlate with differences in behavior (in language usage, for example). In fact, so strong is the hold upon today's educators of this sociologically simplistic philosophy, with its "all children are the same" credo, that many educators and teachers even find uncomfortable the anthropologist's contention that correlations between ethnicity and behavior are not only possible but probable, when one considers that ethnicity is more of a social phenomenon than a physiological one, and that so much of human behavior is socially conditioned rather than genetically determined. And instead of seeing the chronic failure of disadvantaged Negroes in integrated school situations as a strong indication that this "sameness" credo is inadequate and counter-productive in terms of the real goals of education, many educators let such unpleasant realities force them into clinging all the more blindly and tenaciously to their simplistic views of the matter.

But the failure to perceive structural differences between the nonstandard dialects of American Negroes and those of American whites has not been unique to English teachers and speech therapists. Some prominent dialectologists also have claimed that Negro dialects represent, at the most, a minor statistical skewing of white dialect features.[17] And still others have passed over the subject altogether.[18]

One further reason why both language teachers and dialectologists have failed to appreciate the extent to which nonstandard Negro dialects may differ from nonstandard white dialects (even in the Deep South) may simply be that such differences now remain mostly in syntax (i.e., grammatical patterns and categories) rather than in vocabulary or lexicophonology (i.e., word forms), and are thus not normally uncovered by the word-comparison techniques which dialectologists and nonlinguists rely on so heavily. Yet, a comparison of the grammatical details of white and Negro nonstandard dialects suggests a very different kind of historical relationship than is evident from a comparison of words alone. This can be illustrated by the comparison of a standard English (STE) conjunctive sentence like "We were eating—and drinking, too" together with its equivalents in representative varieties of Southern white nonstandard basilect (WNS), Negro nonstandard basilect (NNS), and Gullah basilect (GUL):[19]

> STE: We were eating—and drinking, too.
> WNS: We was eatin'—an' drinkin', too.
> NNS: We was eatin'—an' we drinkin', too.
> GUL: We bin duh nyam—en' we duh drink, too.

[17] As one dialect geographer expressed his view of the matter, "the range of variants is the same in Negro and in white speech, though the statistical distribution of variants has been skewed by the American caste system." Raven I. McDavid, Jr., "American Social Dialects" *College English*, Vol. 26, No. 4 (January 1965), p. 258, fn. 7. In an even more recent article, McDavid rejects the idea of a pidgin or creole background for American Negro dialects, saying "To a naive social scientist, what is generally known about the operations of the domestic slave trade should be sufficient to refute such an argument." Raven I. McDavid, Jr., "Needed Research in Southern Dialects" in Edgar T. Thompson, editor, *Perspectives on the South: Agenda for Research* (Durham, N.C.: Duke University Press, 1967), p. 122. In view of the numerous attestations of the actual use of pidgin and creole forms of English by American Negro slaves in the contemporary literature (see my "Sociolinguistic Factors in the History of American Negro Dialects" *loc. cit.*, for a few references), it is difficult to imagine any historical basis for McDavid's statements. Since he must have seen at least the reprintings of some of these in scholarly books and articles, it can only be that he has not considered the linguistic implications of their rather non-European grammatical structure. Furthermore, if there is anything in what is known about the slave trade, slave life, or plantation social stratification in America which would call into question these early attestations of pidgin and creole English, it is strange that it has never been articulated in such standard works on American Negro slavery as Philip Alexander Bruce, *Economic History of Virginia in the Seventeenth Century* (New York: The MacMillan Co., 1895); Ulrich B. Phillips, *American Negro Slavery* (New York: D. Appleton and Co., 1918) and his *Life and Labor in the Old South* (Boston: Little, Brown and Co., 1929); Marcus William Jernegan, *Laboring and Dependent Classes in Colonial America: 1607-1783* (University of Chicago Press, 1931); Frederick Bancroft, *Slave-Trading in the Old South* (Baltimore: J. H. Furst Co., 1931); Kenneth M. Stampp, *The Peculiar Institution: Slavery in the Ante-Bellum South* (New York: Alfred A. Knopf, Inc., 1956); Herbert S. Klein, *Slavery in the Americas: A Comparative Study of Virginia and Cuba* University of Chicago Press, 1967).

[18] None of the four recent publications on American dialects which have been written for the use of English teachers contain any substantive reference to Negro dialect—not even a simple statement of the historical and definitional issues involved in the concept. This omission is probably due to the tacit acceptance on the part of the various authors of the theory that most Negro speech is identical to Southern varieties of white speech, and therefore that the description of the latter in their manuals takes care of Negro speech as well. These four publications are: Jean Malmstrom and Annabel Ashley, *Dialects—USA* (Champaign, Ill.: National Council of Teachers of English, 1963); Jean Malmstrom, *Language in Society* (New York: The Hayden Book Co., 1965); Carroll E. Reed, *Dialects of American English* (Cleveland: World Publishing Co., 1967); Roger W. Shuy, *Discovering American Dialects* (Champaign, Ill.: National Council of Teachers of English, 1967).

[19] The term *basilect* refers to that variety of a particular dialect which is structurally the most deviant from standard English. See William A. Stewart, "Urban Negro Speech: Sociolinguistic Factors Affecting English Teaching" *loc. cit.*, particularly pp. 15-17.

If one compares only the forms of the equivalent words in these sentences, NNS (Negro nonstandard) appears to be virtually identical to WNS (white nonstandard), with both of them about equally different from STE (standard English).[20] Judged by the same criteria, GUL (Gullah) appears to be radically different from all the others, including NNS.

Because of such word-form similarities and differences, many dialectologists have concluded that, while Gullah itself may be a creolized form of English (rather than a direct descendant of any British dialect or dialects), there is no evidence that other kinds of American Negro speech are related to it in any direct way.[21] For, according to the same kind of word-form comparisons, these represent little more than the use by Negroes of dialect patterns which are also used by (and presumably borrowed from) whites in the Deep South.

However, a comparison of the sentence structure of these dialects shows a somewhat different kind of relationship. In the foregoing equivalent sentences, this is evident in the treatment of the subject pronoun and the tense-marking auxiliary (or copula). For, although STE, WNS, NNS, and GUL can all repeat the subject pronoun and auxiliary in a conjunctive clause (e.g., STE "We were eating—and we were drinking, too"), this is not generally done in any of them. Instead, one or both will usually be omitted (provided, of course, that the subject and temporal referents remain the same). But in terms of what they omit, these dialects split along lines which are different from those indicated by word-form similarities and differences. Both STE and WNS normally omit both the subject pronoun and the auxiliary in a conjunctive clause, although the tense-marking auxiliary must be present if the subject is not omitted. But NNS, like GUL, often repeats the subject pronoun in a conjunctive clause while omitting the auxiliary—even when this indicates past tense.[22]

An example of the same phenomenon in American Negro speech at the beginning of the nineteenth century is to be found in A. B. Lindsley's play *Love and Friendship* (New York: 1807). A Negro

[20] The literary dialect spellings which I have used in these examples may well make the individual words in WNS and NNS seem more alike than they actually are when pronounced. But, for the sake of argument, I would just as soon allow for the possibility that some words might have identical phonological forms in the different dialects.

[21] This concession as to the creole nature of Gullah was largely forced upon an intensely Anglo-centric American dialect-studies tradition by Lorenzo Dow Turner's *Africanisms in the Gullah Dialect* (University of Chicago Press, 1949) which, though it concentrated more on African survivals than on creole influences and dealt more with naming practices than with linguistic structure, did at least make the point rather strongly that Gullah is a creolized form of English.

[22] Those who have had enough contact with Negro nonstandard dialects to know that constructions like *We tryin'* usually indicate the present tense (i.e., STE "We are trying") might assume that the superficially similar construction *we drinkin'*

says: "I tink dey bin like sich a man de boss, for dey like for be tumel 'bout." Side by side with *dey bin like* in the first clause is *dey like* in the second one, even though the context makes it reasonably clear that both mean "they liked."[23]

If, in such features as the omission of a redundant auxiliary (while retaining the redundant subject pronoun), Gullah and other nonstandard Negro dialects part company with standard English and nonstandard white dialects (of both America and Great Britain), they do have counterparts in a number of pidgin and creole forms of English which, though used far from the shores of the United States and in widely separated places, are all the legacy of the African slave trade. To illustrate how much these forms of English resemble Gullah and other nonstandard Negro dialects with respect to auxiliary omission, the same equivalent sentences are given in Jamaican Creole (JMC), Sranan (SRA), the creole English of Surinam in South America, and West African Pidgin English (WAP):[24]

JMC: We ben a nyam—an' we a drink, too.
SRA: We ben de nyang—en' we de dringie, too.
WAP: We bin de eat—an' we de dring, too.

in the NNS sentence *We was eatin'—an' we drinkin', too* also indicates the present tense—the whole thereby meaning "We were eating—and we are drinking, too" with an erroneous lack of tense agreement between the two clauses. Although it is true that *we drinkin'* does mean "we are drinking" in most circumstances (cf. NNS *We drinkin' right now*), in the sentence cited the phrase really represents *we was drinkin'* with the past tense marker *was* omitted. By the same token, GUL *we duh drink*, can mean "we are drinking" as well, but represents *we bin duh drink*, with the past tense marker *bin* omitted, in the sentence cited.

[23] Quoted in George Philip Krapp, *The English Language in America* (New York: The Century Co., 1925), Vol. I, pp. 258-259.

[24] For comparative purposes, I have written these languages in a spelling which is as close to that of standard English as the literary dialect spellings used in the preceding set of equivalent sentences. Scientific (phonemic) orthographies have been devised for these languages, however, and in them the same sentences would appear as: JMC *We ben a nyam—an we a dringk, tu;* SRA *we ben njam—en we de dringi, toe;* WAP *Wi bin de it—an we de dring, tu.* See Frederic G. Cassidy, *Jamaica Talk* (London: Macmillan Co., Ltd., 1961); Beryl L. Bailey, *Jamaican Creole Syntax* (Cambridge University Press, 1966); A. Donicie, *De Creolentaal van Suriname* (Paramaribo: Radhakishun and Co., 1959); Gouvernement van Suriname, Bureau Volkslectuur, *Woordenlijst van het Sranan-Tongo* (Paramaribo: N. V. Varekamp & Co., 1961); Gilbert D. Schneider, *West African Pidgin English* (Ph.D. Thesis, Hartford Seminary Foundation, 1966); David Dwyer, *An Introduction to West African Pidgin English* (African Studies Center, Michigan State University, 1967).

[25] The past tense markers in this series are *ben* (JMC, SRA) and *bin* (WAP), the latter having a common variant—*be.* The preverbal *a* in JMC is a modern reduction of an older *da*, obviously related historically to GUL *duh*, as well as to SRA and WAP *de.* In fact, the preverbal *a-* in some Southern Negro dialects (e.g., *he a-workin'*) may well derive from just such a source, rather than from the verbal prefix *a-* of many white dialects. This seems likely in view of the fact that, in those white dialects in which such a prefix is used functionally, there is usually a contrast between its presence and its absence (e.g., *he's workin'* "he is working within view" vs. *he's a-workin'* "he is off working somewhere"), while Negro dialects with preverbal *a-* use it like Gullah uses preverbal *duh*—for the simple durative. Finally, Gullah actually has *a* (or *uh*) as a variant of *duh*, especially after *bin.*

In addition to the grammatical correspondences, the word-form similarities of these languages with Gullah will be apparent.[25]

These correspondences are much too neat to be dismissed as mere accident. Rather, they seem to indicate that at least some of the syntactic features of American Negro dialects are neither skewings nor extensions of white dialect patterns, but are in fact structural vestiges of an earlier plantation creole, and ultimately of the original slave-trade pidgin English which gave rise to it.

This kind of evidence—existing in abundance for those who will admit it—calls for a complete reassessment of the relationships between British dialects, white American dialects, Negro American dialects (including Gullah), and the pidgin and creole English of Africa and the Caribbean. In particular, a new and more careful look at the question of American Negro dialects needs to be taken by those working within orthodox American dialectology—most of all by those who have made an almost exclusive use of American Dialect Atlas materials and techniques. High on the list of priorities for determining Negro and white dialect relationships should be: (1) the relationship between Gullah and other Negro dialects, and (2) the relationship between Negro dialects (other than Gullah) and white dialects. In such a reassessment, many new insights into the history of these relationships will be gained from studies of the syntax, not only of present-day dialects, but also of literary attestations of early Negro and white nonstandard dialect, and by comparative studies of European, pidgin, and creole dialects of English.

All-in-all, it looks very much like the word-form similarities between nonstandard Negro dialects and nonstandard white dialects are the result of a relatively superficial merging process, in which creole-speaking Negroes tried to make their "broken" (i.e., creole) English become more like that of the whites by means of minor pronunciation changes and vocabulary substitutions. But the creole grammatical patterns of these Negroes' speech, being less amenable to conscious manipulation, remained more resistant to this substitution process.[26] In an earlier article on urban Negro dialect in Washington,

---

[26] Even persons who are quite familiar with American Negro dialects may be led, by dissimilarities in word-forms, to overestimate the difference between them. For example, as keen an observer of dialect as E. C. L. Adams stated in *Nigger to Nigger* (New York: Charles Scribner's Sons, 1928), p. viii, that the speech of the Congaree Negroes of inland South Carolina was "absolutely distinct" from the coastal Gullah. Actually, the many striking syntactic similarities between the two dialects would suggest that the former is only a slightly de-creolized form of the latter. Observers of Gullah, from John Bennett on, have all remarked on how the older "pure" form of the language has been undergoing modification (i.e., decreolization), particularly in the cities and towns. Seeing this "modified Gullah" always as a new phenomenon, they never expressed any awareness of the possibility that they might have been watching a continuation of the same process which earlier gave rise to the contemporary forms of other American Negro dialects.

D.C., I pointed out how Negro children who reach school age speaking a radically nonstandard dialect often modify it in the direction of standard English in a similarly superficial fashion as they grow older.[27] It is interesting to consider that, in the language-socialization process of their individual lifetimes, many American Negroes may actually repeat something of the larger process of Negro dialect history.

Now, the pedagogical implications of a historical relationship of this kind between Negro and white nonstandard dialects and, more particularly, between nonstandard Negro dialects and standard English ought to be clear. For, if American Negro dialects have evolved in such a way that structural similarities with other dialects of American English (including standard English) are greatest at the superficial word-form level, then it is possible for these similarities to mask any number of grammatical differences between them. And the teacher, concentrating on the more obvious word-form differences, is quite likely to miss the grammatical differences in the process— thereby leaving them to persist as apparent malapropisms, awkward turns of phrase, and random "mistakes" in speech and composition through grade school, high school, and frequently even through higher education.

As the grammatical study of nonstandard Negro dialect progresses, it is quite probable that many more differences will be found between Negro and white speech patterns, and it may well turn out that at least some of these will also be traceable to a creole English, pidgin English, or even African language source. Of course, such discoveries are bound to cause embarrassment to those superficially liberal whites who will accept the Negro for what he is only if his behavioral patterns prove to be as European as their own, and they will be disquieting to those racial image-conscious Negroes who are so often preoccupied with the question "What will the white folks think?" But quite apart from whether he thinks they are a help or a hindrance in integration, good or bad for the Negro's racial image, the dedicated educator should welcome the discovery and formulation of such ethnically correlated dialect differences as do exist. For, only when they are taken into account in the teaching process will the linguistic cards cease to be stacked against the disadvantaged Negro pupil in the nation's classrooms.

[27] William A. Stewart, "Urban Negro Speech: Sociolinguistic Factors Affecting English Teaching" loc. cit., p. 17.

PART THREE

BLACK LANGUAGE TODAY

Ossie Davis

"THE ENGLISH LANGUAGE IS MY ENEMY"

I stand before you, a little nervous, afflicted to some degree with stage fright. Not because I fear you, but because I fear the subject.

The title of my address is, "Racism in American Life— Broad Perspectives of the Problem," or, "The English Language Is My Enemy."

In my speech I will define culture as the sum total of ways of living built up by a group of human beings and transmitted by one generation to another. I will define education as the act or process of imparting and communicating a culture, developing the powers of reasoning and judgment and generally preparing oneself and others intellectually for a mature life.

AN EDUCATION IN WORDS

I will define communication as the primary means by which the process of education is carried out.

I will say that language is the primary medium of communication in the educational process and, in this case, the English language. I will indict the English language as one of the prime carriers of racism from one person to another in our society and discuss how the teacher and the student, especially the Negro student, are affected by this fact.

The English language is my enemy.

Racism is a belief that human races have distinctive characteristics, usually involving the idea that one's own race is superior and has a right to rule others. Racism.

The English language is my enemy.

But that was not my original topic—I said that English was my goddamn enemy. Now why do I use "goddamn" to illustrate this aspect of the English language? Because I want to illustrate the sheer gut power of words. Words which control our action. Words like "nigger," "kike," "sheeny," "Dago," "black power"—words like this. Words we don't use in ordinary decent conversation, one to the other. I choose these words deliberately, not to flaunt my freedom before you. If you are a normal human being these words will have assaulted your senses, may even have done you physical harm, and if you so choose, you could have me arrested.

Those words are attacks upon your physical and emotional well being; your pulse rate is possibly higher, your breath quicker; there is perhaps a tremor along the nerves of your arms and your legs; sweat begins in the palms of your hands, perhaps. With these few words I have assaulted you. I have damaged you, and there is nothing you can possibly, possibly do to control your reactions—to defend yourself against the brute force of these words.

These words have a power over us; a power that we cannot resist. For a moment you and I have had our deepest physical reactions controlled, not by our own wills, but by words in the English language.

WHAT ROGET REVEALS

A superficial examination of Roget's *Thesaurus of the English Language* reveals the following facts: The word "whiteness" has 134 synonyms, 44 of which are favorable and pleasing to contemplate. For example: "purity," "cleanness," "immaculateness," "bright," "shiny," "ivory," "fair," "blonde," "stainless," "clean," "clear," "chaste," "unblemished," "unsullied," "innocent," "honorable," "upright," "just," "straightforward," "fair," "genuine," "trustworthy,"—and only 10 synonyms of which I feel to have been negative and then only in the mildest sense, such as "gloss-over," "whitewash," "gray," "wan," "pale," "ashen," etc.

The word "blackness" has 120 synonyms, 60 of which are distinctly unfavorable, and none of them even mildly positive. Among the offending 60 were such words as "blot," "blotch," "smut," "smudge," "sullied," "begrime," "soot," "becloud," "obscure," "dingy," "murky," "low-toned," "threatening," "frowning," "foreboding," "forbidding," "sinister," "baneful," "dismal," "thundery," "wicked," "malignant," "deadly," "unclean," "dirty," "unwashed," "foul," etc. In addition, and this is what really hurts, 20 of those words—and I exclude the villainous 60 above—are related directly to race, such as "Negro," "Negress," "nigger," "darkey," "blackamoor," etc.

"THINKING IS SUBVOCAL SPEECH"

If you consider the fact that thinking itself is subvocal speech (in other words, one must use words in order to think at all), you will appreciate the enormous trap of racial prejudgment that works on any child who is born into the English language.

Any creature, good or bad, white or black, Jew or Gentile, who uses the English language for the purposes of communication is willing to force the Negro child into 60 ways to despise himself, and the white child, 60 ways to aid and abet him in the crime.

Language is a means of communication. This corruption, this evil of racism, doesn't affect only one group. It doesn't take white to make a person a racist. Blacks also become inverted racists in the process.

A part of our function, therefore, as teachers, will be to reconstruct the English language. A sizeable undertaking, but one which we must undertake if we are to cure the problems of racism in our society.

DEMOCRATIZING ENGLISH

The English language must become democratic. It must become respectful of the possibilities of the human spirit. Racism is not only reflected in words relating to the color of Negroes. If you will examine some of the synonyms for the word Jew you will find that the adjectives and the verb of the word Jew are offensive. However, if you look at the word Hebrew you will see that there are no offensive connotations to the word.

When you understand and contemplate the small difference between the meaning of one word supposedly representing one fact, you will understand the power, good or evil, associated with the English language. You will understand also why there is a tremendous fight among the Negro people to stop using the word "Negro" altogether and substitute "Afro-American."

You will understand, even further, how men like Stokely Carmichael and Floyd McKissick can get us in such serious trouble by using two words together: Black Power. If Mr. McKissick and Mr. Carmichael had thought a moment and said Colored Power, there would have been no problem.

We come today to talk about education. Education is the only valid transmitter of American values from one generation to another. Churches have been used from time immemorial to teach certain values to certain people, but in America, as in no other country, it is the school that bears the burden of teaching young Americans to be Americans.

Schools define the meaning of such concepts as success. And education is a way out of the heritage of poverty for Negro people. It's the way we can get jobs.

THE ONE-BY-ONE ROUTE

Education is that which opens that golden door that was so precious to Emma Lazarus. But education in the past has basically been built on the theory that we could find those gifted individuals among the Negro people and educate them out of their poverty, out of their restricted conditions, and then, they would, in turn, serve to represent the best interests of the race; and if we concentrated on educating Negroes as individuals, we would solve the problem of discrimination by educating individual Negroes out of the problem. But I submit that that is a false and erroneous function and definition of education. We can no longer, as teachers, concentrate on finding the gifted black child in the slums or in the middle-class areas and giving him the best that we have. This no longer serves the true function of education if education indeed is to fulfill its mission to assist and perpetuate the drive of the Negro community to come into the larger American society on the same terms as all other communities have come.

Let us look for a brief moment at an article appearing in *Commentary* in February, 1964, written by the associate director of the American Jewish Committee. "What is now perceived as the revolt of the Negro amounts to this," he says. "The solitary Negro seeking admission into the white world through unusual achievement has been replaced by the organized Negro insisting upon a legitimate share for his group of the goods of American society. The white liberal, in turn, who, whether or not he is fully conscious of it, has generally conceived of progress in race relations as the one-by-one assimilation of deserving Negroes into the larger society, now finds himself confused and threatened by suddenly having to come to terms with an aggressive Negro community that wishes to enter en masse.

"Accordingly, in the arena of civil rights, the Negro revolution has tended to take the struggle out of the courts and bring it to the streets and the negotiating tables. Granting the potential for unprecedented violence that exists here, it must also be borne in mind that what the Negro people are now beginning to do, other ethnic minorities who brought to America their strong traditions of communal solidarity did before them. With this powerful asset, the Irish rapidly acquired political strength and the Jews succeeded in raising virtually an entire immigrant population into the middle class within a span of two generations. Viewed in this perspective, the Negroes are merely the last of America's significant ethnic minorities to achieve communal solidarity and to grasp the role of the informal group power structure in protecting the rights and advancing the opportunities of the individual members of the community."

LIBERAL "GRADUALISM"

Teachers have a very important function. They have before them the raw materials of the future. And if we were satisfied by the job that was being done in our country and in our culture it would not be necessary to call a protest conference. It would be necessary only to call a conference to celebrate.

I submit that racism is inherent in the English language because the language is an historic expression of the experience of a people; that racism, which is the belief that one group is superior to the other and has the right to set the standards for the other, is still one of the main spiritual policies of our country as expressed in the educational process.

Those of us who are concerned, those of us who are caught up, those of us who really want to be involved, must be prepared at this conference to tear aside our most private thoughts and prejudices, remembering that we have been taught them because we are all born to the English language.

Let us not feel personally guilty or personally responsible for the fact that we may not like Negroes. Let us remember that we are participating in the culture which has taught us not to like them, so that, when we are tempted to teach a child from above his position, or to say that "I represent white Anglo-Saxon gentility and culture, and out of the gratitude and graciousness of my heart I am going to reach down and lift you up to my level," we know that is the incorrect attitude.

We cannot reach down and lift up anymore, we must all get down together and reciprocate one to the other and come up together.

Let us, above all, be honest one to the other. Let us pursue truth though it hurts, though it makes us bleed. I said in the beginning that my purpose in using those lacerating words was to expose our innermost feeling. We must dig even deeper for the roots in our own consciousness, black and white, of the real fact of racism in our culture, and having faced that in ourselves, go back to the various schools from which we came and look upon the children before us as an opportunity, not only to practice the craft of teaching and the imparting of knowledge but, equally important, as an opportunity to learn from a subjugated people what its value, its history, its culture, its wealth as an independent people are. Let there be in our classrooms a sharing of the wealth of American democracy.

WHY TEACHERS FAIL

Liberal opinion in the North and in the South thus continues to stand upon its traditions of gradualism—that of one-by-one admission of deserving Negroes into the larger society and rejection of the idea that to help the Negro it must help first the Negro community.

Today in America, as elsewhere, the Negro has made us forcefully aware of the fact that the rights and privileges of an individual rest upon the status obtained by the group to which he belongs.

In the American pattern, where social power is distributed by groups, the Negro has come to recognize that he can achieve equal opportunities only through concerted action of the Negro community. We can't do it one by one anymore, we must do it as a group.

Now, how is education related to the process not of lifting individuals but of lifting a whole group by its bootstraps and helping it climb to its rightful place in American society?

One of the ways is by calling such meetings as this to discuss Negro history—to discuss those aspects of Negro culture which are important for the survival of the Negro people as a community. There is nothing in the survival of the Negro people as a community that is inherently hostile to the survival of the interests of any other group.

So when we say Black Power and Black Nationalism we do not mean that that is the only power or that that is the only nationalism that we are concerned about or that it is to predominate above all others. We merely mean that it should have the right of all other groups and be respected as such in the American way of life.

"A BOOTLEG TEACHER"

I have had occasion (and with this I'll come to a close) to function as a teacher—I'm a bootleg teacher, I teach Sunday school, it's the closest I can get to the process—I teach boys from nine to twelve, and I have the same problem with getting them to appreciate the spoken and written word, as you do, in your daily classrooms. Most of them can't read. I don't see how they're going to get, not only to Heaven—I don't see how they're going to get to the next grade unless they can command some of these problems that we have.

But, more importantly, I am also involved in the educational process. And those of us who are involved in culture and cultural activities, do ourselves and our country and our cause a great injustice not to recognize that we, too, are communicators and have therefore a responsibility in the process of communication. I could be hired today to communicate to the great American public my great delight in smoking a cigarette, but I know that a cigarette would cause you cancer and I could be paid for that. I could be used to do many other things in the process of communications from the top to the bottom.

I have a responsibility to show that what I do, what is translated through me, is measured by the best interest of my country and my people and my profession. And in that I think we are all together.

Joan C. Baratz

THE LANGUAGE OF THE GHETTO CHILD

What the psychologist who is studying the ghetto child and his learning patterns needs, among other things, is a sense of the child's language system. In this area the three major professions are the educators, the psychologists (mainly child-development types), and the

linguists. The educators were the first to contribute a statement
about the language difficulties of these children, a statement amount-
ing to the fact that the children were virtually verbally destitute—they
couldn't talk; if they did, it was deviant speech, filled with "errors."
The next group to get into the fray, the psychologists, initially confirmed that the children didn't talk, and then added the sophisticated
wrinkle that if they did talk, their speech was such that it was a deterrent to growth. The last group to come into the picture were the
linguists, who, though thoroughly impressed with the sophisticated
research of the psychologist, were astonished at the naiveté of his
pronouncements concerning language. The linguist began to examine the language of black children and brought us to our current
conception—that black children speak a well-ordered, highly structured, highly developed language system which in many aspects is
different from standard English.

The linguist takes as basic that all human beings develop language. After all, there is no reason to assume that black African bush
children develop a language and black inner-city Harlem children do
not. Subsumed under this is that the language is a well-ordered system with a predictable sound pattern, grammatical structure, and
vocabulary (in this sense, there are no "primitive" languages). The
linguist assumes that any such verbal system used by a community
is a language. The linguist also contends that children learn language
in the context of their environment—that is to say, a French child
learns French not because his father is in the home or his mother
reads books to him but because that is the language he hears continually inside and outside the home and that is the language individuals
in his environment respond to. Another assumption the linguist
works with is that by the time a child is five he has developed language—he has learned the rules of his linguistic environment.

The syntax of low-income Negro children differs from standard
English in many ways, but it has its own internal consistency. Unfortunately, the psychologist, not knowing the rules of Negro nonstandard English, has interpreted these differences not as the result
of well-learned rules but as evidence of "linguistic underdevelopment." He has been handicapped by his assumption that to develop
language is synonymous with the development of the psychologist's
own form of standard English. Thus he has concluded that if black
children do not speak like white children they are deficient. One of
the most blatant errors has been a confusion between hypotheses
concerning language and hypotheses concerning cognition. For this
reason, superficial differences in language structures and language
styles have been taken as manifestations of underlying differences
in learning ability. To give one example, a child in class was asked, in
a test of simple contrasts, "Why do you say they are different?" He

could not answer. Then it was discovered that the use of "do you say," though grammatically correct, was inappropriate to his culture. When he was asked instead, "Why are they different?" he answered without any hesitation at all.

There is a widespread notion among psychologists that some environments are better than others for stimulating language and learning growth. This assumption is, I believe, an outgrowth of the psychologist's confusion between general language development and the acquisition of standard English, which causes him to think that he must explain a "language deficit." According to researchers of this school, among the most detrimental factors is the "inadequacy" of the ghetto mothering patterns. The ghetto mother, they say, is so taken up with survival—"subsistence behaviors"—that she is too exhausted to talk to her children. Such a notion tells us more about the psychologist's lack of knowledge about the ghetto mother than it does about her real role. It also assumes that there is a minimal amount of language that must be present for language to be learned and that Negro mothers do not give this to their children. Part of this notion is that language is only learned from one's mother and that the language learned from her is underdeveloped. It is also presumed that the mother of a black child does not know how to stimulate or reinforce her child so that learning can occur. Under that assumption is the idea that such things as reading a book and singing to a child are essential behaviors in order for language to develop. Finally, it is presumed that she encourages passive, withdrawn behavior in her children because verbal ability is not highly valued in the ghetto community.

It seems as if all these assumptions have evolved because of misconceptions of what language is and how it functions. The psychologist has constructed elaborate environmental and psychological explanations of differences in language behavior but the elaborateness is unnecessary. The assumptions have been used after the fact to explain data erroneously—they have no experiential base.

Samuel D. Crawford and Robert H. Bentley

AN INNER-CITY "IQ" TEST

The test which follows may seem frivolous to some, but we hope to accomplish two things with it: (1) to demonstrate how ignorant most middle-class Americans (the class from which we traditionally draw teachers) are of the black sub-culture, and (2) to allow the reader to get an idea of what it feels like to take a test from another culture (assuming, of course, that the reader is not particularly familiar with black culture already).

The first point should be especially important to teachers and prospective teachers. For years, blacks have been described in the professional literature of education as "disadvantaged," and "culturally deprived," and a host of other euphemistic labels all of which imply that blacks have existed in America without the benefits of "culture." It seems to us that such is not the case at all: many young blacks may indeed not be said to possess the dominant middle-class "culture," but they certainly possess a counter- or sub- "culture" which is reflected in the lexicon by such terms as "playin' the dozens," "buying a hog" (not the animal), "pullin' my coat off to it," and the concept of "soul." The following statements reflect the lexicon as it appears in certain sections of black communities:

1) Say man, the eagle flies on Friday, and I'm gonna buy some bad new threads and be sho' nuf clean.

2) Man dig it, I'm gonna pull your coat tail to this, this chick's shuckin' and jivin', and that dude gonna go up side her head.

The second point has been receiving a good deal of attention in recent years (see Part Six of this book, "22,000 Retarded Children Face Second Chance"). If tests and textbooks are to evaluate and instruct, respectively, they must take the child from the known to the unknown, and too many tests and textbooks assume that middle-class culture is "known" and shared by minority sub-cultures. It makes little sense to ask a child whether T-bone or round steak is the better cut of meat if his diet has consisted only of "chitluns, neckbones, or oxtails." To decide that the child is stupid because he cannot answer the question is at odds with professional ethics, if not personal ethics as well.

The authors know of a case where a young black child was having difficulty working some story problems for his math class. The teacher was surprised, as the child usually did well in math, and called the father in for a conference. One of the problems had to do with adding and subtracting the number of knobs on a chest of drawers. The father pointed out to the teacher that the child had worked the problem correctly if the word "drawers" was substituted for "knob," and explained that his was very poor household, that they had very little furniture, and that the child had never seen a chest of drawers—and the teacher learned something about middle-class assumptions.

Similarly, stories in books that portray well-fed white children feeding their dog are of little interest to a poor black child who doesn't own a dog and may not have had breakfast that morning. "Helping Daddy Fix the Airconditioner" may be an appropriate story line for suburbia, but not for a child who lives in a house where there is no father, and broken windows let in the heat of summer and the cold of winter.

This "IQ" test is as up-to-date as we could make it as of this writing. The items, of course, date rapidly as slang terms and meaning change. The answers follow the test.

NAME _____

I. Completion
Fill in the blank space with the correct word or words.

1. Wow! did you see Bob Gibson _____ the ball?

       a) throw   b) toss   c) chunk

2. The guys on the block were really _____ after the Ali-Frazier thing.

       a) talkin it up   b) runnin it down   c) conversing

3. The country preacher usually can be found in _____.

       a) the South   b) the Windy City   c) any rural area

4. The birthplace of Malcolm X is _____.

       a) Detroit   b) Cottonwood, Ala.   c) Omaha, Nebraska

5. The brother got _____ because he ripped off with a short.

        a) rapped   b) busted   c) bimped

6. To make out with a female a dude has to _____.

        a) put down a heavy rap   b) run a game   c) find a lame

II. Matching

1. Jackson Five   _____a. James Brown
2. Soledad Brothers   _____b. L.A. Ram
3. Mr. Dynamite   _____c. doing time in prison
4. The Deacon   _____d. country blues singer
5. Charlie Pride   _____e. teenage singing group
                                      _____f. a Muslim

III. True and False:
Mark "T" or "F" after each sentence:

1. A hog is a hustler._____
2. To get a blow-out is to refer to an afro hair style. _____
3. A chine is an automobile. _____
4. A capping dude is a fellow who never complains and is very easy-going.

_____

5. *Checkin, chargers* is an expression used when a group of guys are admiring females' legs._____
6. A Prat is some sort of a Con game._____

IV. Multiple Choice

1. In the sentence below, *main squeeze* refers to:

        a) cigaret   b) book   c) girl

The other day I was standing on the corner and I saw Willie in his hog with his *main squeeze.*

2. Which word in the sentence below has reference to a *Job?*

Life is a drag man!! Why?   a) No bread   b) No gig and no way of getting one.

3. Which organization was responsible for labeling the white man as the *Devil?*

    a) the Black Panthers   b) Chicago 7   c) the Black Muslims

4. The expressions *Holy Ghost* and *Tarrying* are most closely associated

        a) Methodist   b) Baptist   c) Holiness

5. When a black person speaks of *Getting it together* he has reference to:

   a) group of people agreeing on an issue   b) expressing different ideas and opinions   c) integration

6. When a brother speaks of *Hat 'n Up* he means:

   a) clothing   b) idea   c) moving on

7. The best definition of *soul* is:

   a) something loud and emotional   b) taking the effects of pain and sorrow and translating them into something beautiful   c) the spiritual as opposed to the secular.

8. If a brother says he is going to *Pull his coat off to it,* he means:

   a) that he wants to start a fight   b) he wants to show respect
   c) explain something thoroughly

9. The expression "He's a *bad* dude" means:

   a) He's a good dude   b) He's a bad dude   c) He's not a good cowboy

10. If a sister says she's going to *Lay her purse upside yo' head,* she means:

    a) she is going to clobber you   b) she is going to give you some money   c) she is going to let you see for yourself that she has no money

11. If a brother is going to get his *fro blown dry,* you know he *doesn't* have:

    a) a car   b) a thirst   c) a conk

12. Who is *MR. C?*

    a) Charlie Parker, a musician   b) a hundred-dollar bill
    c) "Mr. Charlie," the Man, the white man.

Answers: (I) 1c, 2b, 3b, 4c, 5b, 6a; (II) 1e, 2c, 3a, 4b, 5d (III) 1f, 2t, 3t, 4f, 5t, 6t;   (IV) 1c, 2b, 3c, 4c, 5a, 6c, 7b, 8c, 9a, 10a, 11c, 12c.

J. L. Dillard

NEGRO CHILDREN'S DIALECT IN THE INNER CITY

As a public description of a language program for inner city Negroes stated recently, "The English used by most socio-economically disadvantaged Negroes in the United States severely limits their opportunities." A semipopular magazine would perhaps classify gleefully under *Department of Fuller Information* the news that disadvantaged people have their opportunities limited, but the lack of an objective delineation of this problem makes it virtually impossible to discuss it in a way free from redundancy and invented terminology.

But it is the study of this language problem which is new, not the language problem itself. There is every reason to believe that the field slave and sharecropper in the South had their opportunities limited, and that a language difference was one factor in that limitation; but no one worried about analyzing their language or about teaching them standard English. It was only when they migrated in great numbers to the large cities of the nation that they came to the attention of leading educators, of congressmen, and of political figures. Only then did the difference between their dialect and standard English become a problem for which it was felt necessary to find a solution—not just a problem which could be ignored. What was basically a rural language problem, of the plantation and of the sharecropper's farm, has since become a full-fledged urban language problem—one which has spawned more than one research project and development program for remedial English.

Perhaps largely by coincidence, at just about the same time that the problems (including the language problems) of the inner city Negro became prominent to educators, a few Caribbeanists were perceiving clear relationships between "Creole" or "Calypso" speech and the dialects of certain Negroes in the United States.[1] This has raised once again the issue of Afro-American-European language relationships which Melville J. Herskovits had raised in the anthropological literature in the 1930s and 1940s. In part, this constituted a challenge to the traditional position of American dialect geographers, who had recognized the existence in the United States of creole languages like

[1] For a recent summary of such relationships, see William A. Stewart, "Sociolinguistic Factors in the History of American Negro Dialects," *Florida FL Reporter*, Vol. 5, No. 2 (Spring 1967).

Gullah and Louisiana French Creole, but had tended to treat them as isolated phenomena—unrelated to any other American Negro dialects. Actually, the linkage had been made in Bloomfield's *Language* (1933, pp. 474-475), and *belles lettres* found the idea familar from such works as Thomas Wentworth Higginson's *Army Life in a Black Regiment* (1870). Furthermore, the long tradition of studying only the dialect of adult Negroes is now being supplanted by the view that what should now be studied is the speech of Negro children.[2] The theoretical issue raised thereby is a considerable one: Is it a general linguistic condition or perhaps a special characteristic of Negro dialect that archaic forms are preserved longer in the speech of children than elsewhere? Obviously, a linguistic study which focuses on the language of children would be much more relevant to the educational process than the older studies which utilized adult informants.

Creolists have long been aware that English-based creole languages often differ from the standard language primarily in syntactic properties (more basic matters from the point of view of the linguist), rather than in local idiosyncrasies of pronunciation and vocabulary (which, in current linguistic terminology, may be derived from the standard language by "low level" rules). Some transformational-generative linguists have joined the creolists in insisting upon a thorough study of the syntax of the speech of Negro children, and the results have been quite surprising. Among other things, these transformationalists, working independently, have found one of the major defining characteristics of Afro-American (and Creole) dialects according to Herskovits and others to be dominance of aspect over tense in the verb system. Thus, in one particular dialect, *He there* contrasts with *He be there;* the difference signalled is not one of past or present action but of *duration* of the action.[3] Speakers of standard English, including English teachers, do not have this category in their grammatical system, and accordingly think that anything besides *He is there* is "bad," concluding that there is a haphazard distribution of these forms in this dialect. They hear *He there* and *He be there* and do not apply the simple linguistic test of co-occurrent adverbs in test frames *(He there right now; He be there all the time).* This test with co-occurrent adverbs is, of course, a mildly artificial device utilized by the linguist and does not mean that the adverbs *must* accompany the verb forms.

The verb system utilized by these children turns out to be a quite complex one, with forms as "bizarre," from the viewpoint of

---

[2] William A. Stewart, "Urban Negro Speech: Sociolinguistic Factors Affecting English Teaching" in Shuy (ed.), *Social Dialects and Language Learning*, NCTE (1964), p. 15.

[3] See *Florida FL Reporter*, Vol. 4, No. 2 (Winter 1965-1966), p. 25.

the standard speakers, as *I been know*, which is an anterior form
something like a preterite. The linguist is not especially surprised,
since he knows that comparable forms occur, for example, in "'Wes
Kos" (the pidgin English of Nigeria and the Cameroun), and in
Sranan (the creole English of Surinam). As the Negro adolescent
finds it necessary to adjust to mainstream American society, he gives
up something of his earlier verb paradigm—either forgetting it completely or, more likely, using it only for special speaking styles and
for special audiences. His acquisition of standard English (which becomes in effect a second language) is handicapped by a lack of awareness of the dialect difference. As a matter of fact, there is not even
a popular name for the dialect from which the Negro speaker starts.
Further complicating the problem is the matter of group loyalty. The
requirement is satisfied, at certain social levels, by the imposition of
ethnic slang upon the often quite standard grammar of certain Negro
groups. This gives rise to the picturesque vocabulary which is often
written up as the "language" of the Negro or of the ghetto. As in
other fields, the public finds the superficialities of language much
more attractive than the elusive solid core.

The typical speaker of the Negro dialect who makes part of the
long trip toward standard English retains some of the less strikingly
different forms. The "zero copula" as in *He there* is often retained,
since it can pass (almost in the racial disguise sense) for *He's there*
with a "lightly articulated" -*s*. Many a speaker who would no longer
say *I been know that already* will say *I been knowing that a long
time*; the latter can pass for *I have been knowing that a long time*
with a "lightly articulated" auxiliary. On the other hand, certain
Negroes who remain low on the social scale actually retain what
Stewart has called basilect in a relatively pure form.[4]

But the emphasis, for the educator, must clearly be on the
child. Since the child's linguistic system may be so radically different
from that of standard English, it makes a great deal of sense to treat
the teaching problem as a second language teaching problem, using
the techniques which have been developed for teaching English as a
foreign language during the past few years. When this has been tried,
it has worked unexpectedly well. Contrary to certain expectations,
the drills, in the hands of a competent teacher, have been very well
received by the student. Eighth-grade students at Kelly Miller School
in Washington, D.C., even made their own drills on a volunteer basis,
so popular was this approach to English teaching. One materials de-
veloper reported that only in the rare case of students with a greater

[4]William A. Stewart, "Urban Negro Speech: Sociolinguistic Factors Affecting
Teaching" in Shuy (ed.), *Social Dialects and Language Learning*, NCTE (1964),
p. 15.

mastery of standard English (perhaps acquired in the home and not at school) was there boredom with this method of teaching.

One of the most suggestive aspects of research on Negro children's dialect concerns the degree of age-grading which affects the dialect's structure.[5] We know already that a great deal of such age-grading does occur in urban Negro dialects, and a prime target of future research ought to be the detailing of its exact characteristics. Consider, for example, the gender of pronouns—again, one of those things which the average speaker of standard English, including the English teacher, is likely to take for a language absolute. It would surprise most educators to learn that many of the world's languages do not distinguish *grammatically* between the third person singular masculine (*he*) and the third person singular feminine (*she*). Among these are the creole dialects in the Caribbean, pidgin English along the west coast of Africa, and certain indigenous West African languages. It is, then, not surprising to creolists that forms like *He a nice little girl* and *I don't know her name* (referring to a man) are sometimes encountered in non-standard Negro dialects among children in the five to six-year-old group. It is also not surprising that the age-grading eliminates this "small-fry" grammatical form (more sophisticated terminology would say that gender differentiation is "introduced") very quickly. Speakers of standard English are likely to be hard on the person who can be considered to have trouble with gender forms. Other forms, which bear no such personal or pseudo-psychological stigmata, disappear more slowly. The undifferentiated form of the pronoun as possessive (*he brother, she book*) apparently disappears somewhere between the ages of nine and fourteen.

If the learning of something like standard English were the only aim of education (remember that the adult Negro typically attempts to approximate standard English), a *laissez faire* attitude toward age-grading might be in order. But, clearly, the child's educational problems are most critical at just that age when his dialect is most different from standard English. The six or seven-year-old who is trying to learn to read standard English texts—usually taught by a teacher who has no idea how different the student's language really is when it is Negro nonstandard—faces much more of a problem than does the middle-class white child who need only master the print-to-sound decoding system of what is essentially his own dialect. One literacy specialist discovered several apparently quite intelligent Negro fourteen-year-olds in Washington, D.C. who were functional illiterates. Even granting the somewhat unlikely premise that the Negro

---

[5] Walter Loban, *Problems in Oral English*, NCTE Report (1966). (This age-grading is fairly well documented by Loban, even though some linguists would disagree with the taxonomy of his work.)

child acquires standard English perfectly somewhere in his teens, one could not proceed to any logical conclusion that he would then be ready to start learning to read. The school system expects him already to have mastered quite complex reading skills in the dialect which only the most advanced have acquired by their late teens. In this context, people like Robert Kendall, author of *White Teacher in a Black School*, who are "shocked by the illiteracy of (his) students" (p. 34) appear culturally naive. The wonder is rather that the student, without guidance based upon an accurate knowledge of what the dialect is, has been able to progress at all. Imagine trying to learn to read German without ever being told that German is not the same language as English!

An age-grading study ought to be an important topic on any research agenda, and the pedagogical implications should be far-reaching. Only then is it justifiable to have materials developers do grade-by-grade pedagogical materials. It will also be necessary to conduct some research into language acquisition matters in the Negro non-standard-speaking community, if only to forestall criticism that the age-grading forms are really language acquisition forms. My position in this matter by no means represents the consensus among linguists, but I will stand by it firmly.[6] The pronoun-gender "problem," for example, is one which is eliminated very early from the language acquisition problems of the white, standard-speaking child. The possibility of age-graded retention of archaic features (many of them being somewhat like Gullah and the creoles of the Caribbean) is a reasonable alternative to explanations of such features as merely the result of "learning to talk."

In addition to the pedagogical utility of such discoveries, this kind of research seems to be revealing a great deal about certain areas of liberal knowledge, such as the history of the English language in the United States. Long ago, the McDavids suggested that it was unwise to look for factors other than the total language environment of the Negro for explanation of the differences between the English of the Negro and of the white in the United States.[7] Actually, one must take into account creole *lingua franca* forms which are rather well attested to as having been current among the plantation field hand population. In a way, a bit of African romanticism may have been lost along with the new creole emphasis; but there has been a great compensating gain in accuracy and clarity.

[6] On the other hand, William A. Stewart is in general agreement with me on this point.

[7] Raven I. and Virginia McDavid, "The Relationship of the Speech of American Negroes to the Speech of Whites" *American Speech*, XXVI (1951), 3-17.

It would be well to put such matters into an accurate light; there is no more reason to read pidginization into everything said by Negroes than there is to find Africanisms behind every cotton plant. Clear archaisms like *ax* for "ask," even though they are found in Trinidad, Jamaica and St. Thomas, as well as among Negroes in the Northern ghettos and in the rural South, should probably be attributed to survivals from earlier stages of English. The lack of distinction between pairs of words such as *pen* and *pin* is also widespread enough among white English dialects to make it unlikely as an "African" importation. But there remains the very strong possibility that even the speech of American whites—and especially of Southerners (perhaps, ironically enough, even some of those Southerners who are most bitterly racist)—has been influenced by the speech of the Negro to a greater degree than historians of the language have been willing to admit. Charles Dickens, in his *American Notes*, expressed the theory of Negro influence on the speech of American whites as long ago as 1849, and a lot of ink has been spilled to prove that he and others like him were wrong. Unfortunately, the purely linguistic problem has been entangled with political problems and matters of race prejudice. Many linguists have in effect given up the study of Negro dialects because statements that some Negroes speak differently from whites can be taken to mean that they have "thick lips" or even "thick brains." But we have apparently reached the point where these absurdities need no longer stand in the way of serious research. When such research is completed, the picture of what went on in the history of American English may be changed a great deal. It may also be that English teaching will have to change.

Riley B. Smith

INTERRELATEDNESS OF CERTAIN DEVIANT GRAMMATICAL STRUCTURES IN NEGRO NONSTANDARD DIALECTS

Research in highly divergent dialects of American English, especially in what has been termed Negro Nonstandard English (NNE), has lately been thriving, and quite a number of hitherto unnoticed divergences have been disclosed and published.[1] The findings themselves have for the most part been categorized in terms of the standard language, and though there is at present a theoretical controversy over descriptive methods,[2] some highly creative work has been done toward explaining certain features of NNE within both models. The data in any case are always valuable, and the explanations themselves are often highly insightful. But there may be relationships between divergent features of a dialect which would tell us more about that dialect, and the researcher should not shrink from speculating about his findings in the dialect's own terms, i.e., of the divergences' relations with each other within the dialect.

Generative-transformational linguists have quite properly used the phenomenon of intracode ambiguity (constructional homonymy within their own dialects, as in "the shooting of the hunters") as a discovery tool and as a rhetorical device. That such intracode ambiguity is a phenomenon in all dialects of all languages should require no defense. But that certain divergent dialects of American English have terminal formatives which grammatically "ambiguate" underlying phrase-markers different from those of standard English (SE), or indeed "ambiguate" phrase-markers not at all ambiguable in SE, should be considered a possibility offering dialectologists a powerful tool.

Notice has admittedly been given to this phenomenon of ambi-

---

[1] An earlier version of this paper was read at the annual meeting of the American Dialect Society, December 28, 1968, in New York.

[2] The bases of this controversy are clearly shown in William Labov and Paul Cohen, "Systematic Relations of Standard and Non-Standard Rules in the Grammar of Negro Speakers," ERIC Document Number ED 016946 (May 1967), and in William A. Stewart, "Continuity and Change in American Negro Dialects," *The Florida FL Reporter*, IV (Spring 1968), 3 ff. Though the controversy is of extreme interest to researchers in Negro Nonstandard English, it does not directly relate to the findings or argument of this paper.

guity peculiar to a dialect, but it has generally been restricted to dialect homophony, as in *stock-stalk* (Western Pennsylvania), *pin-pen* (South Midland and Western South),[3] and *right-rat* (NNE), this last still the subject of controversy.[4] And though the locative-existential transformation *it + be*, as in *It's a lot of wires down here*, was pointed out as early as 1953 with reference to the speech of West Virginia and the Chesapeake Bay area,[5] has since been randomly noticed as a feature of certain South Midland dialects (especially in Oklahoma and Texas), and has subsequently been checklisted as a feature of NNE,[6] the potential intracode ambiguity of this structure with the extrapositional *it + be*, as in *It was six of the boys what saw a lizard*, has not been pursued. Thus, *It was a man under the bed* is ambiguous in NNE and in some other American English dialects in a way that it is not in SE, reflecting the SE translations *There was a man under the bed* and *It was a man under the bed (who + VP)*.

The unavailability of the dialect-informant qua dialectologist is, of course, the principal and rather overwhelming reason why this technique of dialect analysis has been hitherto ignored. But it is also true that speakers of dialects of SE, under certain conditions at least, are quite deaf to grammatical divergences of nonstandard dialects. Aretha Franklin's hit song of last spring is labeled *Ain't No Way*, but it is almost always referred to by white disc-jockeys as *There Ain't No Way*, seldom as *It Ain't No Way (for me to love you if you won't let me*—the lyric actually repeated in the "refrain"), except by those whose dialects generate this structure. But researchers who have worked intensively with a particular dialect are able to recognize structural ambiguation within the dialect, and the analytical tools this recognition offers them are invaluable.

Few linguists have dealt at all with the phenomenon of crosscode ambiguity, a phenomenon doubtless peculiar to the domain of dialectology. It has usually been treated as a curiosity of fortuitous skewing, resulting in the near homophony of lexical items across dialect boundaries, such as in *hard* (eastern New England) - *hide* (certain

---

[3] Variously attested. See Uriel Weinreich, William Labov, and Marvin I. Herzog, "A Theory of Language Change," *Directions for Historical Linguistics*, eds. W. P. Lehmann and Yakov Malkiel (Austin, Tex., 1968), p. 152, n. 41.

[4] Ruth I. Golden, "Changing Dialects By Using Tapes," *Social Dialects and Language Learning*, ed. Roger W. Shuy (Champaign, Ill., 1964), p. 63. For a disclaimer, see Raven I. McDavid, Jr., "A Checklist of Significant Features for Discriminating Social Dialects," *Dimensions of Dialect*, ed. Eldonna L. Evertts (Champaign, Ill., 1967), p. 9, n. 3.

[5] E. Bagby Atwood, *A Survey of Verb Forms in the Eastern United States* (Ann Arbor, 1953), p. 30.

[6] Beryl Loftman Bailey, "Some Aspects of the Impact of Linguistics on Language Teaching," *Elementary English*, XLV (May 1968), 576.

South Midland dialects).[7] But the phenomenon exists also at the syntactic level, as in *It was a man under the bed,* and such types of ambiguations perhaps result in serious barriers to communication and
learning, especially in those areas where there has been recent ethnic
resettlement. The inability of the disc-jockey to hear Aretha Franklin's locative-existential transformation, *It Ain't No Way,* can be
attributed, I think, not so much to the divergence itself, but to the
cross-code ambiguation it would cause with a structure in his own SE
dialect.

The persistence of some "ungrammatical" forms of NNE has
been accounted for by citing causes of ethnic identity, self-conceptu-
alization within the subculture, and language loyalty. Though these
are certainly important factors, the English teacher's frustrations
perhaps attest that they are not completely satisfactory explanations.[8] The phenomenon of cross-code ambiguation is offered in this
paper as a collateral explanation of the persistence of certain "ungrammatical" forms of NNE.

The two deviant grammatical structures of a dialect of NNE to
be discussed in this paper are 1) the pleonastic subject pronoun, and
2) the deletion of the subject relative pronoun. A relationship between the two structures within the dialect will be shown, and some
conjecture about interference phenomena attributable to the relationship will be made. And it is hoped that this discussion will have more
general ramifications for future research and analysis in dialectology.

Among Negro informants of East Texas,[9] the frequency of the

---

[7] A perhaps more vivid example of such "cross-code" ambiguity was related to
me by Professor Rudolph C. Troike of the University of Texas at Austin. A lady
from Houston, named Kaiser, having arrived at a hotel in Boston to claim her
reservation, said her name to the clerk, who carefully wrote "Carser."

[8] It is certainly not the intent here to downgrade the importance of functional
interference. See William Labov and Paul Cohen, "Some Suggestions for Teaching Standard English to Speakers of Non-Standard Dialects," ERIC Document
Number ED 016 948 (July 1967) for a discussion of the distinction between
"structural" and "functional" interference.

[9] The fieldwork and analysis were one phase of a project to reevaluate English
instructional material and curricula in the wake of integration in five independent
school districts of East Texas: Atlanta, Clarksville, Marshall, Nacogdoches, and
Tyler. The project was sponsored by the school districts under grants from ESEA
and NDEA, and by the Texas Education Agency. All the interviews were conducted between August and December, 1967.

The 253 informants, of whom 170 were Negro, were selected to include a
wide range of ages, and of ethnic and educational backgrounds. Because grammatical as well as phonological data were of interest to the project, the interviews
were in general topical and did not follow a standardized worksheet. With modifications, the interviews followed techniques suggested in Roger W. Shuy,
Walter A. Wolfram, and William K. Riley, *Linguistic Correlates of Social Stratification in Detroit Speech* (East Lansing, Mich., 1967), and in William Labov,
The Social Stratification of English in New York City (Washington, D.C., 1966).

pleonastic subject pronoun is extremely high among speakers of all age-groups, and its occurrence is quite widespread.[10]

So the older peoples *they* got herbs and stuff and holp made medicine theirself.   (67, Atlanta, No. 122)[11]

My mother *she* used to wash and iron and cook.
(46, Marshall, No. 101)

And then my daughter *she* is a secretary for a store manager.
(46, Marshall, No. 101)

My brother from Lubbock *he* visit to get his wife and baby.
(17, Tyler, No. 085)

Some of them *they* put the needle in the fire.
(9, Tyler, No. 041)

Teenager(s) *they* don't much like his rock.
(14, Nacogdoches, No. 065)

Among this same group of informants, the frequency of the deletion of the subject relative pronoun (usually *what* in this dialect of NNE), not optionally deletable in SE as it is in this dialect, is extremely high and its occurrence is widespread.

He look like a little man have on a hat with a round circle on it.
(8, Marshall, No. 021)

This here is one family eat anything.
(53, Nacogdoches, No. 121)

I have a brother work at Ralston Purina here in town.
(13, Nacogdoches, No. 061)

She be the kind like to go.   (17, Tyler, No. 085)

It's a bush grow up like that, and it's good for fever.
(67, Atlanta, No. 122)

---

[10] I do not wish to suggest that all Negro informants used particular deviant grammatical structures with the same frequency in all cases. The data have in some measure been selected to reflect what I consider to be "basilect" structures. See William A. Stewart, "Urban Negro Speech: Sociolinguistic Factors Affecting English Teaching," *Social Dialects and Language Learning*, op. cit., pp. 10-18, for a discussion of basilect reconstruction to account for structural interference in the learning of standard English. Further, this discovery technique is not entirely incompatible with the position of Labov, *The Social Stratification*.

[11] The age of the informant, city of domicile, and my informant number follow the responses cited, in that order.

Further, in strings where both of these structures occur in this dialect, the pleonasm is highly stable even where the relative pronoun is present.

The one stay here in Clarksville *she* don't do anything at all.
(44, Clarksville, No. 101)

The one who lives here in Clarksville doesn't do anything at all.
(SE translation)

The man *what* own(ed) the land *he* come over.
(18, Clarksville, No. 084)

The man who owned the land came over.   (SE translation)

The boy won *he* did a three.   (15, Tyler, No. 069)

The boy who won did a three.   (SE translation)

My other sister *she* fourteen go to Dogan   (10, Tyler, No. 047)

My other sister is fourteen who goes to Dogan.   (SE translation)

Not: My other sister who is fourteen goes to Dogan.

These strings, which consist of *one* sentence, not two, suggest that there is an interrelatedness between the two structures such that the high frequency of the deletion of the relative pronoun exerts an influence in some way on the stability of the pleonastic subject pronoun, or that the pleonasm is in some sense itself a disambiguating formative.[12]

The string *I saw the man did it* is ambiguous in NNE in a way that it cannot be in SE. In the shorthand derivations below, the second sentences of both A and B are embedded, but in A they are relativized, in B they are nominalized. (The dotted line indicates a possible but infrequent deletion transformation.)

---

[12] On the phonemic level, the mere notion of a disambiguating marker was rather thoroughly discredited by the neo-grammarians, who showed that what their opponents had maintained were exceptions to sound laws on the basis of their importance to the maintenance of semantic distinctions could be accounted for on the basis of other perfectly regular phenomena. See Leonard Bloomfield, *Language* (New York, 1933), pp. 346 ff., for a discussion. This controversy and its outcome certainly still have relevance for modern generative theory, but it is not clear that the notion of disambiguation is without validity on the syntactic level, even though our present grammatical model seems unable to handle it. To account for the phenomenon on the basis of stylistic variation certainly seems to beg the question.

Negro Nonstandard English

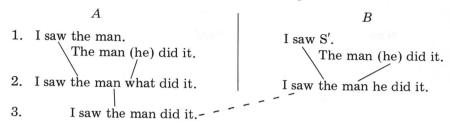

A	B
1. I saw the man. The man (he) did it.	I saw S'. The man (he) did it.
2. I saw the man what did it.	I saw the man he did it.
3. I saw the man did it.	

Standard English

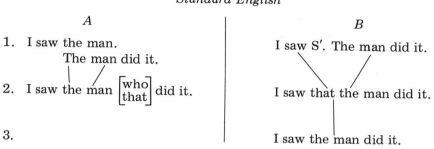

A	B
1. I saw the man. The man did it.	I saw S'. The man did it.
2. I saw the man [who/that] did it.	I saw that the man did it.
3.	I saw the man did it.

It will be noted that though the *what* in NNE above (A2) could be retained—i.e., the deletion transformation could be blocked—to disambiguate, the relative *what* is a rare formative in any terminal string, and the pleonasm usually takes over this function, i.e., its deletion is usually blocked. The relatives *who* and *that* in SE (A2 above) are not deletable and therefore the string never ambiguates with B3. It will be futher noted that there is cross-code ambiguity between the terminals (3) of NNE and SE, such that the speakers of the two dialects may decode different underlying phrase-markers for the terminal string *I saw the man did it.*

To the speaker of NNE, the SE string *My sister plays the piano* may reflect not a sentence, but a noun-phrase with an embedded relative clause: i.e., *My sister who plays the piano.* The pleonastic pronoun is usually present in NNE, as in *My sister she play the piano,* to disambiguate the two structures. Thus both intracode and cross-code ambiguation militate against the NNE speaker's learning to leave out the subject pronoun pleonasm, which seems to have more a grammatical than a strictly stylistic function in his dialect.

There is at present no clear way to describe what appear to be synchronic influences of transformational rules upon each other, rules apparently unrelated except that they have the potential of generating ambiguous terminal strings within a dialect.[13] Optionally deletable markers occasionally, though rarely, perform such a disambiguating function in standard English. *I see the men do it* is ambiguous in SE, reflecting phrase-markers which are clearly different when we pronominalize *the men:* (1) *I see they do it*, and (2) *I see them to it.* But the SE speaker normally disambiguates with the clause marker *that* when he wants to reflect the structure of 1): *I see that the men do it.*

Analogously, the NNE string *The man did it* is ambiguous; *The man he did it* disambiguates with the pleonasm. Whatever the generative provenience of the pleonastic subject pronoun (it appears to be neither a clause marker nor a relative pronoun in the SE sense), it is a marker in the sense that it marks nonrelativization of the following verb phrase, a function stabilized by the regular deletion of the relative pronoun in this dialect of NNE.

Acrolect pressure on the basilect compounds the communication and pedagogical problems further. The failure of the NNE speaker to recognize the complexity of certain ambiguations between divergent dialects is certainly no more serious than this same failure on the part of the SE Speaker. The dialectologist should look for relationships within a dialect which may be indispensable to a proper description of it. And the English teacher, in her struggle against "ungrammatical" forms, should begin to recognize that some of her students' failures may be identical to her own, resulting from a blockage of understanding of the grammatical structures of the unfamiliar dialect because of ambiguity across dialect boundaries.

William Labov

LANGUAGE CHARACTERISTICS: BLACKS

One of the most extraordinary failures in the history of American education is the failure of the public school system to teach black children in the urban ghettos to read. The fact of reading failure is so general, and so widespread, that no one school system, no one method, and no one teacher can be considered responsible. We are plainly dealing with social and cultural events of considerable magnitude in which the linguistic factors are the focal points of trouble or centers

[13] See footnote 12.

of difficulty rather than the primary causes. Before considering specific linguistic problems, it will be helpful to look at the general reading problem of disadvantaged blacks in its cultural setting.

Since 1965, research has been conducted into the structural and functional differences between the nonstandard vernacular used by black speakers in the urban ghettos and the standard English of the classroom.[1] One of the first studies was a series of seventy-five interviews with black boys in randomly selected "Vacation Day Camps" in Harlem in the summer of 1965. These day camps were conducted in recreation centers and schools, and each child's parents had to enroll him personally in the program; there was therefore a large factor of selection for intact homes and favorable family attitudes. In these interviews we found that the great majority of these boys, aged ten to twelve, had considerable difficulty in reading second- or third-grade-level sentences such as the following:

> Last month I read five books.
> When I passed by, I read the posters.
> When I liked a story, I read every word.

In the course of the next two years, the language and behavior of a number of preadolescent and adolescent peer groups in South Central Harlem were systematically investigated. The researchers avoided contact with the home and the school, the adult-dominated environments; instead, they worked through participant-observers in the area to reach the boys on the streets, in their own territories, in environments dominated by peer-group interaction. In the same areas, marginal members of the groups and isolated individuals were studied. The latter included boys from the Vacation Day Camps and boys from the immediate neighborhood of the peer groups, who were "lames"—definitely not participants in the vernacular street culture. Reading tests showed that reading skills were very low for most boys—close to zero for many. More important, reading was truly irrelevant to the

---

[1] The research reported here was supported by the United States Office of Education as Cooperative Research Project 3091 and 3288. The most complete report is provided in W. Labov, P. Cohen, C. Robins, and J. Lewis, *A Study of the Non-Standard English of Negro and Puerto Rican Speakers in New York City*, Final Report on Cooperative Research Project 3288 (Washington, D.C., 1968; available through ERIC, Center for Applied Linguistics, Washington, D.C.). The sections of this chapter entitled "The Problem of Black Dialect," "Relevant Patterns of Black Speech," "Some Phonological Variables and Their Grammatical Consequences," "Changes in the Shapes of Words," "Grammatical Correlates of the Phonological Variables," and "Consequences for the Teaching of Reading" were adapted from William Labov, "Some Sources of Reading Problems for Negro Speakers of Nonstandard English," in A. Frazier, ed., *New Directions in Elementary English* (Champaign, Ill.: N.C.T.E., 1967), pp. 140-167, and are used by permission of the National Council of Teachers of English. Some of the treatment in this chapter is derived from William Labov, "A Note on the Relation of Reading Failure to Peer Group Status," *Teachers College Record*, Vol. 70 (1969), pp. 395-405.

Figure 1. Grade and reading achievement of thirty-two nonmembers of street groups in south central Harlem.

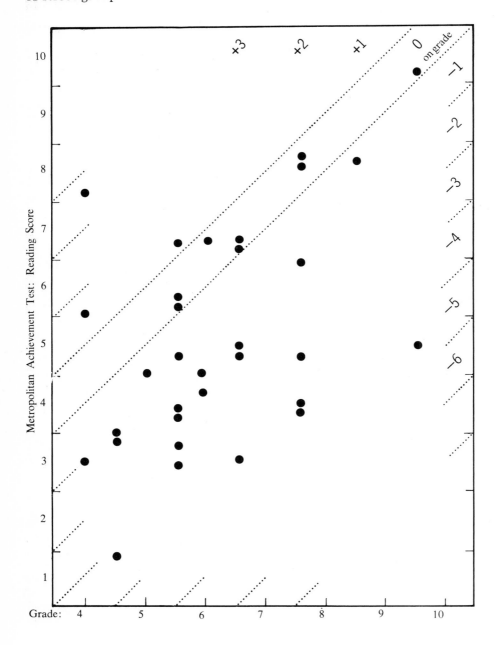

Figure 2. Grade and reading achievement of forty-six members of street groups in Harlem.

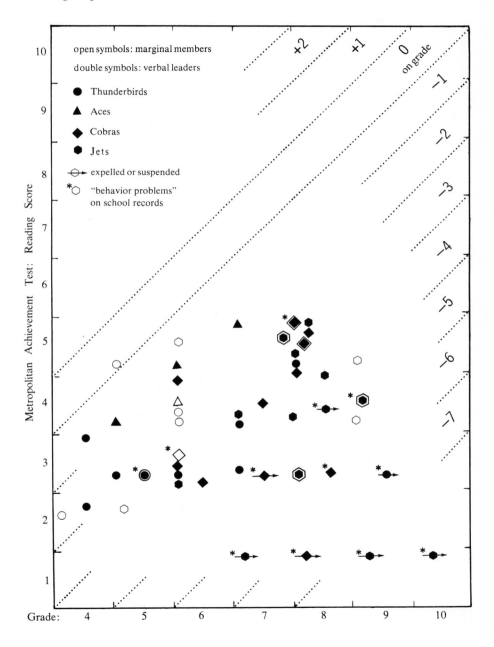

daily life of these boys. For example, two boys who were best friends and saw each other every day had very different reading abilities. One could read the last page in Gray's Oral Reading Test, and the other could not read the second-grade-level sentences; the first was astonished to find that his friend could not read, and the second was even more surprised to find that the first boy could read so well.

With the cooperation of the New York City Board of Education, the school records were examined for most of the individuals studied.[2] Figure 1 shows the relation of reading level to grade level for thirty-two isolated individuals. The horizontal axis is the actual grade at the time the investigators were in contact with the boys; the vertical axis is the average Metropolitan Achievement Test score. The central diagonal, from lower left to upper right, represents reading on grade: the pair of symbols at the upper right of the diagram, for example, shows two boys in the eighth grade reading at the eighth-grade level.

In Figure 1, we see that most of the children studied from South Central Harlem are indeed below grade in reading, though there are some who are doing quite well. The general movement of the population from lower left to upper right indicates that learning is taking place.

We can contrast Figure 1 with Figure 2, which shows the same relations for forty-six children who are members of various gangs, clubs, or hang-out groups—fully participating members of the street cultures. The overall pattern is very different from Figure 1: only one person is reading on grade, and the great majority are not learning to read at all. Year by year, the boys belonging to these groups fall further below grade—four, five, six years, until they finally drop out.

The sharp difference between these two figures represents information that could not have been gathered by research within the schools, since teachers have no means of knowing which children are indeed fully identified with the street culture. The linguistic differences between the two groups are minor, but the difference in acceptance or rejection of school as an institution is very great indeed.

These figures make it fairly evident that there are factors operating that are more important than native intelligence or verbal ability—culturally-determined values and attitudes that interfere with the process of learning to read. The fundamental problem revealed in Figures 1 and 2 should be kept in mind so that the relative importance of functional and structural problems is not obscured. At the present time we can give a number of concrete suggestions on linguistic problems and some of these are presented in the following pages.

---

[2] Data given here are based on a relatively small sample of seventy-five boys, since many had moved or been transferred, suspended, or discharged during this period.

As helpful as these may be, it should be clear that they deal with only one (and certainly not the major) problem interfering with the learning of reading.

THE PROBLEM OF BLACK DIALECT

One of the first questions to which we must address ourselves is whether or not there is a single definite pattern of speech used by blacks in urban ghetto areas. This question has provoked a great deal of discussion in the last few years, much more than it deserves. At many meetings on educational problems of ghetto areas, time that could have been spent in constructive discussion has been devoted to arguing the question as to whether black dialect exists. The debates have not been conducted with any large body of factual information in view, but rather in terms of what the speakers wish to be so, or what they fear might follow in the political arena.

For those who have not participated in such debates, it may be difficult to imagine how great are the pressures against the recognition, description, or even mention of black speech patterns. For various reasons, many teachers, principals, and civil rights leaders wish to deny that the existence of patterns of black speech is a linguistic and social reality in the United States today. The most careful statement of the situation as it actually exists might read as follows: *Many features of pronunciation, grammar, and lexicon are closely associated with black speakers—so closely as to identify the great majority of black people in the northern cities by their speech alone.*

The correspondence between this speech pattern and membership in the black ethnic group is of course far from complete. Many black speakers have none—or almost none—of these features. Many northern whites, living in close proximity to blacks, have these features in their own speech. But this overlap does not prevent the features from being identified with black speech by most listeners: we are dealing with a stereotype that provides correct identification in the great majority of cases, and therefore with a firm base in social reality. Such stereotypes are the social basis of language perception; this is merely one of many cases where listeners generalize from the variable data to categorical perception in absolute terms. Someone who uses a stigmatized form twenty to thirty percent of the time will be heard as using this form all the time. It may be socially useful to correct these stereotypes in a certain number of individual cases, so that people learn to limit their generalizations to the precise degree that their experience warrants; but the overall tendency is based upon very regular principles of human behavior, and people will continue to identify as black speech the pattern that they hear from the great majority of the black people they meet.

The existence of a black speech pattern must not be confused of course with the myth of a biologically, racially, exclusively black speech. The idea that dialect differences are due to some form of laziness must be rejected with equal firmness. Anyone who continues to endorse such myths can be refuted easily by such subjective-reaction tests as the Family Background Test, which we are using in our current research in Harlem. Sizable extracts from the speech of fourteen individuals are played in sequence for listeners who are asked to identify the family backgrounds of each. So far, we find no one who can even come close to a correct identification of black and white speakers. This result does not contradict the statement that there exists a socially based black speech pattern; it supports everything that I have said above on this point. The voices heard on the test are the exceptional cases: blacks raised without any black friends in solidly white areas; whites raised in areas dominated by black cultural values; white southerners raised in predominantly black areas; blacks from small northern communities untouched by recent migrations; college-educated blacks who reject the northern ghetto and the South alike. The speech of these individuals does not identify them as black or white because they do not use the speech patterns that are characteristically black or white for northern listeners. The identifications made by these listeners, often in violation of actual ethnic membership categories, show that they respond to black speech patterns as a social reality.

RELEVANT PATTERNS OF BLACK SPEECH

One approach to the study of nonstandard black speech is to attempt a complete description of this form of language without direct reference to standard English. This approach can be quite revealing, and can save us from many pitfalls in the easy identification of forms that are only apparently similar. But as an overall plan, it is not realistic. We are far from achieving a complete description of standard English, to begin with; the differences between nonstandard black speech and standard English are slight compared to their similarities; and finally, some of these differences are far more relevant to reading problems than others. Let us therefore consider some of the most relevant patterns of black speech from the point of view of reading problems.

Some black-white differences are plainly marked and easy for any observer to note. In the following examples, the black forms are patterns that frequently occur in our recordings of individual and group sessions with boys from ten to seventeen years old—ranging from careful speech in face-to-face interaction with adults to the most excited and spontaneous activity within the primary (closed network) group:

Black	*White*
It don't all be her fault.	It isn't always her fault.
Hit him upside the head.	Hit him in the head.
The rock say "Shhh!"	The rock went "Shhh!"
I'm a shoot you.	I'm g'na shoot you.
I wanna be a police.	I wanna be a policeman.
Ah 'on' know. [a o no]	I d'know. [a^I dno^U]

Now consider the following examples, in which black-white differences are less plainly marked and very difficult for most people to hear:

Black	*White*
He [pæsɪm] yesterday	He [pæsdɪm] yesterday.
Give him [ðeᴵ] book.	Give him [ðɛə:] book.
This [jɔ:ɫ] place?	This [jɔ:ə] place?
[ðæs] Nick boy.	[ðæᵗs] Nick's boy.
He say, [kæːᵗɫ] is.	He says, [kærəǀ] is.
My name is [bu].	My name is [bu?].

This second series represents a set of slight phonetic differences, sometimes prominent, but more often unnoticed by the casual listener. These differences are much more significant than the first set in terms of learning and reading standard English. In truth, the differences are so significant that they will be the focus of our attention. The slight phonetic signals observed here indicate systematic differences that can lead to reading problems and problems of being understood.

Corresponding to the phonetic transcriptions on the left, we can and do infer such grammatical constructions and lexical forms as

He pass him yesterday.
Give him they book.
This you-all place?
That's Nick boy.
He say, Ca'ol is.
My name is Boo.

Each of these sentences is representative of a large class of phonological and grammatical differences that distinguish nonstandard black speech from standard English. The most important are those in which large-scale phonological differences coincide with important grammatical differences. The result of this coincidence is the existence of a large number of homonyms in the speech of black children that are different from the set of homonyms in the speech system used by the teacher. If the teacher knows about this different set of homonyms, no serious problems in the teaching of reading need occur; but if the teacher does not know about it, there are bound to be difficulties.

The simplest way to organize this information seems to be under the headings of the important rules of the sound system that are affected. By using lists of homonyms as examples, it will be possible to avoid a great deal of phonetic notation and to stay with the essential linguistic facts. In many cases, the actual phonetic form is irrelevant: it is the presence or absence of a distinction that is relevant. Thus, for example, it makes no difference whether a child says [pɪn] or [pɪ n] or [pe: n] or [p n] for the word *pen;* what counts is whether or not this word is distinct from *pin.* The linguistic fact of interest is the existence of contrast, not the particular phonetic forms that are heard from one time to another. A child might seem to distinguish [pɪn] and [p n] in northern style in one pair of sentences, but if the basic phonemic contrast is not present, the same child might reverse the forms in the next sentence, and say [pɪn] for *ink pen* and [p n] for *safety pin.* A linguistic orientation will not supply teachers with a battery of phonetic symbols, but rather encourage them to observe what words can or cannot be distinguished by the children they are teaching.

SOME PHONOLOGICAL VARIABLES
AND THEIR GRAMMATICAL CONSEQUENCES

R-lessness

There are three major dialect areas in the eastern United States where the *r* of spelling is not pronounced as a consonant before other consonants or at the ends of words: eastern New England, New York City, and the South (upper and lower). Thus white speakers from Boston, New York, Richmond, Charleston, or Atlanta will show only a lengthened vowel in *car, guard, for,* and usually an obscure centering glide [schwa] in place of *r* in *fear, feared, care, cared, moor,*

moored, bore, bored, and so on. This is what we mean by *r*-less pronunciation. Most of these areas have been strongly influenced in recent years by the *r*-pronouncing pattern that is predominant in
broadcasting, so that educated speakers, especially young people,
will show a mixed pattern in their careful speech. When the original
r-less pattern is preserved, we can obtain such homonyms as the following:

guard	= god	par	= pa	
nor	= gnaw	fort	= fought	
sore	= saw	court	= caught	

and we find that *yeah* can rhyme with *fair, idea* with *fear.*

Black speakers show an even higher degree of *r*-lessness than
white New Yorkers or Bostonians. The *r* of spelling becomes a schwa
or disappears before vowels as well as before consonants and pauses.
Thus in the speech of most white New Yorkers, *r* is pronounced when
a vowel follows, as in *four o'clock;* even though the *r* is found at the
end of a word, if the next word begins with a vowel, it is pronounced
as a consonantal [r]. For most black speakers, *r* is still not pronounced
in this position, and so never heard at the end of the word *four.* The
white speaker is helped in his reading or spelling by the existence of
the alternation in which the underlying *r* comes out before a vowel,
as in four o'clock, but the black speaker has no such clue to the underlying (spelling) form of the word *four.* Furthermore, the same
black speaker will often not pronounce intervocalic *r* in the middle
of a word, as indicated in the dialect spelling *inte'ested, Ca'ol.* He has
no clue, in his own speech, to the correct spelling form of such
words, and may have another set of homonyms besides those listed
above:

Carol	= Cal
Paris	= pass
terrace	= test

L-lessness

The consonant *l* is a liquid very similar to *r* in its phonetic nature. The chief difference is that with *l* the center of the tongue is up
and the sides are down, whereas with *r* the sides are up but the center
does not touch the roof of the mouth. The pattern of *l*-dropping is
very similar to that of *r*, except that it has never affected entire dialect areas in the same sweeping style. When *l* disappears, it is often replaced by a back unrounded glide, sometimes symbolized [ ],
instead of the center glide that replaces *r;* in many cases, *l* disappears

entirely, especially after the back rounded vowels. The loss of *l* is
much more marked among the black speakers we have interviewed
than among whites in northern cities, and one therefore finds much
greater tendencies toward such homonyms as

toll	= toe	all	= awe
help	= hep	Saul	= saw
tool	= too	fault	= fought

Simplification of Consonant Clusters

One of the most complex variables appearing in black speech is
the general tendency toward the simplification of consonant clusters
at the ends of words. A great many clusters are involved, primarily
those ending in /-t/ or /-d/, /-s/ or /-z/.[3] We are actually dealing with
two distinct tendencies: (1) a general tendency to reduce clusters of
consonants at the ends of words to single consonants, and (2) a more
general process of reducing the amount of information provided after
stressed vowels, so that individual final consonants are affected as
well. The first process is more regular and requires more intensive
study in order to understand the conditioning factors involved.

The chief /-t, -d/ clusters that are affected are (roughly in order
of frequency) /-st, -ft, -nt, -nd, -ld, -zd, -md/. Here they are given in
phonemic notation; in conventional spelling we have words such as
*past, passed, lift, laughed, bent, bend, fined, hold, poled, old, called,
raised, aimed.* In all these cases, if the cluster is simplified, it is the
last element that is dropped. Thus we have homonyms such as

past	= pass	mend	= men
rift	= riff	wind	= wine
meant	= men	hold	= hole

If we combine the effect of *-ld* simplification, loss of *-l*, and monoph-
thongization of /av/ and /aw/, we obtain

[i wa:]   She wow! = She wild!

and this equivalence has in fact been found in our data. It is important to bear in mind that the combined effect of several rules will

---

[3] When the /-t/ or /-d/ represents a grammatical inflection these consonants are
usually automatic alternants of the same abstract form *-ed*. Phonetic rules delete
the vowel (except after stems ending in /-t/ or /-d/), and we then have [t] following voiceless consonants such as /p, s, t, k/ and [d] in all other cases. In the same
way, [s] and [z] are coupled as voiceless and voiced alternants of the same *-s*
inflections, but in clusters that are a part of the root word we do not have such
automatic alternations.

add to the total number of homonyms, and even more, to the un-
expected character of the final result:

told = toll = toe

The /-s, -z/ clusters that are often simplified occur in such words
as *axe* /æks/, *six* /siks/, *box* /baks/, *parts* /parts/, *aims* /eymz/, *rolls*
/rowlz/, *leads* /liydz/, *besides* /bisaydz/, *John's* /džanz/, *that's* /æts/,
it's /its/, *its* /its/. The situation here is more complex than with the
/-t, -d/ clusters, since in some cases the first element of the cluster is
lost, and in other cases the second element.[4]

In one sense, there are a great many homonyms produced by
this form of consonant-cluster simplification, as we shall see when we
consider grammatical consequences. But many of these can also be
considered grammatical differences rather than changes in the shapes
of words. The /-t, -d/ simplification gives us a great many irreducible
homonyms, so that a child has no clue to the standard spelling differences from his own speech pattern. Though this is less common in
the case of /-s, -z/ clusters, we can occasionally have

six	= sick	Max	= Mack
box	= bock	mix	= Mick

as possible homonyms in the speech of many black children.

Weakening of Final Consonants

It was noted above that the simplification of final consonant
clusters was part of a more general tendency to produce less information after stressed vowels, so that final consonants, unstressed final
vowels, and weak syllables show fewer distinctions and more reduced
phonetic forms than initial consonants and stressed vowels. This is a
perfectly natural process in terms of the amount of information required for effective communication, since the number of possible
words that must be distinguished declines sharply after we select the
first consonant and vowel. German and Russian, for example, do not
distinguish voiced and voiceless consonants at the ends of words.
However, when this tendency is carried to extremes (and a nonstandard dialect differs radically from the standard language in this respect), it may produce serious problems in learning to read and spell.

This weakening of final consonants is by no means as regular as
the other phonological variables described above. Some individuals

---

[4] The loss of the first element—that is, assimilation of the following *s*—is most
common in forms where the *-s* represents the verb *is* or the pronoun *us* in *it's*,
that's and *let's*. In none of these cases is there a problem of homonymy.

appear to have generalized the process to the point where most of their syllables are of the CV type, that is, consonant plus vowel, and those we have interviewed in this category seem to have the most serious reading problems of all. In general, final /-t/ and /-d/ are the most affected by the process. Final /-d/ may be devoiced to a [t]-like form or disappear entirely. Final /-t/ is often realized as glottal stop, as in many English dialects, but more often disappears entirely. Less often, final /-g/ and /-k/ follow the same route as /-d/ and /-t/: /-g/ is devoiced or disappears, and /-k/ is replaced by glottal stop or disappears. Final /-m/ and /-n/ usually remain in the form of various degrees of nasalization of the preceding vowel. Rarely, sibilants /-s/ and /-z/ are weakened after vowels to the point where no consonant is heard at all. As a result of these processes, it is possible to have such homonyms as

Boot = Boo	seat = seed	= see
road = row	poor = poke	= pope
feed = feet	bit = bid	= big

It is evident that the loss of final /-l/ and /-r/, discussed above, is another aspect of this general weakening of final consonants, though of a much more regular nature than the cases considered in this section.

Other Phonological Variables

In addition to the types of homonymy singled out in the preceding discussion, there are a great many others that may be mentioned. They are of less importance for reading problems in general, since they have little impact on inflectional rules, but they do affect the shapes of words in the speech of black children. There is no distinction between /i/ and /e/ before nasals in the great majority of cases. In the parallel case before /-r/, and sometimes /-l/, we frequently find no distinction between the vowels /ih/ and /eh/. The corresponding pair of back vowels before /-r/ are seldom distinguished; that is, /uh/ and /oh/ fall together. The diphthongs /ay/ and /aw/ are often monophthongized, so that they are not distinguished from /ah/. The diphthong /oy/ is often a monophthong, especially before /-l/, and sometimes cannot be distinguished from the vowel /oh/, so that *oil = all.*

Among other consonant variables, we find the final fricative /-Θ/ is frequently merged with /f/, and similarly final /- / with /v/. Less frequently, /Θ/ and / / become /f/ and /v/ in intervocalic position. Initial consonant clusters that involve /r/ show considerable variation: /str/ is often heard as /skr/; / r/ as [sw, sr, s]. In a more complex series of shifts, /r/ is frequently lost as the final element of an initial cluster.

As a result of these various phonological processes, we find that the following series of possible homonyms are characteristic of the speech of many black children:

pin	= pen	beer	= bear	poor	= pour
tin	= ten	cheer	= chair	sure	= shore
since	= cents	steer	= stair	moor	= more
		peel	= pail		
Ruth = roof		stream	= scream	boil	= ball
death = deaf		strap	= scrap	oil	= all
find	= found = fond				
time			= Tom		
	pound = pond				

CHANGES IN THE SHAPES OF WORDS

The series of potential homonyms given in the preceding sections indicate that black children may have difficulty in recognizing many words in their standard spellings. They may look up words under the wrong spellings in dictionaries and be unable to distinguish words that are plainly different for the teacher. If the teacher is aware of these sources of confusion, he may be able to anticipate a great many of the children's difficulties. But if neither the teacher nor the children are aware of the great differences in their sets of homonyms, it is obvious that confusion will occur in every reading assignment.

However, the existence of homonyms on the level of a phonetic output does not prove that the speakers have the same sets of mergers on the more abstract level that corresponds to the spelling system. For instance, many white New Yorkers merge *guard* and *god* in casual speech, but in reading style they have no difficulty in pronouncing the /r/ where it belongs. Since the /r/ in *car* reappears before a following vowel, it is evident that an abstract *r* occurs in their lexical understanding of the word. Thus the standard spelling system finds support in the learned patterns of careful speech and in the alternations that exist within any given style of speech.

The phonetic processes discussed above are often considered to be "low level" rules—that is, they do not affect the underlying or abstract representations of words. One piece of evidence for this view is that the deletable final /-r, -l, -s, -z, -t, -d/ tend to be retained when a vowel follows at the beginning of the next word. This effect of a following vowel would seem to be a phonetic factor, restricting the operation of a phonetic rule; in any case, it is plain that the final consonant must "be there" in some abstract sense if it appears in this prevocalic position. If this were not the case, we would find a variety of odd final consonants appearing, with no fixed relation to the standard form.

For all major variables that we have considered, there is a definite and pronounced effect of a following vowel in realizing the standard form.

The same argument, however, can be applied to show that black speakers have underlying forms considerably different from those of white speakers. The white speakers showed almost as much overall simplification of the clusters before a following consonant, but none at all before a following vowel; in other words, their abstract forms were effectively equivalent to the spelling forms. The black speakers showed only a limited reduction in the degree of simplification when a vowel followed.

GRAMMATICAL CORRELATES
OF THE PHONOLOGICAL VARIABLES

As we examine the various final consonants affected by the phonological processes, we find that these are the same consonants that represent the principal English inflections. The shifts in the sound system therefore often coincide with grammatical differences between nonstandard and standard English, and it is usually difficult to decide whether we are dealing with a grammatical or a phonological rule. In any case, we can add a great number of homonyms to the lists given above when we consider the consequences of deleting /-r, -l, -s, -z, -t, -d/.

The Possessive

In many cases, the absence of the possessive *s* can be interpreted as a reduction of consonant clusters, although this is not the most likely interpretation. The *-s* is absent just as frequently after vowels as after consonants for many speakers. Nevertheless, we can say that the overall simplification pattern is favored by the absence of the *-s* inflection. In the case of *-r*, we find more direct phonological influence: two possessive pronouns that end in /-r/ have become identical with the personal pronoun:

[eɪ] book   not [:] book

In rapid speech, one can not distinguish *you* from *your* from *you-all*. This seems to be a shift in grammatical forms, but the relation to the phonological variables is plain when we consider that *my*, *his*, *her*, and *our* remain as possessive pronouns. Only in areas under strong Creole influence will one hear *I book*, *she book*, or *we book*, for there is no phonological process that would bring the possessives into near-identity with the personal pronouns.

The Future

The loss of final /-l/ has a serious effect on the realization of future forms:

you'll = you	he'll = he
they'll = they	she'll = she

In many cases, therefore, the colloquial future is identical with the colloquial present. The form *will* is still used in its emphatic or full form, and various reductions of *going to* are frequent, so there is no question about the grammatical category of the future. One con- tracted form of the future heard only among black speakers is in the first person, *I'm a shoot you*; there is no general process for the de- letion of this *m*.

The Copula

The finite verb forms of *be* are frequently not realized in sen- tences such as *you tired* and *he in the way*. If we examine the para- digm as a whole, we find that phonological processes have obviously been at work. In the first person, we find that either the full or con- tracted form is normal; such forms as *I here* or *I is here* are extremely rare except perhaps among very young children, but because they are so striking many casual observers have reported them as common. The third-person form *is* represents a true variable for all vernacular speakers. We have found that the deletion of *is* ranges from twenty or thirty percent to seventy or eighty percent, but it is never absent entirely even in the most casual speech. On the other hand, the second-person singular and plural form *are* is deleted much more fre- quently and is almost completely absent for many speakers. It is evident that the phonological processes that affect *are* are much stronger than those that affect *is*.

It may seem strange at first to speak of phonological processes operating to effect the deletion of a whole word. However, our recent studies of the copula have revealed that in every situation in which standard English cannot contract to 's, the nonstandard vernacular does not permit deletion of *is*.[5] Thus contraction precedes deletion in the rules operating here; the rules of consonant-cluster simplification, discussed above, apply in part to this situation.

The Past

Again, there is no doubt that phonological processes are active in reducing the frequency of occurrence of the /-t, -d/ inflection.

pass = past = passed	pick = picked
miss = mist = missed	loan = loaned
fine = find = fined	raise = raised

At the same time, there is no question about the existence of a past tense category. The irregular past tense forms, which are very frequent in ordinary conversation, are plainly marked as past no matter what final simplification takes place.

I told him   [atoɪm]   he kept mine   [hik pmaɪn]

The problem that confronts us concerns the form of the regular suffix *-ed*. Is there such an abstract form in the structure of the nonstandard English spoken by black children? The answer will make a considerable difference both to teaching strategy and to our understanding of the reading problems that children face. We have carried out a number of quantitative studies of consonant clusters and the *-ed* suffix on this point.[6] The behavior of speakers in spontaneous group interaction has been studied, as well as their ability to recognize *-ed* in reading as a past tense signal and to detect nonstandard forms in printed material. Our conclusion is that there are many black children who do not have enough support in their linguistic system to identify *-ed* as a past tense signal, and they must be taught the meaning of this form from the outset. There are many others who

---

[5] Thus in *He is here, He ain't here, is he? Yes he is, I'm smarter than he is, That's what it is,* and many other cases we find that *is* can neither be contracted or deleted. See William Labov, "Contraction, Deletion and Inherent Variability of the English Copula," *Language,* Vol. 44 (1969), pp. 718-722.

[6] See "Some Sources of Reading Problems" cited in note 1 and Cooperative Research Report 3288 for quantitative data.

have no difficulty in *reading -ed* even though they do not pronounce it. In our investigations, we use test sentences such as

1. Tom read all the time.
2. Last month I read five books.
3. Now I read and write better than my brother.
4. When I passed by, I read the sign.

The unique homograph *read* helps us to discover the status of the *-ed* suffix for the reader. If he correctly reads aloud sentences 1 and 2 with the past tense form [r d], and sentence 3 in the present tense form [ri:d], then we know that he can interpret this homograph in a standard manner depending on whether it is placed in a past or present context. Then in sentence 4, he should give us the pronunciation [r d] *if* he deciphers the *-ed* in *passed* as a signal of the past tense, whether or not he pronounces it.

An Overview of the Nonstandard Vernacular

We have contrasted the casual speech of peer groups of ten- to twelve-year-olds with that of groups of fourteen- to sixteen-year-olds. We find that the rules for the basic vernacular become more consistent and regular rather than more mixed with standard English. Some phonological conditions become more consistent, and the spelling forms of individual words, such as *box*, come closer to the standard forms. But the basic grammatical patterns (no third-person singular *-s*, no possessive *-s*, weak *-ed* suffix, stylistic deletion of the copula, and so on) remain well fixed. Whereas the dropping of the plural *-s* is never more than an occasional feature, the third-person singular *-s* has no more support among sixteen-year-olds than among twelve-year-olds.

The most striking evidence of these underlying grammatical facts is the effect of a following vowel on the consonant cluster concerned. When a vowel follows *-ed*, as in *messed up*, the percentage of simplified forms drops moderately. When a vowel follows clusters that are a part of a word, as in *act* or *box*, we see a regular decrease in simplification. This effect becomes stronger with the increasing age of the speakers; and when a vowel follows plural clusters, as in *books*, there is a marked decrease in simplification as well. But when a vowel follows the third-person singular *-s*, as in *works*, or possessive *-s*, as in *John's*, we do not find the *-s* remaining more often. On the contrary, it appears *less* often than when a consonant follows. For this reason, we can argue that there is no phonological process involved here at all. In the underlying grammar, there simply is no morpheme -*s* representing the third-person singular of the verb, and no morpheme -*s* representing the possessive. To be sure, there is a possessive category in *my*, *our*, *his*, and *mine*, and so on, but the particular use of -*s* to mean the possessive after nouns must be taught from the beginning.

CONSEQUENCES FOR THE TEACHING OF READING

Let us consider the problem of teaching a youngster to read who has the general phonological and grammatical characteristics just described. The most immediate way of analyzing his difficulties is through the interpretation of his oral reading. As we have seen there are many phonological rules that affect his pronunciation, but not necessarily his understanding of the grammatical signals or his grasp of the underlying lexical forms. The two questions are distinct: the relations between grammar and pronunciation are complex and require careful interpretation.

If a pupil is given a certain sentence to read, say *He passed by both of them*, he may say [hi pæs baᴵ bof ə dɛm]. The teacher may wish to correct this bad reading, perhaps by saying, "No, it isn't [hi pæs baᴵ bof ə dɛm], it's [hi pæst baᴵ boθ əv dɛm]." One difficulty is that these two utterances may sound the same to many children—both the reader and those listening—and they may be utterly confused by the correction. Others may be able to hear the difference, but have no idea of the significance of the extra [t] and the interdental forms of *th-*. The most embarrassing fact is that the child who first read the sentence may have performed his reading task correctly, and understood the -*ed* suffix just as it was intended. In that case, the teacher's correction is completely beside the point.

We have two distinct cases to consider. In one case, the deviation in reading may be only a difference in pronunciation on the part of a child who has a different set of homonyms from the teacher. Here, correction might be quite unnecessary. In the second case, we may be dealing with a child who has no concept of -*ed* as a past tense marker, who considers the -*ed* a meaningless set of silent letters. Obviously the correct teaching strategy would involve distinguishing between these two cases and treating them quite differently.

How such a strategy might be put into practice is a problem that educators may be able to solve by using information provided by linguists. As a linguist, I can suggest several basic principles derived from our work that may be helpful in further curriculum research and application.

1. In the analysis and correction of oral reading, teachers must begin to make the basic distinction between differences in pronunciation and mistakes in reading. Information on the dialect patterns of black children should be helpful toward this end.

2. In the early stages of teaching reading and spelling it may be necessary to spend much more time on the grammatical function of certain inflections that may have no function in the dialect of some of the children. In the same way, it may be necessary to treat the final elements of certain clusters with the special attention given to silent letters such as *b* in *lamb*.

3. A certain amount of attention given to perception training in the first few years of school may be extremely helpful in teaching children to hear and make standard English distinctions. But perception training need not be complete in order to teach children to read. On the contrary, most of the differences between standard and nonstandard English described here can be taken as differences in the sets of homonyms that must be accepted in reading patterns. On the face of it, there is no reason why a person cannot learn to read standard English texts quite well in a nonstandard pronunciation. Eventually, the school may wish to teach the child an alternative system of pronunciation. But the key to the situation in the early grades is for the teacher to know the system of homonyms of nonstandard English and to know the grammatical differences that separate her own speech from that of the child. The teacher must be prepared to accept the system of homonyms for the moment if this will advance the basic process of learning to read, but not the grammatical differences. Thus the task of teaching the child to read *-ed* is clearly that of getting him to recognize the graphic symbols as a marker of the past tense, quite distinct from the task of getting him to say [pæst] for *passed.*

If the teacher has no understanding of the child's grammar and set of homonyms, she may be arguing with him at cross purposes. Over and over again, the teacher may insist that *cold* and *coal* are different, without realizing that the child perceives this as only a difference in meaning, not in sound. She will not be able to understand why he makes so many odd mistakes in reading, and he will experience only a vague confusion, somehow connected with the ends of words. Eventually, he may stop trying to analyze the shapes of letters that follow the vowel and guess wildly at each word after he deciphers the first few letters. Or he may completely lose confidence in the alphabetic principle and try to recognize each word as a whole. This loss of confidence seems to occur frequently in the third and fourth grades, and it is characteristic of many children who are effectively nonreaders.

The sources of reading problems discussed here are only a few of the causes of poor reading in black ghetto schools. But they are quite specific and easily isolated. The information provided here may have immediate application in the overall program of improving the teaching of reading to children in these urban areas.

PART FOUR

DOWN HERE
WHERE IT'S AT:
REPORTS FROM FIVE TEACHERS

The five brief selections below were written as a response to a course in dialectology. In these essays five in-service, inner-city teachers discuss problems of teaching in the ghetto and methods of implementing the subject matter of the dialects course into their everyday teaching.

Larry Bowers

PROBLEMS IN THE GHETTO SCHOOL

I am presently teaching science in junior high school. This is my first professional teaching assignment since graduating from college. The students I have in my six classes range from the very quick learners to the very slow and emotionally handicapped. They are in the seventh and eighth grades. The student enrollment is almost ninety-nine percent black.

While attending college, I expressed an interest in working in the ghetto or hard-core area, and when I received my student-teaching assignment I found myself assigned to an all-white upper-middle-class school. Thus, during my first year of actual teaching I have suffered from the usual difficulties that most first-year teachers in any school suffer from, but I also feel that some special preparations should have been offered while I was in the university. It is my opinion that courses dealing with the teaching of children in the ghetto should be

offered in every teachers' college. There might even be merit in requiring these courses for everyone in education.

I teach about one hundred and thirty students, and at least
seventy-five percent have a below-average reading level. My experiences reinforced the saying "every teacher is a reading teacher."
However, when preparing at a university, a person in secondary education seldom takes a course in the teaching of reading. I was not
required to take a teaching-of-reading course, and I do not think such
a course, not to mention a course in reading instruction for slow
learners, was available for all secondary teachers. It is my opinion
that it is necessary for us to change the education of our teachers in
order that they may change and improve the education of their students.

At my school, the students are tested and placed into homogeneous groups. My groups range, as I stated before, from the very
intelligent to the groups labeled EMH (Educable Mentally Handicapped) and Emotionally Disturbed. I must confess that I have no
training in the last two areas. My immediate superiors are untrained
in these areas also. We have discussed the problems but have not yet
found any major solutions.

Many problems arise from having such a wide range of student
abilities. Much more preparation is required by the teacher, and the
subject matter and course content suffer when required to be presented in four or five different ways. One possible solution proposed
by one of our special-education instructors was that we have one
teacher to handle all special-education science classes. One teacher
would take some courses on teaching EMH students and then teach
only "sped" (special education) science. This would be much better
than having each science teacher teaching one or two EMH groups in
addition to his regular classes. I should point out that there are ten
or twelve students in the EMH core rooms, but when the students
come to science or math or some other special-area class they come
in groups of twenty to twenty-eight. This makes it difficult to work
with individual students rather than the group.

With materials and textbooks one runs into similar problems.
The wide range of student ability in one class makes it difficult to
use the same textbook. I have spent close to $30 this semester on
materials to supplement the text. I did this on my own, because I
needed the materials right away. I could have had some materials
made at the audio-visual center. This center does very good work,
and I am now trying to get some ideas for projects that they could
prepare. But I should have five different textbooks for my six classes.
The textbooks that we use now are adequate for the fast groups but
are still too advanced for the low-average and EMH groups.

Up to this point I have not made any definite points concerning the introduction of methods learned in this course into my instruction. Many of the points I have mentioned were discussed in detail in class. This has just helped me to confirm and slightly alter some of my beliefs about teaching the young people in the ghetto. I do feel that the course leaned toward the point of instruction on the elementary level, but many of those methods still apply to the junior high grades. The course helped bring out some very good practical and theoretical points. Some of those points that come to mind: recognizing that there is a black dialect, as well as a white dialect; learning not to correct or try to change a student's pronunciation; being very conscious not to "tune" a student out, but rather bending a little to try to "tune" him in.

Some people might not feel that many of the subjects we discussed during class were of importance in educating or further educating teachers. However, many of us are not really aware of the problems and surrounding circumstances that our students come into contact with, and this type of informal discussion proves to be very beneficial when teaching and interacting with the children. There is merit in learning what a new slang term means and learning, or at least being exposed to, some of the names of soul food. It is time that our educational institutions start trying to bridge the existing void in preparing people to teach in the ghetto area.

Another point that I had thought about previously that was mentioned during our discussions was that of educating the white person to the black person's ways. Our society has been trying to teach the blacks the ways of the whites, but it seems to me that it is about time for the whites to learn about the blacks. This is the first class in five years of college that I have had that dealt with the black race. It was only in my last year in college that a course in black history was taught, and I have learned from teaching and from this course that in order to be an effective teacher one must first learn about the people he or she are teaching. I have mentioned only the black race because this is where my main interest is now, but the idea is applicable to all minority groups.

I came into ghetto teaching quite ignorant and am slowly learning more about how to be an effective teacher. This course was enjoyable if only because it presented a chance to throw back and forth ideas and attitudes openly with other teachers in the same situation, to discuss problems and little tricks of the trade that sometimes help to meet these problems, not only with the idea of solving the problem, but to help get some insight as to why the problem may exist. I feel that a school staff could profit from having similar informal talk sessions during which teachers could discuss student problems, and exhibit and explain professional materials or other items they use to help solve teaching problems.

Joan Gayle Wilson Chapin

TEACHING IN A GHETTO SCHOOL

The World, the United States, the City—every place we see or read about or hear about is faced with a serious problem: education. The solution lies in the problem. People name the problems as war, crime, racism, disease, ghettos, and so on. The key to solving all of these problems is education. Of course, the world cannot have one ideal system of education. I do not even believe there is one ideal system of education because, obviously, people, their needs, desires, capabilities, and ambitions are all so diversified that one system would be ridiculous even to think about. However, education is still the answer.

I teach a sixth grade at a Title I school; this is my first full year of teaching. I did teach summer-school math at another Title I school; the difference is that the latter is a "white ghetto" school while the former is in the "black ghetto." All of my students are black except for one boy who came to us in the middle of the semester. He is accepted fairly well by the eight other boys in my class; the thirteen girls do not like him and they make no effort to disguise their dislike. This is the first time I have ever been around Blacks for any length of time, and the first week did present problems. To be blunt, my first dilemma on opening day was that all of my children looked alike! This situation remedied itself as I grew more familiar with my children. More important, though, was the fact that I could not understand what they said. Their language was not so different from mine, but their inflections, intonations, expressions, and lack of what is referred to as standard English threw me. Before I enrolled in the dialects course, I did not realize that the blacks spoke their own language and were responsible for many of our colloquial expressions.

There are many changes that must be made in education, especially in the ghetto schools. Straying from the academic level for a moment and discussing nonacademic problems, I feel that we have to show or make these children find a place and purpose in life. To understand this reasoning fully, a teacher must be familiar with the background of most ghetto children. Many come from broken homes, live with relatives, do not have adequate food, shelter, clothing, or the opportunities to play, read, or work. Often their parents are uneducated—sometimes even illiterate—and many are on ADC. A child raised in this atmosphere sees little else. Often there is little love shown. The child is left to make his own life—the best way he can. This is not true for all black children, but these conditions do exist. Many black children are undisciplined and do not realize there is a life better than the one they are leading. Even if they do realize it, they do not know how, or oftentimes do not have the ability, to raise themselves out of their situations. They need help; they need love, discipline, and attention. They need teachers they can respect. That word—respect—is one key to the answer. In any class a mutual respect is imperative to learning. Just as a child must respect a teacher, so must the teacher respect that child—not only as a student, but as a human being.

Part of the role of the school must be to fill the gap found in a ghetto home. It is a small foundation, but a good place to start. We should build the foundation with elementary counselors. I believe this is a coming concept in education. Many of these children have problems that untrained personnel cannot understand, and that problem might be one reason that the child is a nonreader. Before one can reach these children academically—with books—one must first reach them with interest, kindness, trust, love, or firmness—whatever it takes to be accepted by them.

The knowledgeability of my superiors varies. My immediate superiors naturally understand the problems of ghetto children. They work with them every day. However, supervisors, department heads, and E-TV (Educational Television) personnel (generally speaking) are ignorant of the situation and the problems that do exist. This is only natural. A person has to meet a problem, become familiar with it, and work with it before he can hope to offer suggestions or criticisms on solving it. I know a supervisor who, out of necessity, had to substitute teach in a ghetto school. After one-half day, she declared she could not take it any more and she left. Yet this same person, who could not work with black children, supervises, corrects, and compliments teachers that do work with black children. How can people who do not work in the ghetto know the problems of black students and set up programs to alleviate those problems? This I cannot understand.

Some people say that working in a Title I school offers a teacher many advantages because of the access to a variety of materials and books and audio-visual aides. In most instances this is correct; however, I am still waiting for readers that I ordered five months ago. Two of my three reading groups do not have workbooks.

This brings me to another problem—reading. What I would change immediately in education is the reading program. The first thing I would recommend teaching is *how* to read. Reading starts in the primary grades and consequently the responsibility lies there. All efforts should be concentrated almost solely on reading. When the child has mastered the most basic reading skills, then he can be introduced to the next step. Reading readiness and mastering skills in the lower grades cannot be overstressed. All phases of education, formal and informal, depend on a person's ability to read, interpret, and understand symbols.

The lower grades are the areas where small classes are important, and primary classes are at present too large for effective teaching of reading. Therefore, many children do not gain the ground-level skills in reading—their foundation is too weak to build upon. If a child has not learned the first-grade skills, he should be retained until he does— if he is capable. If the child does not have the capability or intelligence, then he should be in a special classroom where trained personnel can help him. I am a firm believer in retaining a child in the lower grades for remedial reading. However, the process would be a waste of time if the same methods of instruction were used over and over again on the same child. If one method was unsuccessful for an entire year, then it would be useless and boring to use the same method again. It is only an "easy out" for a teacher to promote a nonreader, and it only lessens the child's chances for success and lowers his self-image.

My low reading group is in a 2.1 reader. They will probably never read beyond the third-grade level. They can't really take an interest in reading; the same material has been presented to them for five years. They have lost interest and do not want to learn. A teacher cannot motivate a child at this point; the child must motivate himself. Sixth graders feel insulted if they are given a second-grade reader. Why do publishers insist on marking their books by grade level? Why not publish the books according to mastery of skills? If nothing else, it would save embarrassment for the student.

We must improve education in all areas. I do believe the solution to poverty and crime and most of the problems that face the world today is in education. The task is almost impossible, though, because we only reach a very small percentage of those with whom we are in contact. The others will be content to live in the ghetto and with the problems of the ghetto—white or black. This is the main reason I teach in the disadvantaged area. If I can lift some of my children out of their environment, then it is a start toward a better world, for them, for me, for everyone.

H. James Anding

COMMUNICATION GAP

There is a wall in every school building which keeps the cold and the rain out and the children in. This wall is made of concrete, steel, wood, asbestos, or glass. We have all seen this wall, can readily acknowledge its existence and usefulness, and therefore need not dwell upon it.

However, there is another wall which separates the school from the outside world—one which is most important in our teaching situation. This is a wall which many people say they cannot see and which many others do not want to see. Research shows that it is seen more easily by students than by their parents or teachers. It prevents students from making any vital connection between what they learn in the classroom and what they know is happening in the smoldering world outside the school. There are many names for this wall, but I choose to call it a "communication gap."

The dialects course is a foundation upon which we can build a bridge to span the gap in relating to our students. It is not the bridge itself, but the anchoring pads which we are able to build upon. It has been said that "you can never really know a man until you stand in his shoes and walk around in them" How can we as teachers teach a child we cannot relate to in any way except as an authority figure? It is essential that we relate and communicate, so that we can teach effectively.

Reading has been defined as a process of recognizing, interpreting, and understanding symbols which trigger off meanings in the light of one's background of experiences. Using this definition, we are compelled to teach in a way which brings together new concepts and old, culminating in a learning experience. To do this we must know how to communicate to our students.

Once we become aware of these needs, we can implement our class findings into many teaching experiences. But first there must be a sensitivity to the situation, and, if necessary, a change of attitude. Otherwise it becomes another facade and our students are the first to know—we find out last because we are slow to admit defeat.

INVOLVEMENT

Get others involved by making them aware. I had an opportunity to speak to a group of white, middle-class high-school seniors from South Dakota. They expressed a desire to get involved for a weekend in the ghetto. This was a prime time to make them aware of the differences in dialectology in different environments.

RISK IS CENTRAL TO THE EXPERIENCE

From class, I have developed a basis upon which to formulate a teaching experience. Thus, I can try out new behaviors and ideas and take a few risks because I have this new experience.

The example of West African Pidgin provided a genuine learning experience as I learned to read this different-sounding tongue in class and as we figured out its meaning together. This knowledge can be incorporated into classes in social studies, English, and cultural understanding.

Book reports used in this class can be used in our other classes as well. In my other classes I would never have brought up the African novel by Achebe. But seeing it around, the students wanted to know why I was reading it, and what it was about. This started a new interest in proverbs. We had a unit on "wise sayings" in reading that was so full of "Birds of a feather . . . " it became boring. But when the students heard African ones (new to them), more beneficial discussions began.

EXPECT RESULTS

Experience does not necessarily lead to brilliant learning situations. We are known to translate new experiences and information so they fit perfectly into our old, narrow, and often prejudicial way of living. That is why it is essential that students have the opportunity to validate their experiences and learning with those of their peers, and to check out these learnings with the accumulated body of knowledge which we can make available to them. This is a right we also have as teachers. We can take our newly acquired ideas and compare them with those of our fellow teachers. In doing this we run the risk of striking out, but we can usually expect results.

Not only is it important to "speak the child's language" but to know and understand why he speaks in a particular way. Better still, it's important to reach these children with learning experiences in the light of their backgrounds. When we accomplish this, we have become involved enough to take the risks facing us as teachers, not only expecting results but being proud of them.

Gary T. Barta

IMPLEMENTING THE DIALECTS COURSE

It should be recognized that culturally deprived children speak differently and listen to a different jargon in their home setting. Most teachers, however, are not aware of the fact that this dialect is deeply rooted in Afro-American heritage. These same teachers are also unaware of the fact that this dialect difference is "legal" and full-blown. This ignorance on the teacher's part leads to the contention that black children use poor English and that their speech needs constant correction to bring it up to the quality of "standard English." This constant correction of speech habits by the educator is usually done in a negative manner. It is believed by most that this constant criticism on the teacher's part tends to make the so-called culturally deprived child fearful of expressing himself verbally in class and in other situations where he is in contact with individuals having a comfortable command of standard English. It is not hard to imagine the frustrations and apprehension in the mind of a student so stifled. The educator is actually curbing the basic communicative process essential to normal intellectual development. Would it be wrong to say, then, that lack of interest in school and excessive nonattendance could actually be promoted by the educators, in their grammatic lust for a "virgin" dialect composed purely of standard English elements? This writer does not maintain that the drop-out problem rests entirely on the misunderstanding of this dialect situation, but sufficient evidence has been brought to light to make it apparent that this is a contributing factor, a factor that deserves more concern than has been awarded it in the past.

If by dissolving this awkward situation, or at least lessening the damage caused by it, educators can keep more students in school, a course in dialectology and developmental reading for the disadvantaged child has great worth. The next logical step would then be the implementation of concepts and ideas gained in a course of this type.

Perhaps it is here where the greatest problem to the educator will arise. A minority of teachers are currently being made aware of the fact that bidialectal education among ethnic groups is a necessity. But consider the major segment of our teaching populace. Courses in dialectology were nonexistent until recently in our area and few of the teachers are concerned enough to take advantage of those currently offered. As a language-arts instructor dealing almost entirely with black students of the lower-income bracket, this writer sees the need for an understanding of the bidialectal system and what it means. But what about the educator who denies the existence of a "legal" black dialect? This educator presents the premier obstacle to progress for it is he who must first be enlightened to the seriousness of his denial. One can imagine the clamor which will arise when this type of teacher is introduced to these new and liberal ideas. Consider his reaction when told "ain't" is an adequate spoken substitute for "aren't," and that ghetto speech is an absolute necessity to the social success of the black child in his home setting.[1] This must be the starting point for the concerned few. The attack must be directed at that afore-mentioned majority of conservative teachers who are unknowingly making it impossible for the black student to express himself.

The dialect differences of black students must be considered in the same light as geographic speech patterns. No one would consider correcting a New Englander when he says "Omahar" instead of "Omaha." That people in different geographic locations use a different jargon is a generally accepted fact, but often unaccepted is the idea that differences in economic strata also have effects on the spoken word. Only after attitudes like these are altered will the real work with black students begin.

The logical progression would take on from this point of new concepts to ideas for immediate action, to what can be done for the black student once his problems in dialect and reading are understood. To begin with, negative reinforcement of speech mannerisms must be abolished completely. This "Bonnie and Clyde"[2] approach is far outdated and, in the opinion of many psychologists, only about one-tenth as effective as positive methods. Perhaps standard English, which many deem necessary in the blacks' dealings with most white people, could be made more palatable if it were offered in the manner of a foreign language rather than jammed at black students.

---

[1] Board of Education of the City of New York, *Nonstandard Dialect* (Champaign, Ill.: National Council of Teachers of English, 1968), p. 4.

[2] Roger W. Shuy, "Bonnie and Clyde Tactics in English Teaching," *Florida FL Reporter* (Special Anthology Issue), 7 (Spring/Summer 1969), p. 81, ff.

As for the new reading programs designed to aid the immediate situation, many aspects must be taken into consideration. First, it is apparent that teachers on the elementary level are ill-prepared to aid the disadvantaged child in bringing his reading ability to a sufficient level for social and economic success. Far too little time has been spent in preparing most elementary teachers for the acute problems found in the urban situation. These teachers use reading programs which are designed for the white middle-class child by members of the white middle class. Most materials used in today's reading courses are aloof from and fail to relate to the black child and the situation which is distinctly his. More black-oriented reading materials must be made available for use on the elementary level if this situation is to be remedied.

Too often in the past, reading has been solely the responsibility of the elementary schools. Again this smacks of the middle-class attitude toward public education. Today's black student at junior-high age needs much work in reading skills, yet reading is relegated to a minor role in grades seven to nine and is usually taught by a teacher whose subject area is far from reading. More and more specialized personnel must be channeled into the reading programs of secondary schools in the ghetto area.

This writer has briefly touched on what he considers to be serious gaps in today's educational system. The misgivings concerning speech mannerisms and reading ability could quite conceivably be rooted in prejudices of antiquity concerning the black person's place in society. Whatever the causes, these attitudes are real and current and are daily taking their toll among a great segment of this country's young people. The job facing concerned educational revolutionaries is certain to be a burdensome yet fulfilling task, for to them is awarded the twofold task of educating their students and awakening their fellow educators.

Mary T. LaBute

THE DIALECTS COURSE

Before attempting to evaluate the implementation of the subject matter of this class in my actual classroom teaching, I must first comment briefly on the atmosphere or climate of the class. The stated intent of the class was the "honest discussion of America's number-one social problem." I must admit that at first I was skeptical about the degree of honesty such a class could have, and also about what could actually be accomplished.

I am happy to acknowledge that my skepticism was unnecessary and unwarranted. I feel that we very openly and sincerely discussed many of the problems behind "the problem," things that needed bringing out. For example, a black female student honestly admitted, both overtly and inadvertently, her many insecurities stemming from her racial background and experience, even though she is presently a very successful teacher in the Omaha inner-city schools. I assimilated many startling bits of information I have never before given thought to—things I had always taken for granted—even after teaching for the past three years in close association with an integrated staff. I view with a new perspective the problem of linguistics and the black dialect and the vast differences in culture between the black community and white middle-class America.

Another thought which came to me many times as I sat in class discussions and listened to older, white middle-class teachers was that a class in modern grammar and linguistics could have enlightened them and helped to clarify many of their traditional grammar-teaching hang-ups. I now place more value on the grammar course, which I studied three years ago, not realizing how much it has helped my understanding in my present teaching position. Before I took the grammar course, I reasoned and taught much as these teachers did (being older, white, and middle-class, also!).

As for the subject matter of the dialects course, I feel that the many fine reports and follow-up discussions, especially those on the lives of black leaders, were very enlightening. (I am now reading *The Autobiography of Malcolm X.*) I feel that now I can better understand the frustrations of blacks with our social structure and why some of them have reacted as they have.

I have gained more understanding of ghetto language and how

it is tied into black culture, attitudes, and values. Knowledge of the kinetic element of black language and connotations of words, good or bad, is very useful information for a teacher of black children, if he or she is to use good judgment in resolving the many disputes and discipline problems which arise daily in the classroom.

The readings on black dialect which we have studied will be of much practical use in the classroom. I am presently trying out the idea of experience story-writing with one of my fourth-grade reading groups. I have found that the children vastly enjoy writing stories without worrying about proper grammar and spelling. Later we have valuable discussions as we translate their stories into standard English. My students have also presented spontaneous, original plays, using a puppet theater we have made for use in our classroom. Students will use many expressions in black dialect when they do not directly face an audience. This has been very beneficial to the shy and backward students. I agree with William Labov that "taboo" words used by a child will open him up, and that unnecessary verbiage does not always serve to help in communication. It is good to know that many well-known educators feel that standard English can be viewed as a second dialect.

Another useful subject brought out in class was one of home visits. The value of home visits should never be underestimated. They teach us much that is helpful in understanding the child's physical and cultural environment. Parents can teach teachers and teachers can teach parents in this way, offering immeasurable help to the child.

In conclusion, being a member of this class has been a rewarding experience. I have acquired knowledge which I will use both directly and indirectly in dealing with my students. Also, I believe the subject matter taught in this class will be receiving much attention in the near future. "America's number-one social problem" can be alleviated to a great extent with acceptance and understanding of the dialects of socially stigmatized groups, including black Americans, Mexican Americans, and American Indians.

PART FIVE

WHERE DO WE GO FROM HERE?

LANGUAGE AND EDUCATION

Thomas B. Kochman

SOCIAL FACTORS IN THE CONSIDERATION OF TEACHING STANDARD ENGLISH

The purpose of this paper is twofold: one, to weigh the educational value of an oral language program which attempts to teach standard dialect to speakers of a nonstandard dialect, and two, to consider the probable success of such a program, given present social trends.

My first quarrel with such a program is that it does not develop the ability of a person to use language which I would further define as performance capability in a variety of social contexts on a variety of subject matter. Instead, we utilize valuable time to set up drill exercises which are designed to get the individual to replace socially stigmatized forms with socially preferred ones. I cannot endorse as valid a program that sacrifices individual language growth in exchange for some nebulous and highly problematic "social security." The child comes to us with some ability to play the horn and no ability to play the piano. This type of program presumes that a mediocre ability to play the piano is to be preferred to a better than average ability to play the horn. I cannot accept this thesis.

Underlying this approach seems to be a misapplication of Basil Bernstein's terms which falsely equates *restrictive code* and *elaborated code* with respectively, nonstandard dialect and standard dialect.

It ought to be noted, as Bernstein uses the term, *code* is not to be equated with *langue*, but *parole*, not with *competence* but *performance*. What is restrictive or elaborated is not in fact the *code* as sociolinguists use the term, but the message.

This false equation is further reinforced by the observation made by some that speakers of standard dialect possess more elaborate users of language than speakers of nonstandard dialect. This coincidence is erroneously interpreted to be casual, viz, that speakers of standard dialect are more capable *because* they speak standard dialect. You hear remarks such as "there are things you can't say in nonstandard dialect." These people overlook the fact that standard dialect speakers are so designated by their educational level which often includes being better educated in the *use* of language. What limitations there are exist in the abilities of the speakers.

I might add that many elaborate users of language perform in the nonstandard dialect of the Black Urban Communities and the Kentucky mountains. People who make observations such as the one cited in the paragraph above generally know little of the high degree of prestige associated with verbal ability and consequent high degree of verbal performance in the above named sub-cultures and my guess is that they care to know even less.

The point here is that you can and do have elaborate performances in nonstandard dialect as well as standard and restrictive performances in standard dialect as well as nonstandard.

My second quarrel with such a program deals with what can be called its efficiency quotient. How much time and drill are required to acquire the new set of language habits necessary to produce even a mediocre and restrictive performance in standard dialect. Speech teachers tell me that with maximum cooperation it takes several months of drill to get a person to say *ask* who formerly said *aks*. My own observation tells me that the input in time and effort is prodigious and the results negligible. Tying in this remark with those made earlier, how might this time be spent in a fashion more beneficial to the language growth and development of the learner?

My third quarrel deals with the exaggerated importance English and Speech teachers attach to being able to perform in a prestige dialect, far beyond its net social worth. How important is it really to getting or keeping a job, to getting the greatest amount of cooperation from your audience, or even to being necessary to the aesthetic of a speech event.

As regards getting a job there are any number of factors that take precedence over ability to perform in standard English such as labor supply and demand, race, membership in the dominant group, educational level, and presently, ability to threaten the establishment. Some factors influencing social and economic success are social background; race, dominant group membership; ability to manipulate people and situations; skill in exploiting others' abilities to personal advantage; acquiring political and social contacts; ability to project personality; ability to demonstrate skills of intelligence, aggressiveness, shrewdness, guile and judgment; and most important, the ability to bluff, i.e., deceive others about one's *actual* knowledge, intelligence, etc. Add to that, being a member of a group that constitutes a present threat to the establishment.

As regards the thesis that standard dialect is necessary to get the greatest cooperation from the audience, I have witnessed too many speech events where the audience accommodated the speaker on *his* terms and others where an accent actually added to the *authoritativeness* of the speaker. Also, it seems to me that speaking a *regional standard* that is different from the audience's might involve the same social handicap as speaking a nonstandard dialect. Educated South Midlanders experience much the same difficulty as uneducated ones in getting housing in Chicago. People from Chicago, New York and elsewhere seem to have different social attitudes towards regional standards and rank them differently on a social scale; yet we don't advocate that regional standard speakers accommodate the audience by modifying their speech. The point is if we are attempting to educate people that one regional standard is as good as another why not educate them that all dialects are equally good.

The final point here is that the aesthetic of a speech event involves a great deal more than the simple use of standard dialect speech forms. I have in mind such qualities as the ability to project personality, style, self-assurance, authoritativeness, native coloring, in a fluent manner, regardless of dialect.

I just read where the BBC in London is permitting the reporting of news events in dialects other than the Received Standard. They have found that news broadcasted on the scene by reporters in local dialect added a touch of "realism" to the presentation.

The second part of this paper proposes to deal with the probable success of such a program, given present social trends. The audience might well wonder why I am pursuing this aspect after I have just apparently concluded that such a program is not educationally fruitful. You ask "If it is not educationally sound, why is it necessary to consider whether it is possible." Your logic is flawless but unhappily it is based on the illusory assumption that what is done in the classroom is done only after it is decided that it is worth doing. My observations at English, Speech and TESOL conventions and in school classrooms in the past persuade me that teachers and supervisors are concerned almost exclusively with methodology—"how to teach it"—and are gratuitously deaf to the logically antecedent question of "whether to teach it at all." This portion of the paper is especially aimed at them.

What are the teaching problems facing the teacher who attempts to teach the prestige form of a dialect to, let us suppose, black children, against whom the focus of such a program is generally directed? The two teaching problems he will have to face are social in origin. They are the problems of motivation and reinforcement. Let us consider motivation first.

There are basically two reasons for wanting to learn a second language or dialect: cultural identification and/or functional need. With respect to the first reason we must take into account the alienation black people feel; with regard to the second reason we must consider the credibility gap that has been created because of the failure of blacks who had skills to get meaningful jobs. How has language teaching contributed to the alienation and credibility gap we now face? How have both contributed to the failure and frustration of students, producing a drop-out rate of 1000 students a month in our Chicago schools?

In the past and generally up to the present time children have encountered in the English and Speech classroom the prescriptive approach. This approach advanced the superiority of the standard dialect and through the process of exclusion, negation and derogation the inferiority of the nonstandard dialect, and by direct implication the inferiority of the speakers who speak it and the inferiority of their culture which produces it. You who are unwilling to accept the implication, ask yourselves why English spoken with a French accent is socially acceptable, even "charming," while English spoken with a black accent is not. The inescapable social truth of the matter is that people's attitudes towards other people's speech are merely an extension of people's attitudes towards their culture and the people of that culture. This point is not missed by the culturally different when they enter the middle class establishment of the schoolroom.

What was the underlying perspective behind this approach? Assimilationist! What was the justification? At worst, it was arrogant ethnocentrism; at best, it recognized that the society is prejudiced and the way to escape discrimination was by losing your group identification. Your perspective and attitude said: obliterate what is culturally different, or if you can't, conceal it; relegate it to the inside of your homes. The penalty for non-assimilation was social ostracism, so the groups that could assimilate did, but often with much bitterness and resentment, and then only partially.

The groups that couldn't assimilate or chose not to, like American Indians, blacks and Mexican-Americans, were and are relegated respectively to the societal oblivion of the reservation and the ghetto. They have been the invisible people of our society.

The assimilationist approach made people resentful, resistant to learning. Now it has made them angry enough to demand, through petition and boycott, an end to this kind of attitude and teaching.

It is to the credit of the linguistic approach that it has at least recognized that the speaker's native dialect has cultural value for him and is not to be tampered with. It advances the teaching of standard English as a second dialect. It is a step in the right direction but it hardly goes far enough. The problem is in its supposedly "realistic" approach. It says, "People make social judgments all the time. We live in a socially stratified and deterministic society. Recognize it! Conform to the existing social order and its rules." Unfortunately, the linguistic approach accepts as social determinant the same obnoxious and racist standards as the prescriptive-assimilationist approach and in so doing merely perpetuates the alienation begun with its predecessor.

If a child does not wish to identify with the larger society, emphasize the *functional* value of performing in standard dialect; "He'll need it to get a better job," or "Teach it to him so that he will be able to decide later on whether he wants to use it or not." This "functional need" motivation falls on unbelieving ears. The black child knows that he pays the social price for being black, not because he does or does not speak standard dialect. He asks, "Why do I have to speak better than the white man to get the same job." Do you need to be able to perform in standard dialect to be a carpenter, plumber, brick layer, construction worker, or printer, or to be any trade or non-trade union employee? How many white collar jobs require the ability to perform in standard dialect? Are blacks going to believe that they are being discriminated against in all of these jobs because they don't speak standard dialect? In 1963 for those blacks who attended college, their median income was only sixty percent of that of whites with comparable education. In 1966 blacks with an eighth grade education earned eighty percent of what whites earned with comparable education. If educational level, which is a far more significant employment factor than ability to perform in standard dialect, has not been effective in reducing the disparity between black and white income why should blacks believe performing in the prestige dialect will. According to a 1967 report[1] entitled *Chicago's Widening Color Gap*, "Negro college graduates in Chicago earn less than white high school drop-outs," (pp. 80-81). It is to be noted also that the higher the educational level, the greater the disparity between black and white income.

With regard to the problem of reinforcement, where is the child going to use, outside of the classroom, the dialect the teacher is attempting to teach him inside? And if he can't find a place to use it, how is he going to acquire a "new set of language habits." The area in which he lives reinforces his native dialect, not the standard. In Chicago, it is not unusual for a black child to have attended one hundred percent black schools up to and through high school. Clearly, the linguistic approach presumes that *integration* will take place; either that black families will move into white areas or that black children will be bussed into white areas where reinforcement of standard dialect can take place. Demographic statistics show a contrary trend, viz., black communities are becoming "blacker" and white communities "whiter." Even in communities such as Maywood, Joliet and Wheaton with which I am partly familiar, with a majority white population, the blacks invariably live in segregated housing, and socialization in the high school is almost invariably *intra*-group with very little chance of reinforcing prestige dialect patterns assuming even that white high school students speak them.

Finally, the linguistic approach is based on a social fallacy, viz., that the social order is immutably stratified, that the social judgments that people are making today are the same judgments that they will be making fifteen or even five years from now. I find this assumption challenged by present social trends. The walls of racism are even today starting to crumble and those teachers using the linguistic-integrationist approach will find themselves accused of having made a pact with the same devil as those using the prescriptive-assimilationist approach.

I see our society experiencing the throes of social reform this very minute. Our cherished prejudices and practices are being assaulted at every turn, besieged with long hair and "bad manners" on the one hand and Black Power and creative disorder on the other. What if blacks succeed in changing the social order so that they and their culture will no longer be regarded as inferior by the larger society? What if, in twenty years, you will regard a black accent comparably to the way you regard today the accent of a German professor, French singer, or British actor? Does it really matter how people of status speak? You say, what if the social order is not changed? Then I ask you, What have you accomplished in your program: the ability to avoid some stigmatized forms which are so stigmatized because the people who speak them are?

Will speaking better remove the stigma attached to that person? At the Democratic convention Julian Bond probably spoke "better" than most people there. Will speaking better make Bond president? I doubt it, but Black Power might.

It ought to be clear by this time that what is emerging in our society today is a resurgence of ethnic pride as well as attempts by ethnic communities to establish control over their own destiny. Not only are the culturally different resisting or rejecting the assimilationist pressure of the present establishment they are also no longer relegating or subordinating their own culture to the inside of their homes. Ultimately, the choice of what is to be taught and how it is to be taught is the learner's, and educators, like everyone else in our society, will have to respond to the challenge of being "relevant" in both our goals and our methods or be faced with empty classrooms and "student schools."

My conclusion is apparent. The present efforts to teach a prestige form of speech to nonstandard speakers are educationally wasteful and the effective realization is socially improbable, unless the express desire and cooperation of those learning it are forthcoming. That decision will be neither yours nor mine to make!

You who will persist in your efforts despite the resistance of your students, their parents and communities, do so at your own peril.

Kenneth R. Johnson

SOCIAL BACKGROUNDS: BLACKS

Minority group membership is not synonymous with being disadvantaged. However, a person's chances of being disadvantaged are increased if he is black instead of white.

ECONOMIC AND CULTURAL DEPRIVATION

Discrimination in employment has caused disproportionate numbers of black people to be economically impoverished. The incomes of black families of every level of education are significantly lower than the incomes of white families. For example, a black college graduate earns about the same amount as a white high school graduate, and a black high school graduate earns about the same as a white elementary school graduate. The discrepancy can only be explained by discrimination.

Poverty affects the achievement of many black children in specific ways. Basic needs—for food, clothing, and shelter—often go unsatisfied, and it is difficult for children affected in this way to achieve in school. Poverty also prevents many black children from having the kinds of experiences that support the instructional efforts of the school. Trips to cultural facilities, books in the home, educational toys—in other words, all the objects and services that are commonly part of the experiential background of middle-class children and that satisfy educational needs outside school—cost money, and many black families cannot afford them.

This does not mean, however, that educational experiences—trips to cultural facilities, books in the home, educational toys—are substitutes for money. The basic problem for many black families is a lack of money. They need money to satisfy basic needs first—educational experiences are secondary. Many educators miss this point.

Membership in a minority group increases a person's chances of being culturally disadvantaged. Culture can be defined as a way of life, a design for living, that consists of the attitudes, beliefs, practices, patterns of behavior, and institutions that a group has developed in response to particular conditions in order to survive. In this country the conditions that existed for the majority of the people have produced the response labeled "the dominant culture." Black people, however, have had to respond to a different set of conditions, and they have developed a subculture that is different in many ways from the dominant culture. One of these differences is the matriarchal family structure of many black families. Another is the nonstandard English dialect spoken by many black people.

Membership in the black subculture contributes to cultural deprivation because it prevents black children from acquiring the middle-class cultural patterns on which almost all school curricula and instructional materials are based. Many black children have not acquired from their subculture the language patterns, the value system, the attitudes and beliefs—the entire experiential background—that the school program demands. The readiness of black children for achievement is *different*, not just deficient. This is another point educators have missed; compensatory education programs have aimed to supply disadvantaged black children with a middle-class experience so that they could conform to the expectations of the standard middle-class curriculum. This is impossible, and it may be the main reason for the only moderate success (some would argue the lack of success) of compensatory education. Instead of this approach, educators should discover what kinds of experiences membership in the black subculture affords and what kinds of concepts these experiences yield. The curriculum for disadvantaged black children should be based on these discoveries.

Not all black children are disadvantaged, even though they are members of the black subculture. Many black children have acquired almost the same experiential background that middle-class white children have acquired. These black children, though not assimilated, are acculturated. They are bicultural. Furthermore, not all disadvantaged black children are disadvantaged to the same degree. The disadvantaged population is not as homogeneous as it is often thought to be.

OTHER CHARACTERISTICS OF DISADVANTAGED BLACKS

In most instances, disadvantaged children live in a negative environment, suffer from family breakdown, lack a tradition of literacy, feel rejected by society, have a poor self-concept, and are linguistically handicapped. Of course, this is not a complete list of characteristics of disadvantaged children; however, it includes those characteristics that affect school achievement most seriously.

Negative Environment

Many disadvantaged black children live in the negative environment of large-city ghettos. This environment is negative because it restricts the experiences of these children, and the concepts their experiences yield are not those on which the school program is based. Again, it must be pointed out that the experiences and concepts gained from this environment are not deficient, but different. Some educators have erroneously concluded that the ghetto environment is unstimulating. In fact, it is over-stimulating. That is, children living in a noisy ghetto under crowded conditions and surrounded by activity are bombarded with stimuli. They learn to shut out stimuli in order to have peace of mind. This habit becomes a hindrance to them in school because they shut out the instructional stimuli provided by teachers. For example, ghetto children frequently do not have the same ability as the majority of children to distinguish meaningful sounds.

Ghetto life generates a value system that is often in opposition to the value system of the school. For example, ghetto children tend to be very aggressive, and they value aggressiveness over intellectualism. Aggressive behavior is a survival pattern in the ghetto; thus, it is

a necessary pattern. One of the reasons that these children often cannot work well in groups is that they are accustomed to using threats
or physical force as a means of persuasion instead of cooperation and
discourse.

The pattern of aggression derived from ghetto living also explains why disadvantaged black children do not like to be touched by
teachers in a stress situation. In a stress situation, teachers should not
touch disadvantaged black children because the children are apt to
interpret any physical contact, even the middle-class "pat on the
back" to communicate concern, as an aggressive act.

Ghetto living also generates anti-intellectualism because ghetto
children see few benefits of intellectualism in their environment.
Therefore, behavior appropriate in school is considered nonfunction-
al. On the other hand, black people recognize that education is a
means for advancement.

In an environment scarred by age, neglect, abuse, and overuse,
it is difficult to develop respect for property. Moreover, economic
deprivation prevents private ownership of property, a common source
of pride for more affluent families.

No disadvantaged black child living in the ghetto can escape
being marked by it. Blacks in the ghettos are trapped behind invisible
social barriers that prevent their escape to a more promising environment—sometimes prevent even their coming into direct contact with
the outside world, the dominant culture. The world presented in textbooks is populated by strangers who inhabit a strange environment
unlike anything in their experience. Because these barriers keep disadvantaged black children out of touch with the dominant culture,
the ghetto subculture is perpetuated with all the handicaps of restricted experiential development.

Family Breakdown

The "Moynihan report," issued by the United States Department of Labor in March, 1965, revealed that male absenteeism is
common among poor black families. Too often, women have had to
become both breadwinners and caretakers for their families.

To understand the development of the matriarchal family structure of disadvantaged black families and the absenteeism or weak position of the black male, it is necessary to examine the institution of
slavery in America. Marriage between slaves was not recognized as a
sacrament. Slave families were frequently separated by the sale of the
father to one buyer and of the mother and children to another. The
father was permitted to visit his family only at the whim of his mas-

ter. The disruption of families through selling and separate plantation living helped to establish the pattern of male absenteeism. In addition, white plantation-owners fathered many children who remained with their black mothers. This frequent miscegenation also contributed to the establishment of the matriarchal structure of the black family as something common. Thus, the institution of slavery very early placed the black woman in a position of prominence and power in the family.

The second factor behind the establishment of the matriarchal structure of black families is the precarious economic position of black males in the American employment market. Black women have always been able to obtain employment more easily than black men, and they have often been able to obtain steadier employment. As a result, they often hold the purse strings in the family, and whoever controls the purse strings usually holds the power.

It is ironic that our wefare systems have supported and perpetuated the matriarchy of disadvantaged black families. Many welfare systems deny families financial help as long as an employable male lives at home. Some black women, realizing that the family income from welfare is greater than the income of the black male working at menial and intermittent jobs, simply force their husbands to leave home. Frequently too, black men realize that their families would be better off financially without them and simply leave voluntarily. It may be that many leave "on paper" to qualify their families for welfare, and that the absenteeism rate may not be as high as it appears.

The father's absence does not necessarily mean that a disadvantaged black child is not able to achieve in school. Many disadvantaged black children come from wholesome families without fathers—families that supply basic needs, love, and security. When these children fail, it is due to other factors. Teachers must realize that a black mother and her children (often, the grandmother and the mother and her children) are a functioning family. When a disadvantaged black child from a fatherless home fails, the direct cause of his failure may be economic: no man is present earning an income to satisfy his basic needs. (Of course, there are other reasons that these children fail; this is just one of the reasons.)

Teachers must understand that since the mother usually holds the power in a disadvantaged black family, even when the father is present, she is the one to deal with when contacting the family.

The absence of the father often has a particularly debilitating effect on boys. Too many black boys grow up in families without a male model and attend schools dominated by females. They learn their male roles the best way the can, often in the streets of the ghetto. The most attractive, and apparently the most successful, male adults in ghetto communities are those who are making money, including the men who have been led perhaps by discrimination in employment to apply their talents to illegal activities. These undesirable models do not make school seem attractive or even necessary to the boys who wish to emulate them. (In fact, education does not make a significant difference in the income of blacks; black high school graduates earn only slightly more than black high school dropouts.)

The precarious economic position and high rate of absenteeism of black fathers and the dominance of black mothers rob black boys of appropriate models. Therefore, ghetto schools—particularly ghetto elementary schools—should hire more male teachers, preferably black males.

Finally, the position of the mother in a black family explains something that teachers—white teachers in particular—are often puzzled about: many black children react violently to any derogatory statement or implication about their mothers. (Talking in a derogatory way about another's mother is "playing the dozens" in the idiom of the black subculture.) Teachers should understand that much more often for a black child than for a white child the mother is the only source of love and security, the one person in life on whom the child can depend. Teachers should avoid making overt negative judgments about the mothers of black children.

Tradition of Illiteracy

The black subculture lacks a tradition of literacy. Before the Civil War it was illegal in many southern states to teach slaves to read, and even after slavery was abolished, black people in the South were not encouraged to become literate. The schooling that was provided for them produced semiliterates. In addition, the sharecropping economy in which most blacks in the South were ensnared prevented them from completing many years of schooling. Illiteracy prevailed among blacks in the South until very recently.

Furthermore, the reality of discrimination, until recent years, has preempted the necessity for many blacks to acquire an education. Even if blacks became educated in academic areas other than teaching, the ministry, medicine, and social work (the professions traditionally open to blacks), they could not easily obtain employment. This situation discouraged academic aspiration and consequently academic achievement. The situation, however, is changing. Black college graduates in every field of study are in great demand now. This demand must be communicated to disadvantaged black children to inspire them to set their academic goals high.

Even though black people lack a long tradition of literacy, they generally have a positive attitude toward education. This appears to be a contradiction. However, black parents realize that education is one way their children can improve their standard of living. Consequently, they encourage their children to go to school. Education probably follows employment and housing on the list of priorities of most black people. However, their own ignorance, lack of education, or economic poverty often prevents them from knowing just how to support the efforts of the school.

Feeling of Rejection and Poor Self-Concept

Many black children rightfully feel that society has rejected them. Furthermore, they have concluded that they have been rejected by society simply because they are black. This feeling of rejection has produced a poor self-concept in many black children. These children learn at an early age that they are black, and that they are somehow inferior because they are black.

Black children develop this self-concept in a social context. In making qualitative judgments about themselves they take cues from those who are unlike them as well as from those who are like them. For example, they observe the way black people in our society are treated by many whites. They respond to our language—specifically, to the negative connotations of the word *black* in many contexts.

For many blacks, the unalterable color of their skin has been an outward sign of their inferiority. This traditional attitude is changing, however. The "Black Revolution" is giving black people—particularly the younger ones—a new dignity and a new pride in themselves. Because of their increased dignity and pride, many black people have adopted a new label for themselves: *black*. They have also adopted a new hair style: the natural or Afro style. They no longer wish to conform to white America's beauty standard of straight hair. These two cultural changes are expressions of a healthy self-concept.

Linguistic Disadvantage

Many black children are linguistically disadvantaged: they speak a nonstandard dialect of English that a number of educators and linguists believe interferes with their attempts to learn to read and to speak standard English.

Teachers often react to the use of nonstandard dialect by telling the children that their language is "bad" or "sloppy." Since language is an identifying label, teachers who reject the language of disadvantaged children reject the children themselves and those who speak the same dialect (their friends and families)—indeed, the whole culture from which the children come.

It is unlikely that these children will accept the language of the school and teacher if the school and teacher do not accept their nonstandard dialect. Disadvantaged children whose native language is not English—Mexican-Americans, Puerto Ricans, and Indians, for example—often receive sympathy from their teachers, whereas black children who have a similar but not so obvious interference problem generally do not. Teachers of disadvantaged black children frequently follow a "don't say it like that, say it like this" approach. Before they are likely to learn standard English, these children need specialized help, not unlike that given pupils learning English as a second language. In other words, the points of interference between their dialect and standard English must be dealt with systematically. This is not often done in language programs.

A similar program should be followed for reading instruction. Children should have a reading program that takes account of the phonological and structural differences between their nonstandard dialect and standard English, in particular those that produce interference. This means that the reading program must be custom-made for disadvantaged black children, and it must be coordinated and conducted concurrently with the language program. Instead, the approach usually followed in teaching reading to disadvantaged black children is to give them a remedial reading program—which too often means the regular reading program administered in smaller doses and in diluted form, with no attention given to the interference caused by their nonstandard dialect.

In order to provide effective language arts and reading programs, teachers should be educated in the phonology and structure of the nonstandard dialect of disadvantaged black children as well as in second-language teaching techniques, and instructional materials must be prepared that take into account the special linguistic and cultural features of this group.

Another common fault of the language program for disadvantaged black children is that standard English is taught as a replacement dialect rather than as an alternate dialect. This approach is faulty because as long as these children live in a cultural environment in which the nonstandard dialect is functional, they will not discard it. The goal of language instruction, then, should be to give pupils language flexibility.

THE BLACK REVOLUTION

Black people cannot be discussed without taking note of the "Black Revolution" that is occurring. This revolution touches the lives of everyone—white and black. For many Americans the phrase "Black Revolution" calls to mind sit-ins, demonstrations, arrests, riots, and destruction. These are some features of the revolution, but their dramatic quality tends to blot out the most significant feature, the search for identity. The essence of the revolution is that black people are now defining themselves. They are looking inward and discovering what kind of people they are, and what they are discovering is their identity—their black identity, their membership in a unique subculture. Furthermore, they are discovering valuable and positive aspects in themselves and their subculture.

The term "black," which they have adopted as their total identifying label, is a racial label and a psychological, sociological, and cultural label. It refers to an individual who shares a common experience with twenty-two million others, characterized in part by a common will to survive in a hostile racist society. This self-discovery, or self-definition, is the most significant feature of the revolution. Black people are asserting that they will no longer allow white people to define them and that they will no longer look upon anything identifiably black as automatically inferior.

As black people look inward, many have grown revengeful as they contemplated the accumulated injustices perpetrated on them by a white racist society for over three hundred and fifty years. Young black people are particularly revengeful, and their attitude toward white society is often violent, as the Kerner Commission revealed in its report on violence in American society, published in March, 1968.

This revengeful attitude causes young blacks to reject, often justifiably, the three authority figures of the white society that they come into contact with most frequently: the white businessman, the white policeman, and the white teacher, who symbolize exploitation, brutality, and neglect. In the near future white teachers will probably find it increasingly difficult to work with black pupils because of their revengeful attitude.

The revolution—the process of self-definition—should become as much a part of the curriculum as math or science or history. It is particularly important as part of the secondary-school English program. Language arts activities—reading, writing, speaking, drama, debating—can be structured around the wealth of materials and topics

presented by the revolution, which is the most significant event in
the lives of many black pupils.

Instead of making the Black Revolution a part of the curriculum, many whites have tried to shut it out. They may feel threatened
because the revolution presents a new image of the black man, not
what many whites want him to be. This tendency is reflected in the
kinds of black people included in textbooks. Although blacks appear
in textbooks in increasing numbers, those included are usually "safe
Negroes," such as Booker T. Washington, Dr. George Washington
Carver, Dr. Percy Julian, Dr. Charles Drew, Marion Anderson, Ralph
Bunche, and Jackie Robinson—"safe" because their achievements are
not concerned with current crises. Instead, their success carries the
message "Be good, be outstanding in one attribute, and white people
will accept you." The fallacy is that only a few black children can become as outstanding as these "safe Negroes." The majority will continue to be unacceptable by these standards. A few revolutionary
blacks, too far removed in history to be relevant to today's revolution, Nat Turner and Denmark Vassey, for example, may be included
in an ineffective attempt at a balance.

But black people esteem other kinds of blacks than those included in textbooks. For example, Adam Clayton Powell, Rap
Brown, Stokely Carmichael, Malcolm X, Muhammad Ali, and the
Reverend Jesse Jackson are black men who have fought oppression,
speaking in a way white people do not want to accept. They present
a much more aggressive model to black children. These men have not
waited for or asked politely for civil rights. Instead, they have spoken
defiantly in response to racism, demanding civil rights for black people. This kind of action has earned them the esteem of fellow blacks.

In addition, the reading curriculum must include black writers
who are relevant to today. In addition to works by Paul Lawrence
Dunbar, Countee Cullen, Phillis Wheatley, and James Weldon Johnson, the reading curriculum should include the writings of W. E. B.
DuBois, Richard Wright, James Baldwin, Malcolm X, Eldridge
Cleaver, Le Roi Jones, and other relevant black writers. These writers
are excluded on the grounds that they are "controversial" or "too
mature." The first excuse is intellectually dishonest, and the second
is nonsense. Many young blacks have already discovered these writers.
In fact, their works are nearly all they are reading with fervent interest. Little else in American literature speaks directly to them.

A study of these writers will not increase black pupils' anger and
revengefulness, as some white educators may fear. Instead, it will help
black pupils to go beyond these feelings to self-definition. Anger and
desire for revenge are temporary emotions, and they will cease when
black people realize that they consume both the subject and the ob-

ject. A study of these writers will speed this realization, by focusing attention on the main issue of defining black people. When this definition is completed, white teachers will be able to work effectively with black children—but it will be a new relationship of equals.

Anita E. Dunn

READING AND THE DISADVANTAGED

Clearly, too many Americans—children, adolescents, and adults— are reluctant readers, but one way to improve the desire to read is that which Mortimer Adler pointed out in *How to Read a Book:*

When they (students) are in love and are reading a love letter, they read for all they are worth. They read every word three ways; they read between the lines and in the margins; they read the whole in terms of the parts, and each part in terms of the whole; they grow sensitive to context and ambiguity, to insinuation and implication; they perceive the color or words, the odor of phrases, and the weight of sentences. They may even take the punctuation into account. Then, if never before or after, they read.[1]

Adler's point—that material to be read should be personal, real, and important to the reader—requires that teachers, school and community librarians, youth counselors, and parents join other community leaders in combined attempts to identify materials which have the interest magnitude described by Adler. Where disadvantaged students are concerned such materials have been scarce in the past, but recent publishing innovations and funds from Title III of the Elementary and Secondary Education Act should provide the means for interested communities to acquire reading materials which will accommodate the reading interests of most disadvantaged students.

[1] Mortimer J. Adler, *How to Read a Book* (New York: Simon and Schuster, 1940), p. 14.

Project Head Start, funded to provide a reading readiness background for disadvantaged youth, cannot help the other million or so who have not had a head start in reading readiness. For some of these students, even at the junior high school level, it will mean beginning at the beginning to learn to read. Pulitzer Prize winner Harrison Salisbury described the dilemma when he pointed out:

It is hard for many of us to imagine how narrow the world must be for youngsters who cannot read well enough to study elementary lessons let alone literature, history, poetry, or philosophy. Yet hundreds of thousands of teenagers are growing toward adulthood with minds which are crippled by their inability to unlock the key to the printed page.[2]

Conant also cites the importance of an all-out attack on the reading problems of disadvantaged youth:

In the slum school the development of reading is obviously of first importance. The earlier the slow readers are spotted and remedial measures instituted, the better.[3]

Some tactics have already proved successful in encouraging reading among disadvantaged students. Specially trained children's librarians, summer reading programs, and the Junior Great Book discussions are having some impact. With their classroom displays of inviting books, their reading aloud to children, and their skillful teaching techniques, kindergarten, primary, and elementary school teachers have also improved the reading tastes of many youngsters.

In spite of these improvements there yet remains the adolescent who has been unable to establish reading as a pleasurable and rewarding habit, and his numbers are legion. Somewhere along the line, children who almost inherently want to learn to read become reluctant or nonreading adolescents. For them, reading has become a drudgery, not a delight. One wonders what occurred to turn these children from reading to reading-allergic adolescents and, later, to nonreading adults?

[2] Harrison E. Salisbury, *The Shook-Up Generation* (Greenwich, Conn.: Fawcett Publications, Inc., 1958), p. 117.

[3] James Bryant Conant, *Slums and Suburbs* (New York: McGraw-Hill Book Company, 1961), p. 23.

THE PROBLEM

One source of answers to this question may be students' comments about assigned reading tasks: "I hate books." "I don't like to read." "We ain't got no books at home." "Reading's hard." "It takes too much time." "I'd rather watch TV." "In school, they won't let ya read the books or magazines ya like." "There ain't any good books in the library; just stuff teachers make ya read."

School policy when applied to the shelving of books, to the selection of reading materials, to study hall procedures, and the like sometimes serves to deter student reading. Some specific examples of these and other rituals as they tend to inhibit student reading are as follows.

(1) Shelving teen-agers' and children's books in the same section of the library is not an appealing arrangement for adolescents who consider themselves almost adults.

(2) Crowding books especially written for adolescents in with an overwhelming collection of adult books is equally unacceptable. The already book-wary young shy away from such an arrangement.

(3) Prohibiting youngsters and teen-agers from reading books and magazines in classrooms, study halls, and homerooms is a real deterrent to reading encouragement.

(4) Neglecting to provide periodically a regularly scheduled class period to read library books misses a chance to develop a reading desire. In too many classrooms, no time is planned for young people to go to the library to select books to read. No provision is made to spend a class hour occasionally in the library. All young people, but especially the disadvantaged youth, need a proper reading climate, a quiet place to read.

(5) Frowning on the books young people select to suit their tastes stifles their reading interest. "They should all read the classics" —not eventually, but now—ready or not. In one instance, an English teacher sent a reluctant reader back to the library to select another book because the girl's choice, *Let the Hurricane Roar* (a worthy piece of literature), was in the teachers's opinion "just a thin book." Would we have called *Lord Jim* "just a thin book"?

(6) Lacking knowledge about books written for young people handicaps teachers in assisting students to find books they will enjoy. Books—good books—which will whet the appetite of the reluctant reader are plentiful. Too many teachers still regard all books written expressly for teen-agers as trashy reading material. For the disadvantaged youth, books such as *Hot Rod; South Town; Shuttered Windows; Knock at the Door, Emmy; Roosevelt Grady; Mary Jane; Skid;*

Joe-Pole; and *A Present for Rosita* are excellent stepping stones on the path to reading.

(7) Failing to provide classroom libraries of attractive books, magazines, and newspapers loses an opportunity to stimulate the habit of reading. Teachers of the disadvantaged need to remember that accessibility is one of the prerequisites for the encouragement of reading. By using the attractive, worthwhile Literature Sampler in the classroom, teen-agers may be enticed to read books via their contact with excerpts which have been tested for adolescent appeal.

(8) Hesitating to read stories or parts of books aloud cheats children and young adults of a pleasurable and necessary aural reading experience. Disadvantaged youths, especially, have missed much because no one has ever read to them.

Reading aloud from carefully selected books that will interest a particular grade level is an almost unbeatable technique for encouraging reading. *Call It Courage, Old Yeller, Bristle Face, A Quiet Hero, Shane, Mrs. 'Arris Goes to Paris*, and others with fast-moving plots and abundant conversation are suitable for oral interpretation and are sure-fire starters. Book lists such as *Fare for the Reluctant Reader, Gateways to Readable Books, Good Books for Poor Readers, Reading Ladders for Human Relations*, and *Your Reading* suggest many other books and magazines for young people who are usually not interested in reading.

SUGGESTIONS

(1) Keep school libraries open throughout the year to serve as community libraries or to supplement the local library. "Schools must become community centers, providing welfare and social services as well as learning" was one of the major conclusions reached by the 1965 White House Conference on Education.

A survey of the public library facilities and services in a city of about 120,000 people in eastern New York State revealed a regrettable condition. Only one library set aside one small room for young adults. That room was labelled "Young People's Room." The children's and young people's libraries in that city were closed most evenings and all day Saturday during the summer, the season when young people have the most leisure time.

(2) Hire boys and girls to work in the library—especially disadvantaged youth. At first, the young hired help could assist in the library workroom. One of their first jobs might be removing the due

dates from some of the books. This is one date that frightens the almost nonreader. He needs more time to read his book.

These aides can be trained to charge out books, check in books,
and shelve books. Some disadvantage students can be taught to com-
pile teen-age book lists. They can enlist the aid of the teen-ager who
finally found a book he liked to read. The young readers can write
brief opinions about their favorite books.

Tape recorders could be made available in the library, and the
disadvantaged youth could record his remarks. Such a tape-recorded
comment would be a fine project for girls enrolled in secretarial
courses to transcribe. Pile a stack of these weekly or monthly "best
seller" lists in prominent places in the school or community library
and label them: "Take one; they're for you."

(3) Erect a library building or add an annex to the community
library exclusively for these young adults—a teen-age "reading
hangout." Young people like to go where the gang goes. Why not
have the gang gather in a teen-age library? The "gang" concept will
gradually change to "club," but the youths must make this thought
transition themselves. An attractively and comfortably furnished
teen-age Utopian Library would match and surpass the lure of the
corner newsstand.

(4) Arrange books in a teen-age "Utopia" in a supermarket
and bookstore style. Why must the books in too many libraries for
children and young adults be arranged only or mainly by the
Dewey Decimal System (DDS), a system designed by a librarian
for the ease and convenience of trained librarians? It is surely not
a system designed for the ease and convenience of adolescents,
especially disadvantaged youth. They are not interested in DDS.
They cannot remember the classifications. Why should they? Such
a system is too time consuming and too confusing. Later, when
these young people have become mature readers, they can learn to
use the card catalog and the Dewey Decimal System in the adult
section of the library. Borrow some of the salesmanship techniques
of the supermarket. These pressure salesmen display books under
clearly readable signs: Mysteries, Sports, Hobbies, Cookbooks. They
put up front what they want to sell. Try such selling techniques in
the young-adult library. Shelve all the sports books in one area.
Youthful artists can prepare clever signs, cartoons, and posters that
point the way to the kinds of books boys want to read. Compete
with and outsell the lurid true romance magazines. Prominently
display books for girls on love and romance, on beauty hints, and
on the She-Manners.

Print the last names of teen-age author idols on fairly large
signs— Felsen, Sperry, Meader, Stolz, Means. Headline the section:
"Here they are; books by your favorite authors."

Arrange a special section of attractive editions of more adult books for the mature reader such as *Red Badge of Courage*, *Kon-Tiki*, and *Moby Dick*. Call attention to these titles via Francis Bacon: "Some books are to be tasted, others to be swallowed, and some few to be chewed and digested . . . ."[4]

(5) Man teen-age "Utopia" with some male librarians especially trained to handle young adults. Boys who are reluctant readers and almost nonreaders need a man who can comment, "That's a good book. You'll like it. I read it."

(6) Follow the fine example set by the Henry Horner Boys Clubs in Chicago and add a well-stocked reading room to Boys' Clubs, Catholic youth societies, and other youth organizations. Citizens of the community could contribute the magazines, paperbacks, and books to these youth centers. Once there, teen-agers could be encouraged to take them home—no strings attached. These magazines, books, and paperbacks could also be placed on shelves in employment offices for adolescents and their parents.

(7) Display book jackets in prominent places in the school: on the first floor bulletin board, in the classrooms, in the cafeteria, and even in the locker rooms. Lay a Hansel and Gretel trail to the library. Trophies awarded for athletic prowess and physical fitness hold a place of honor and prominence. Why not reading fitness awards, trophies, and compensations?

(8) Advertise and review books for young adults in the local newspaper on the sports page, in the comic section, or in a unique column devoted exclusively to teen-agers and young adults. Such announcements of popular adolescent literature will more than pay dividends in selling reading to youth. Local editors and merchants might be willing to underwrite the cost of so worthy an advertisement. Hawaii's *Honolulu Advertiser* added a special Sunday supplement entitled "Hawaii's Youth," written and edited primarily by teen-agers themselves, which included reviews of new books.

(9) Park bookmobiles next to the children's playground, the Little League field, the sand-lot baseball diamond, the teen-age hangouts, or the shopping center. Man these vehicles, too, with competent teen-age reading specialists to help encourage reading interests among the disadvantaged.

(10) Provide a reading clinic as part of every community library to supplement reading clinics in school! Developmental and remedial reading skills could be taught to disadvantaged youngsters, adolescents, and adults in an atmosphere surrounded by books, in a place

[4] Robert U. Jameson, *Essays Old and New* (New York: Harcourt Brace Jovanovich, 1955), pp. 8-10.

conducive to nourishing the desire to learn to read well. The following opinion of Edwin and Marie Smith stresses the necessity if improving the reading ability of many Americans.

Americans buy more books and newspapers than any other peoples of the world, yet a great many Americans read less than a book a year. This curious condition has come about because many Americans have difficulty in reading with ease and pleasure. Some, of course, cannot read at all. Skill in reading is perhaps the single most important intellectual skill needed by everyone today. Radio and television are effective means of spreading news quickly, but they cannot and will not replace the persistent everyday need for the ability to read with ease and understanding.[5]

(11) Heed the appeal of the paperbacks. Set up a paperback stand in the young adult library, in the school library, and in the classroom library, or promote a teen-age paperback bookstore in the school. Use a classroom collection of paperbacks. Make it possible to purchase paperbacks at a cheaper rate than the newsstand and supermarket competitors. Hire a teen-ager or let students handle the paperback stand or store. Every young person should be enabled once in his life to own his own book. For every four paperbacks or books a young adult reads and on which he has recorded or written a brief comment, he might be awarded a free copy. In this way he can begin to build his own personal library.

NEXT STEPS

This article has suggested possible steps for encouraging reading among adolescents, especially among disadvantaged youth. Parents, teachers, librarians, and community leaders can apply some of the suggestions. Appeals to other local, state, and national political figures to join the effort should be a next step for expanding reading horizons. Ask for their support—socially, morally, and financially. In the past, America has failed to provide enough money for educating its youth. But today, both Titles I and III of the Elementary and Secondary Education Act provide generous funds for the implementation of imaginative reading programs, programs that augur well for the reading skills needed by the disadvantaged.

[5] Edwin H. and Marie P. Smith, *Teaching Reading to Adults* (Washington, D.C.: National Association of Public School Adult Educators, 1962), p. 7.

Joan C. Baratz

TEACHING READING IN AN URBAN NEGRO SCHOOL SYSTEM

The inner-city Negro child is failing in our schools. His inability to read is a major challenge to contemporary educators because of its relationship to the child's self-esteem and his ultimate social effectiveness.

Failure to acquire functionally adequate reading skills not only contributes to alienation from the school as a social institution (and therefore encourages dropping out), but it goes on to insure failure in mainstream job success. There is certainly a relationship between reading success or failure on the one hand, and receptivity to or alienation from the society in which those reading skills are highly valued (Labov and Robins, 1967). It is almost impossible to underestimate the chain of reactions which can be touched off by early and continued educational failure which so many disadvantaged Negro children experience in even the most well-intentioned schools. Because the educational system has been ineffective in coping with teaching inner-city children to read, it treats reading failure (in terms of grading, ranking, etc.) as if this failure were due to intellectual deficits of the child rather than to methodological inadequacies in teaching procedures. Thus the system is unable to teach the child to read, but very quickly teaches him to regard himself as intellectually inadequate, and therefore, of low self-worth and low social value.

Despite the enormous expenditure of energy in remedial reading programs, children in the ghetto are still not learning to read (National Advisory Council on Education of the Disadvantaged, 1966). Although the difficulties of teaching reading to a portion of the population is a unique problem for the United States, the problem itself is not unique. The parallels are quite clear between the difficulty we are experiencing in teaching reading to the disadvantaged Negro child with those of emergent countries which are attempting to make a multi-cultured population literate in a single national tongue.

In his recent report on the Washington, D.C. School System, Passow (1967) indicated that the central question that must be answered is: "What are the educationally relevant differences which the District's pupils bring into the classroom and what kinds of varied

educational experiences must be provided by the schools to accommodate these differences?" One major educationally relevant difference for Washington, D.C., as for ghettos across the nation, is that
of language. The Negro ghetto child is speaking a significantly different language from that of his middle-class teachers. Most of his
middle-class teachers have wrongly viewed his language as patho-
logical, disordered, "lazy speech." This failure to recognize the interference from the child's different linguistic system, and consequent
negative teacher attitudes towards the child and his language, lead
directly to reading difficulties and subsequent school failure. Understanding that the inner-city child speaks a language that is well-
ordered, but different in many respects from standard English, is
crucial to understanding how to educate him. Unfortunately, there
is a tendency for the educator to think of the black child with his
non-standard speech as a "verbal cripple" whose restricted language
leads to, or is caused by, cognitive deficits.

If we look briefly at the research and research assumptions concerning the language of Negro children, we can see how this erroneous
notion of verbal inadequacy evolved.

When reviewing the literature, one finds three major professions
concerned with describing the language and cognitive abilities of
black children: educators, psychologists (mainly child development
specialists), and linguists. The educators were the first to contribute
a statement about the language difficulties of these children—a statement that amounted to the assertion that these children were virtually verbally destitute, i.e., they couldn't talk, and if they did, it was
deviant speech, filled with "errors." The next group to get into the
foray—the psychologists—reconfirmed initially that the children
didn't talk, and then added the sophisticated wrinkle that if they did
talk, their speech was such that it was a deterrent to cognitive growth.
The last group to come into the picture were the linguists, who,
though thoroughly impressed with the sophisticated research of the
psychologist, were astonished at the naïveté of his pronouncements
concerning language. The linguist began to examine the language of
black children and brought us to our current conceptions of the language abilities of these children, namely, that they speak a well-
ordered, highly structured, highly developed language system which
in many aspects is different from standard English.

We have a fascinating situation here where three professions are
assessing the same behavior—the child's oral language production and
comprehension—but with varying assumptions, so that they see different things. However, it is not merely another example of the parable of the six blind men describing the elephant and asserting that
an elephant equaled that portion of the elephant that the blind man
happened to be touching—for in the parable all men were partially

correct, and an elephant could be adequately described in the sum total of their "observations." But when we look at the assumptions of the educator, the psychologist, and the linguist, we find that there are actually some premises held by one profession, e.g., the psychologists' view that a language system *could* be underdeveloped, that another profession sees as completely untenable, e.g., linguists, who consider such a view of language so absurd as to make them feel that nobody could possibly believe it and therefore to refute it would be a great waste of time. The educator worked under the assumption that there is a single correct way of speaking and that everyone who does not speak in this "grammar book" fashion is in error. (Indeed, although the psychologist may not recognize it, he tacitly adheres to this principle when he defines language development in terms of "correct" standard English usage.) This assumption is also untenable to the linguist, who is interested in the structure and function of an utterance. To him the discussion of a hierarchical system that says that a double negative, e.g., *they don' have none*, is inferior to a single negative, e.g., *they haven't any*, is meaningless. The linguist simply wishes to describe the rules of the system that allow a speaker of that system to generate a negative utterance—or any other complex structure—that is considered grammatical and is understood as intended, by the speakers of the system.

The linguist takes it as basic that all humans develop language—after all, there is no reason to assume that black African bush children develop a language and black inner-city Harlem children do not! Subsumed under this is that the language is a well-ordered system with a predictable sound pattern, grammatical structure and vocabulary (in this sense, there are no "primitive" languages). The linguist assumes that any verbal system used by a community that fulfills the above requirements is a language and that no language is structurally better than any other language, i.e., French is not better than German, Yiddish is not better than Gaelic, Oxford English is not better than standard English, etc. The second assumption of the linguist is that children learn language in the context of their environment—that is to say, a French child learns French not because his father is in the home or his mother reads him books, but because that is the language that he hears continually from whatever source and that is the language that individuals in his environment respond to. The third assumption that the linguist works with is that by the time a child is five he has developed language—he has learned the rules of his linguistic environment.

What are those rules and how have they been determined? By using ghetto informants, linguists such as Stewart (1964, 1965, 1967, 1968), Dillard (1966, 1967), Bailey (1965, 1968), Labov (1967),

Loman (1967) and Shuy, Wolfram and Riley (1968) have described
some of the linguistic parameters of Negro nonstandard English. Differences between standard English and Negro nonstandard occur to
varying degrees in regard to the sound system, grammar and vocabulary.

Although Negro nonstandard has many phonemes similar to
those of standard English, the distribution of these phonemes varies
from standard English. For example, /i/ and /e/ may not be distinguished before nasals, so that a "pin" in Negro nonstandard may be
either an instrument for writing a letter or something one uses to
fasten a baby's diaper. Sounds such as "r" and "l" are distributed so
that "cat" may mean that orange vegetable that one puts in salads—
standard English *carrot*—as well as the four-legged fuzzy animal, or a
"big black dude." The reduction of /l/ and /r/ in many positions may
create such homonyms as "toe" meaning a digit on the foot, or the
church bell sound—standard English *toll*. Final clusters are reduced
in Negro nonstandard so that "bowl" is used to describe either a ves-
sel for cereal or a very brave soldier—standard English *bold*.

These are but a few of the many instances where Negro nonstandard sound usage differs from standard English. It is no wonder then,
that Cynthia Deutsch (1964) should find in her assessment of auditory discrimination that disadvantaged black children did not "discriminate" as well as white children from middle-class linguistic
environments. She administered a discrimination task that equated
"correct responses" with judgments of equivalences and differences
in standard English sound usage. Many of her stimuli, though different for the standard English speaker, e.g., *pin-pen*, are similar for the
Negro nonstandard speaker. She attributed the difference in performance of disadvantaged children to such things as the constant blare of
the television in their homes and there being so much "noise" in their
environment that the children tended to "tune out." However, black
children make responses based on the kind of language they consider
appropriate. In the same way that *cot* (for sleeping), *caught* (for ensnared); or *marry* (to wed), *Mary* (the girl), and *merry* (to be happy)
are not distinguished in the speech of many white people (so that
they would say on an auditory discrimination test that *cot* and
caught were the same), *pin* and *pen* are the same in the language of
ghetto blacks. The responses that the black child makes are on the
basis of the sound usage that he has learned in his social and geographical milieu, and do not reflect some difficulty in discriminating.

The syntax of low-income Negro children also differs from standard English in many ways (unfortunately the psychologist, not
knowing the rules of Negro nonstandard has interpreted these differences not as the result of well-learned rules, but as evidence of "lin-

guistic underdevelopment"). Some examples of the differences are provided below:

1. When you have a numerical quantifier such as two, seven, fifty, etc., you don't have to add the obligatory morphemes for the plural, e.g., *fifty cent; two foot.*
2. The use of the possessive marker is different. For example, the standard English speaker says "John's cousin"; the nonstandard Negro speaker says *John cousin.* The possessive is marked here by the contiguous relationship of *John* and *cousin.*
3. The third person singular has no obligatory morphological ending in nonstandard, so that "she works here" is expressed as *she work here* in Negro nonstandard.
4. Verb agreement differs, so that one says *she have a bike, they was going.*
5. The use of the copula is not obligatory—*I going; he a bad boy.*
6. The rules for negation are different. The double negative is used: standard English "I don't have any" becomes *I don' got none* in Negro nonstandard.
7. The use of "ain't" in expression of the past—Negro nonstandard present tense is *he don't go*, past tense is *he ain't go.*
8. The use of "be" to express habitual action—*he working right now* as contrasted with *he be working every day.*

These are just a few of the rules that the nonstandard speaker employs to produce utterances that are grammatical for other speakers in his environment.

Baratz and Povich (1967) assessed the language development of a group of five-year-old black Head Start children. They analyzed speech responses to photographs and to CAT cards, using Lee's (1967) developmental sentence types model. A comparison of their data and Menyuk's (1964) restricted and transformational types of white middle-class children was performed. Results indicated that the Negro Head Start child is not delayed in language acquisition—the majority of his utterances are on the kernel and transformational levels of Lee's developmental model. His transformational utterances are similar to those appearing above—he has learned the many complicated structures of Negro nonstandard English.

But how did the psychologist manage to come to the erroneous conclusion that the black child has an insufficient or underdeveloped linguistic system? The psychologist's basic problem was that his measures of "language development" were measures based on standard English (Bereiter, 1965; Thomas, 1964; Deutsch, 1964; Klaus and Gray, 1968). From these he concluded that since black children do not speak standard English, they must be deficient in language development.

Despite the misconceptions of the educator and psychologist concerning language and linguistic competence, the linguists for their part have described the differences between Negro nonstandard and standard English in some detail. The following is a list of some of the syntactic differences between the two systems:

Variable	Standard English	Negro Nonstandard
Linking verb	He is going.	He __ goin'.
Possessive marker	John's cousin.	John_ cousin.
Plural marker	I have five cents.	I got five cent_ .
Subject expression	John_ lives in New York.	John he live in New York.
Verb form	I drank the milk.	I drunk the milk.
Past marker	Yesterday he walked home.	Yesterday he walk_ home.
Verb agreement	He runs home.	He run_ home.
	She has a bicycle.	She have a bicycle.
Future form	I will go home.	I'ma go home.
"If" construction	I asked if he did it.	I ask did he do it.
Negation	I don't have any.	I don' got none.
	He didn't go.	He ain't go.
Indefinite article	I want an apple.	I want a apple.
Pronoun form	We have to do it.	Us got to do it.
	His book.	He book.
Preposition	He is over at his friend's house.	He over to his friend house.
	He teaches at Francis Pool.	He teach_ Francis Pool.
Be	Statement: He is here all the time.	Statement: He be here.
Do	Contradiction: No, he isn't.	Contradiction: No, he don't.

But what of these differences? All the linguists studying Negro non-standard English agree that these differences are systematized structured rules within the vernacular; they agree that these differences can interfere with the learning of standard English, but they do not always agree as to the precise nature of these different rules. This leads to varied disagreements as to why a particular feature exists (i.e., phoneme deletion vs. creolization), but it does not dispute the fact that the linguistic feature is present. No one would fail to agree that standard English has a grammatical structure and uniqueness, and many descriptions of that structure have been written. Yet it is probably true that no two linguists would agree in all details on how to write the grammar. This equally explains the current controversy among linguists as to how one writes the grammar of Negro nonstandard English.

This language *difference*, not deficiency, must be considered in the educational process of the black ghetto child. In 1953, the UNESCO report regarding the role of language in education stated that: "It is axiomatic that the best medium for teaching a child is his mother tongue. Psychologically, it is the system of meaningful signs that in his mind works automatically for expression and understanding. Sociologically, it is a means of identification among the members of the community to which he belongs. Educationally he learns more quickly through it than through an unfamiliar medium."

Since 1953, studies implementing the recommendations of the UNESCO report have clearly illustrated the importance of considering the vernacular in teaching reading in the national language (Modiano, 1965). It seems clear that a structural knowledge of nonstandard vernacular and the ways it can interfere with learning to speak and read standard English are indispensable to teaching ghetto Negro children. Goodman (1965) and Bailey (1965), along with Stewart, have all discussed the possibility of interference from the dialect on acquiring the ability to read. Labov (1967) has also stressed that the "ignorance of standard English rules on the part of the speakers of standard English" and the "ignorance of nonstandard English rules on the part of teachers and text writers" may well be the cause for the reading failures that occur in the schools. In addition, Wiener and Cromer (1967) in their article on reading and reading difficulty discussed the need to determine the relationship between language differences and reading problems, because a failure to be explicit about the relationship between reading and previously acquired auditory language often leads to ambiguities as to whether a particular difficulty is a reading problem, language problem, or both.

But does the black nonstandard speaker have to contend with interference from his own dialect on his performance in standard English? The following experiment clearly suggests that he does.

The subjects in this experiment were third and fifth graders from two schools in the Washington, D.C. area. One was an inner-city, impact-aid school; all the children in this school were Negroes. The other was a school in Maryland, located in an integrated low-middle-income community; all the children from that school were white.

	Negro	White	Total
Third Grade	15	15	30
Fifth Grade	15	15	30
	30	30	60

A sentence repetition test was constructed that contained thirty sentences, fifteen in standard English and fifteen in Negro nonstandard. The sentences were presented on tape to each subject, who was asked to repeat the sentence after hearing it once. Two random orders of the sentences were constructed to control for an order effect. The sentences were as follows:

1. That girl, she ain't go ta school 'cause she ain' got no clothes to wear.
2. John give me two books for me to take back the libery 'cause dey overdue.
3. I's some toys out chere and the chil'run they don' wanna play wid dem no more.
4. Does Deborah like to play with the girl that sits next to her in school?
5. The teacher give him a note 'bout de school meetin' an he 'posed to give it ta his mother to read.
6. John he always be late for school 'cause he don't like ta go music class.
7. My aunt who lives in Baltimore used to come to visit us on Sunday afternoons.
8. Do Deborah like to play wid da girl that sit next to her at school?
9. I asked Tom if he wanted to go to the picture that was playing at the Howard.
10. John gave me two books to take to the library because they were overdue.
11. Can Michael make the boat by hisself or do we gotta he'p him do it?
12. Henry lives near the ball park but can't go to the games because he has no money.
13. Where Mary brovah goin' wif a raggedy umbrella and a old blue raincoat?
14. There are some toys out here that the children don't want to play with any more.

15. If I give you three dollars will you buy me the things that I need to make the wagon?

16. When the teacher asked if he had done his homework, Henry said, "I didn't do it."

17. I aks Tom do he wanna go to the picture that be playin' at the Howard.

18. Henry live beside the ball park but he can't go to the games 'cause he ain' got no money.

19. The teacher gave him a note about the school meeting to give to his mother.

20. She was the girl who didn't go to school because she had no clothes to wear.

21. John is always late to school because he doesn't like to go to music class.

22. Patricia sits in the front row so that she can hear everything the teacher says.

23. If I give you three dollar you gonna buy what I need to make the wagon?

24. When the teachah aks Henry did he do his homework, Henry say I ain't did it.

25. My aunt, she live in Baltimore, and she useda come visit us Sunday afternoon.

26. Gloria's friend is working as a waitress in the Hot Shoppes on Connecticut Avenue.

27. Can Michael build the boat all by himself or should we help him with some of the work?

28. Where is Mary's brother going with a raggedy umbrella and an old blue raincoat?

29. Patricia all the time be sittin' in the front row so she can hear everything the teacher say.

30. Gloria frien', she a waitress, she be working the Hot Shoppes on Connecticut Avenue.

Each subject was asked to repeat exactly what he heard as best he could. After the subject had responded to all the stimuli on the tape, he was asked to listen to two stimuli, one in standard English and the other in nonstandard English. After each of these stimuli, the subject was asked to identify who was speaking from among a group of pictures containing Negro and white men, women, boys and girls, and an Oriental girl.

The data were analyzed to ascertain what happened to the following constructions:

Standard Constructions	Nonstandard Constructions
Third person singular	Non-addition of third person -s
Presence of copula	Zero copula
Negation	Double negation; and "ain't"
If + subject + verb	Zero "if" + verb + subject
Past markers	Zero past morpheme
Possessive marker	Zero possessive morpheme
Plural	Use of "be"

1. Analysis of variance on repetition of standard constructions.

The data concerning repetition of the seven standard constructions were subjected to a Winer (1962) multifactor repeated measures analysis of variance (Table 1). The factors under study were: A, race—Negro vs. white performance; B, age—third graders vs. fifth graders; and C, grammatical feature—the seven standard constructions listed above. The analysis of variance indicated that race, grammatical feature and the interaction of race and grammatical feature were significant beyond the .001 level. The interaction of age and grammatical feature was significant.

Table 1   Analysis of Variance of Standard English Sentences

	ss	df	ms	f
Between subjects				
A	128.48	1	128.48	285.51*
B	.09	1	.09	.20
A x B	1.00	1	1.00	2.22
Subjects within groups	25.22	56	.45	
Within subjects				
C	69.98	6	11.66	31.61*
A x C	39.49	6	6.58	21.23*
B x C	4.46	6	.74	2.39**
A x B x C	2.51	6	.41	1.32
C x subjects within groups	103.74	336	.31	
Total	374.97	419		

 * Significant beyond .001 level
**Significant at the .05 level

White subjects were significantly better than Negro subjects in repeating standard English sentences. A Scheffé test (Edwards, 1962) for multiple comparisons of factor C, grammatical features, indicated that most of the significant variance could be ascribed to the differential performance of subjects on the "if" construction. In addition, the plural feature was significantly more accurate than the third person singular and the possessive. The significant A x C interaction, race and grammatical feature, was most readily explained by the significant difference between Negro and white performance on the following grammatical categories: third person singular, copula, "if" construction, and negation. The B x C interaction, age and grammatical feature, was mostly due to the significant difference in performance at grade three and grade five of the "if" construction and the plural marker (Table 2).

2.   Analysis of variance on repetition of nonstandard constructions.
The data concerning repetition of the seven nonstandard constructions were subjected to a Winer multifactor repeated measures analysis of variance (Table 3). The factors under study were the same as those in the previous analysis of variance: A, race; B, age; and C, grammatical feature. The analysis of variance indicated that race, grammatical feature, and the interaction of race and grammatical feature were all significant beyond the .001 level.

Negro subjects did significantly better than white subjects in repeating Negro nonstandard sentences. A Scheffé test for multiple comparisons of factor C, grammatical features, indicated that most of the significant variance could be ascribed to the differential performance of subjects on the "if" construction. The significant A x C interaction, race and grammatical feature, was most readily explained by the differential performance of Negro and white subjects on the "if" and the double negative constructions (Table 4).

3.   Identification of race of the speaker.
Of the third graders, 73.3 percent identified the standard sentence as being spoken by a white man, and 73.3 identified the nonstandard sentence as being spoken by a Negro. Of the fifth graders, 83.3 percent judged the standard sentence as being spoken by a white man, while 93.3 percent judged the nonstandard sentence as being spoken by a Negro. Eighty percent of the white children and 76.6 percent of the Negro children identified standard sentences as being spoken by a white man. Nonstandard sentences were judged to be spoken by a Negro 83.3 percent of the time by both Negro and white children.

In responding to standard English sentences, white speakers did significantly better than black speakers. However, in examining the black child's "errors," it became evident that he didn't fail utterly to

Table 2 Scheffé Results of Standard English Sentences Analysis

Factor C

Third person	"To be"	"If"	Past Marker	Possessive	Plural	Negation
143.40	155.67	76.65	152.67	140.07	167.96	152.67

Third person is significantly different from the plural and the possessive at the .05 level. The "if" construction is significantly different from all other constructions at the .05 level.

Factor A x C

	Third person	"To be"	"If"	Past Marker	Possessive	Plural	Negation
Negro	51.00	65.88	6.33	69.21	66.30	77.14	54.90
White	92.40	89.79	80.32	89.79	48.44	90.82	85.17

Performance of Negro and white students was significantly different on the third person, "to be," "if," and negation constructions at the .05 level.

Factor B x C

	Third person	"To be"	"If"	Past Marker	Possessive	Plural	Negation
Grade 3	72.46	76.73	39.55	74.60	82.39	86.11	65.63
Grade 5	70.94	78.94	47.10	78.07	72.35	81.85	74.44

Performance of third and fifth-graders on the "if" construction was significantly different from their performance on the plural and the possessive.

Table 3   Analysis of Variance of Negro Nonstandard Sentences

	ss	df	ms	f
Between subjects				
A	73.20	1	73.20	66.55*
B	.53	1	.53	.48
A x B	.01	1	.01	.009
Subjects within groups	61.63	56	1.10	
Within subjects				
C	44.34	6	7.39	13.19*
A x C	39.49	6	6.58	11.75*
B x C	.82	6	.14	.25
A x B x C	3.42	6	.57	1.02
C x subjects within groups	188.83	336	.56	
Total	412.27	419		

*Significant beyond the .001 level

complete the sentence; he didn't jumble his response, nor did he use a "word salad." His "error" responses were consistent, e.g., in response to the stimulus: "I asked Tom *if he wanted* to go to the picture that was playing at the Howard," 97 percent of the children responded with: "I aks Tom *did he wanna* go to the picture at the Howard." In response to: "*Does* Deborah like to play with the girl that *sits* next to her in school," 60 percent of the Negro children responded: "*Do* Deborah like to play wif the girl what *sit* next to her in school."

This same behavior was evident in the white subjects when asked to repeat Negro nonstandard sentences. Black children were superior to white children in repeating these stimuli. Here again the "error" responses followed a definite pattern, e.g., in response to the stimulus: "I aks Tom do he wanna go to the picture that be playin' at the Howard," 78 percent of the white children said: "I asked Tom if he wanted to go to the picture that was playing at the Howard." Similar "translations" to standard English occurred on the other Negro nonstandard constructions.

The fact that the standard and nonstandard speakers exhibited similar "translation" behaviors when confronted with sentences that

Table 4 Scheffé Results of Negro Nonstandard English Sentences Analysis

Factor C

Third person	Be	Zero Copula	"If"	Past Marker	Double Negative	Possessive
86.79	54.48	106.61	109.30	80.93	109.57	73.06

The use of "Be" was significantly different from performance in regard to the zero copula, the third person singular, the "if" construction, and the double negative.

Factor A x C

	Third person	Be	Zero Copula	"If"	Past Marker	Double Negative	Possessive
Negro	52.88	35.27	57.16	87.87	53.39	67.90	42.57
White	33.91	19.21	49.45	21.43	26.54	31.67	30.49

Most of the significance was due to the difference in performance between Negro and white students on the double negative and on the "if" constructions.

were outside of their primary code indicates quite clearly that the
"language deficiency" that has so often been attributed to the low-
income Negro child is not a language deficit so much as a difficulty
in code switching when the second code (standard English) is not as
well learned as the first (nonstandard English).

The kinds of "errors" the two groups made (e.g., white subjects
adding the third person -s to nonstandard stimuli and Negroes deleting the third person -s on standard stimuli) represent an intrusion of
one language code (the dominant system) upon the sturcture of the
other code (the newly-acquired system). If, indeed, nonstandard were
not a structured system with well-ordered rules, one would expect
that Negro children would not be able to repeat the nonstandard
structures any better than did the white children, and one would also
expect that nonstandard patterns would not emerge systematically
when lower-class Negroes responded to standard sentences. Neither
of these expectations was upheld. The Negro children were in fact
able to repeat nonstandard structures better than were the white children, and they did produce systematic nonstandard patterns when
responding to standard sentences. The converse was true for the
whites; they responded significantly better to standard structures and
exhibited systematic standard patterns when responding to nonstandard stimuli.

The results of this research clearly indicate that (1) there are two
dialects involved in the education complex of black children (especially in schools with a white middle-class curriculum orientation); (2)
black children are generally not bidialectal; and (3) there is evidence
of interference from their dialect when black children attempt to use
standard English.

Since the disadvantaged Negro child, as the previous study suggests, like the Indian having to learn Spanish in Mexico, or the African having to learn French in Guinea, has to contend with the
interference from his vernacular in learning to read, how does his
task of learning to read differ from that of the middle-class "mainstream American" child? When the middle-class child starts the process of learning to read, his is primarily a problem of decoding the
graphic representation of a language which he already speaks. The
disadvantaged black child must not only decode the written words,
he must also "translate" them into his own language. This presents
him with an almost insurmountable obstacle, since the written words
frequently do not go together in any pattern that is familiar or meaningful to him. He is baffled by this confrontation with (1) a new language with its new syntax; (2) a necessity to learn the meaning of
graphic symbols; and (3) a vague, or not so vague, depending upon
the cultural and linguistic sophistication of the teacher, sense that
there is something terribly wrong with his language.

Although both the middle-class child and the disadvantaged Negro child are at the beginning faced with the task of relating their speech to a graphic representation that appears to be arbitrary and without a direct one-to-one correspondence to their speech (e.g., the "silent *e*" in *love*, the "silent *k*" in *knife*, the "k" as represented in *cut* and *kite*, and the "s" as represented in *Sue*, *cement*, etc.), the cards are stacked against the inner-city Negro child because his particular phoneme patterning is not considered in the curriculum at this early phase, so that when he reads *hep* for "help," *men'* for "mend," *boil* for "ball," the teacher presumes that he cannot read the word. *Hep* and *help*, *men'* and *mend*, and *boil* and *ball* are homonyms in the inner-city child's vernacular.

Despite the obvious mismatching of the "teachers and text writers" phoneme system and that of the inner-city child, the difficulties of the disadvantaged Negro child cannot be simplified solely to the pronunciation and phoneme differences that exist in the two systems. There is an even more serious problem facing the inner-city child, namely, his unfamiliarity with the syntax of the classroom texts. Although the middle-income child also must read texts that are at times stilted in terms of his own usage, there is no question that the language of the texts is potentially comparable to his system. That is to say, although he does not speak in the style of his reading text, he has the rules within his grammar to account for the occurrence of the textbook sentences. However, the textbook style is more unfamiliar to the ghetto child than it is to his middle-class standard-speaking age mate because much of the reading text is not a part of his "potential" syntactic system.

Because of the mismatch between the child's system and that of the standard English textbook, because of the psychological consequences of denying the existence and legitimacy of the child's linguistic system, and in the light of the success of vernacular teaching around the world, it appears imperative that we teach the inner-city Negro child to read using his own language as the basis for the initial readers. In other words, first teach the child to read in the vernacular, and then teach him to read in standard English. Such a reading program would not only require accurate vernacular texts for the dialect speaker, but also necessitate the creation of a series of "transition readers" that would move the child, once he had mastered reading in the vernacular, from vernacular texts to standard English texts. Of course, success of such a reading program would be dependent upon the child's ultimate ability to read standard English.

The advantages of such a program would be threefold. First, success in teaching the ghetto child to read. Second, the powerful ego-supports of giving credence to the child's language system and therefore to himself, and giving him the opportunity to experience success in school. And third, with the use of transitional readers, the child would have the opportunity of being taught standard English (which cannot occur by "linguistic swamping," since his schoolmates are all vernacular speakers) so that he could learn where his language system and that of standard English were similar and where they were different. Such an opportunity might well lead to generalized learning and the ability to use standard English more proficiently in other school work.

The continued failure of programs of reading for ghetto children that offer more of the same, i.e., more phonics, more word drills, etc., have indicated the need of a new orientation towards teaching inner-city children to read. Any such program must take into account what is unique about the ghetto child that is impairing his ability to learn within the present system. This paper has suggested that one of the essential differences to be dealt with in teaching inner-city Negro children is that of language. The overwhelming evidence of the role that language interference can play in reading failure indicates that perhaps one of the most effective ways to deal with the literacy problems of Negro ghetto youth is to teach them using vernacular texts that systematically move from the syntactic structures of the ghetto community to those of the standard English-speaking community.

BIBLIOGRAPHY

Bailey, B. Linguistics and Nonstandard Language Patterns. NCTE paper, 1965.

──── . Some Aspects of the Impact of Linguistics on Language. On Teaching in Disadvantaged Communities. *Elementary English*, 1968, 45, 570-579.

Baratz, J. and Povich, E. Grammatical Constructions in the Language of the Negro Preschool Child. *ASHA* paper, 1967.

Bereiter, C. Academic Instruction and Preschool Children. In R. Cobin and M. Crosby (eds.), *Language Programs for the Disadvantaged*, Champaign, Ill.: National Council of Teachers of English, 1965.

Deutsch, C. Auditory Discrimination and Learning: Social Factors. *Merrill Palmer Quarterly*, 1964, 10, 277-296.

Dillard, J. The Urban Language Study of the Center for Applied Linguistics. *Linguistic Reporter*, 1966, 8 (5), 1-2.

──── . Negro Children's Dialect in the Inner City. *Florida FL Reporter*, 1967, 5 (3).

Edwards, A. *Experimental Design in Psychological Research*. New York: Holt, Rinehart & Winston, 1962.

Goodman, K. Dialect Barriers to Reading Comprehension. *Elementary English*, 1965, 42, 853-860.

Klaus, R. and Gray, S. The Early Training Project for Disadvantaged Children: A report after five years. *Society for Child Development, Monograph 33,* 1968.

Labov, W. Some Sources of Reading Problems for Negro Speakers of Nonstandard English. In A. Frazier (ed.), *New Directions in Elementary English,* Champaign, Ill.: National Council of Teachers of English, 1967.

_____ and Robins, C. A Note on the Relation of Reading Failure to Peer-group Status. Unpublished paper, 1967.

Lee, L. Developmental Sentence Types: A Method for Comparing Normal and Deviant Syntactic Development. *Journal of Speech and Hearing Disorders,* 1966, 31, 311-330.

Loman, B. *Conversations in a Negro American Dialect.* Washington, D.C.: Center for Applied Linguistics, 1967.

Menyuk, P. Syntactic Rules Used by Children from Preschool Through First Grade. *Child Development,* 1964, 35, 533-546.

Modiano, N. A Comparative Study of Two Approaches to the Teaching of Reading in the National Language. U.S. Office of Education, Final Report, 1965.

National Advisory Council on the Education of Disadvantaged Children. March 1966, p. 7.

Passow, A. *Toward Creating a Model Urban School System: A Study of the District of Columbia Public Schools.* New York: Teachers College, Columbia University, 1967.

Shuy, R., Wolfram, W. and Riley, W. *Field Techniques in an Urban Language Study.* Washington, D.C.: Center for Applied Linguistics, 1968.

Stewart, W. Foreign Language Teaching Methods in Quasi-Foreign Language Situations. In W. Stewart (ed.), *Non-standard speech and the teaching of Enlish,* Washington D.C.: Center for Applied Linguistics, 1964.

_____ . Urban Negro Speech: Sociolinguistic Factors Affecting English Teaching. In R. Shuy (ed.), *Social Dialects and Language Learning,* Champaign, Ill.: National Council of Teachers of English, 1965.

_____ . Sociolinguistic Factors in the History of American Negro Dialects. *Florida FL Reporter,* 1967, 5 (2).

_____ . Continuity and Change in American Negro Dialects. *Florida FL Reporter,* 1968, 6 (2).

Thomas, D. Oral Language Sentence Structure and Vocabulary of Kindergarten Children Living in Low Socio-economic Urban Areas. *Dissertation Abstracts* XXIII (1962), 1014 (Chicago).

Wiener, M. and Cromer, W. Reading and Reading Difficulty: A Conceptual Analysis. *Harvard Educational Review,* 1967, 37, 620-643.

Winer, B. *Statistical Principles in Experimental Design.* New York: McGraw-Hill, 1962.

Walter A. Wolfram and Ralph W. Fasold

TOWARD READING MATERIALS FOR SPEAKERS OF BLACK ENGLISH: THREE LINGUISTICALLY APPROPRIATE PASSAGES

Within the last half century the populations of many urban areas in the United States have been drastically restructured. Extensive in-migration by Southern Negroes has resulted in the growth of many large isolated Negro ghettos. The segregated rural populations of the South have thus become the isolated Negro communities of our metropolitan areas. Although sociologists, psychologists, and anthropologists have pointed out the cultural gap that exists between the so-called ghetto culture and the culture of mainstream middle-class American society, it has been only recently that the linguistic consequences of this cultural difference have been examined. Previously, the speech behavior of many lower socio-economic class Negroes was simply considered comparable to that of lower socio-economic white citizens who spoke a variety of nonstandard English. Even some dialectologists simply assumed that the speech of the uneducated Negro was no different from that of the uneducated Southern white. Recent descriptive and sociolinguistic studies of the variety of English spoken by urban ghetto dwellers (i.e., Black English[1]), however, have indicated that there are important systematic differences between Black English and standard English.

At this point, one may ask why the speech behavior found in these isolated Negro communities should differ significantly from the nonstandard variety of English spoken by the lower socio-economic class white. In Northern urban areas, one source of difference can be found in the influence that Southern dialects have on these speech communities. But even in the rural South, Black English is characteristically different from the speech of the lower socio-economic class white, and one must ask why. For an explanation, one need only look at the distinct history of the Negro in

[1] "Black English" is appropriate as a label for the dialect of lower socioeconomic-class Negroes for at least three reasons. First, there is a precedent for designating dialects with color names (Black Bobo, Red Tai, White Russian). In the second place, the current use of the term "black" in throwing off pejorative stereotypes of Negro life matches our efforts to overcome the stereotype that this dialect is simply bad English. Finally, the name "Black English" avoids the negative connotations of terms which include words like "dialect," "substandard," and even "nonstandard."

American life, both in terms of his original immigration and his subsequent segregation. Recently, creole specialists have been particularly occupied with pointing out the historical derivation of Black English, tracing its origin to a rather widespread creole spoken in the Caribbean area. For example, William A. Stewart notes:

Of those Africans who fell victim of the Atlantic slave trade and were brought to the New World, many found it necessary to learn some kind of English. With very few exceptions the form of English they acquired was a pidginized one, and this kind of English became so well-established as the principal medium of communication between Negro slaves in the British colonies that it was passed on as a creole language to succeeding generations of the New World Negroes, for whom it was their native tongue.[2]

Present-day Negro dialect, according to Stewart, has resulted from a process which he labels "decreolization." That is, some of the original features characterizing the creole variety of English spoken by the early Negro slaves were lost through a gradual merging of the creole with the British-derived dialects with which they came in contact. The lexical inventory of this language variety became, for all practical purposes, identical with English (a process called "relexification" by Stewart). Due to the persistence of segregation, however, the process of decreolization was neither instantaneous nor complete. Thus, the nonstandard speech of present day Negroes still exhibits structural traces of a creole predecessor.

Present research by linguists has focused on Black English both as a system in itself and as a variety of English which systematically differs from standard English. Some of the differences between standard English and Black English, though seemingly small, have important consequences for the communication of a message. Furthermore, many of the systematic differences between standard English and Black English have been overlooked by psychologists, sociologists, and educators, who simply dismiss Black English as an inaccurate and unworthy approximation of standard English. To illustrate, we may briefly cite the Black English use of the form *be* as a finite verb, in a sentence such as *He be at work*. This characteristic use of *be* in Black English has been dismissed as simply an inaccurate attempt by the lower socio-economic class Negro to approximate the standard English speech norm. But such is clearly not the case. A study of the grammatical and semantic function of this construction employing the descriptive technique of modern linguistic theory reveals that one function of "finite *be*" has an "habitual" or "iterative"

---

[2] William A. Stewart, "Sociolinguistic Factors in the History of American Negro Dialects," *The Florida FL Reporter*, Vol. 5, No. 2 (1967), pp. 22.

meaning for the Black English speaker. There is no equivalent category in standard English and such a meaning can only be conveyed by a circumlocution (e.g., *He is at work all the time*). Thus, we see a clear-cut difference between the two grammatical systems. As will be seen in the annotated passages at the end of this article, there are a number of consequential systematic differences between Black English and standard English.

Now let us consider the implications of the above on the preparation of reading materials in the school system. We observe clear-cut differences between Black English and standard English on several different levels (i.e., phonological, grammatical, semantic) of language organization. The normal processes which account for dialect differences have been augmented by a creole substratum. We obviously have a dialect situation which is unique vis-à-vis other dialect varieties of American English. Some educators have assumed that one set of reading materials, perhaps "simplified" (however that may be defined) to avoid structural conflict between standard English and Black English, is adequate for the general school population. Certainly some lower socio-economic class speakers read extant materials and with some apparent understanding. We would not argue that the Black English speaker is going to understand as little standard English as a monolingual German speaker reading English, but we do suggest that there will be an inevitable information loss. This leads to the question of what type of reading materials are needed in the inner-city classroom.

Recently, publishers have introduced reading materials that attempt to relate to the culture of the ghetto. They have begun to include stories about Negro families in a ghetto setting, but despite the change in context, the dialogue in these texts is a variety of standard English which does not very closely approximate the actual language usage of black ghetto youth. Somehow, in the cultural adaptation publishers have largely ignored the linguistic consequences of cultural differences. Educators are thus faced with an anomaly which may be greater than the original mismatch of white middle-class-oriented narratives for black ghetto youth. One can imagine what the response would be if the white suburban youth were characterized by Black English dialogue. Yet, it is precisely this type of anomaly which is perpetuated by reading material which attempts to establish a cultural context indigenous to the ghetto but retains the language of white middle-class suburbia. What appears to be needed, then, is a linguistic adaptation or translation of reading materials to a language system which more closely approximates the child's oral language behavior.

Although adaptation or translation of materials is linguistically justifiable, there remain a number of factors which must be taken into account. One has to do with orthography. We have opted for standard orthography and conventional spelling. Conceivably this could lead to difficulties if Black English pronunciations prove different enough from standard English, so that there is a serious mismatch between conventional orthography and the phonology of the dialect. However, research on Black English phonology has indicated that conventional orthography is as adequate for Black English as it is for standard English.[3]

Another factor in the use of the proposed adaptations is that of applicability. There are many black ghetto residents who have learned standard English. For these people, the Black English materials would scarcely be more applicable than they would be to any other speaker of standard English. Because of this, the use of the proposed materials cannot be indiscriminate, even within ghetto schools. These materials should be used only with those children who actually use Black English.

A third factor has to do with the acceptability of the materials to black people themselves. The degree to which the adaptations would be acceptable, even to *bona fide* Black English speakers, is an unanswered question. Sociolinguistic research has shown that speakers who use socially stigmatized speech forms sometimes have the same low opinion of such forms as do speakers who do not use them. As a result, even though the Black English materials might be clearer and more natural to some, they may not be acceptable because of the presence of these stigmatized forms. One consideration which may tend to neutralize rejection, however, is the new feeling of racial pride among black Americans. This pride leads Negroes to seek those parts of their background, both in Africa and America, which are distinctive to them. There is an emphasis on black history, "African bush" hair styles, and neo-African clothing styles. So far this emphasis has not been extended to language. If a realization develops that this dialect, an important part of black culture, is as distinctively Afro-American as anything in the culture, the result may well be a new respect for Black English within the community.

The fourth factor has to do with the acceptability of the materials by educators. One possible objection would be the apparent discrepancy between the use of such materials and widely-advocated plans to teach disadvantaged children spoken standard English. If a child is given books to read in his socially stigmatized dialect at the same time as he is being taught to replace his Black English with a dialect of standard English, the two efforts would appear to be at cross-purposes. There are a number of reasons why this difficulty is

[3] Ralph W. Fasold, "Orthography in Reading Materials for Black English Speaking Children." In *Teaching Black Children to Read*, ed. Joan C. Baratz and Roger W. Shuy (Washington, D.C.: Center for Applied Linguistics, 1969), pp. 68-91.

more apparent than real. First, learning to read another language or dialect and learning to speak it are two different tasks. When the child who speaks Black English is required to learn to read using standard English materials, he is given two tasks at once: learning to read and learning a new dialect. The standard English-speaking child, by contrast, is only required to learn to read. The success in learning to read is greater when the skill is taught in the mother tongue of the child.[4] In the second place, because of the social dynamics involved, there is some question about the degree to which standard English can be taught to the ghetto child in the classroom at all. The most successful language learning has, as a component, meaningful interaction between the learner and speakers of the language he is trying to learn. Most Negro children, segregated by race and poverty, will have little opportunity to develop close acquaintanceships with standard-English speakers. There seems to be no reason why we should withhold from inner-city children materials which may help them learn to read simply because the use of these materials might interfere with teaching them spoken standard English, especially when it may not be possible to teach spoken standard English in the classroom in the first place. In any event, it seems that some of the usual reasons for teaching spoken standard English, e.g., to enhance employment opportunities, are not very relevant to elementary-school children at the age at which reading is taught. Furthermore, there is some evidence that a young person is well into adolescence before he becomes aware of the social dimensions of language,[5] a fact which would seem to indicate that formal efforts to teach standard English would be most effective if delayed until junior high school or later—well after reading skills should have been established.

The best proposals for teaching standard English to speakers of nonstandard dialects have as their goal adding a new dialect to the pupil's linguistic ability, rather than trying to eradicate his "bad" speech. In programs of this type, the students are assured that there is nothing wrong with their speech if it is used in appropriate contexts. If these assurances are sincere, a good way to demonstrate this would be to use the dialect in the educational process, specifically in reading materials.

As an example of how this could be done, we present in what follows three linguistically appropriate passages. First, we have taken

[4] Evelyn Bauer mentions several experiments involving North American Indians in which superior results were obtained when Indian children were taught to read in their own language before attempting to read the national language. (Evelyn Bauer, "Teaching English to North American Indians in BIA Schools," *The Linguistic Reporter*, Vol. 10, No. 4 [1968], p. 2.)

[5] William Labov, *The Social Stratification of English in New York City* (Washington, D.C.: Center for Applied Linguistics, 1966), p. 421.

an original Black English passage, which is a dramatized enactment of a situation occurring in the ghetto. In this passage we have simply transcribed and edited a section from a phonograph record[6] and arranged it as a quasi-drama. The record contains the reasonably spontaneous speech of six pre-adolescent Harlem boys. We have made no grammatical changes in the text so that at places it may appear that certain forms are importations from standard English. The second passage is a dialect translation of reading material which was designed for use in inner-city schools.[7] In the third passage we have taken an established piece of literature, the Bible, and translated a passage into idiomatic Black English. In this passage we have not attempted to change the Biblical cultural setting, which is very different from both mainstream middle-class society and the black ghetto. We have approached this translation with the same rigor expected of any serious translation task. That is, we have attempted to be faithful to the form and content of the original manuscript (which, of course, is Greek and not English). Our translation of the Bible passage must therefore be distinguished from attempts to paraphrase the Bible into contemporary cultural parallels of the original message. We have included a standard English translation of the passage for contrast with the Black English translation. Our annotations indicate those places where there exist clear-cut contrasts between the grammatical systems of standard English and Black English.[8] Phonological differences are not annotated except where they affect grammatical form. Differences in the semantic content of lexical items have not generally been noted.

DUMB BOY

Scene I
   Calvin: One day I was walking. Then I met Lennie. Lennie say, [1, 2]
"Calvin, what happened[3] to your lip?" I said, "Nothing." And
then Lenn came over to me and he say, [1, 2] "What[4] you mean by
nothing?" Like he always say[2] because he's always interested in

---

[6] *Street and Gangland Rhythms* (Folkways 5589 [1959]).

[7] Writers' Committee of the Great Cities School Improvement Program of the Detroit Public Schools, Gertrude Whpple, Chairman, *Four Seasons with Suzy* (Chicago: Follet Publishing Co., 1964), pp. 48-50. Used by permission. (In preparing reading materials for the ghetto we certainly do not recommend working from a standard English text to a Black English version, but in this case we have done so in order to point out some contrasts between the two versions of the story.)

[8] It will be apparent that some of the features discussed here are shared both by Black English and other nonstandard dialects of English.

me and me and him[5] is[6] good friends. So I told him what happened.[3] "This guy named[3] Pierre, he[7] about fifteen . . ."

Lennie: Yeah?

Calvin: He came over to me. . .

Lennie: Uh huh.

Calvin: And he hit me in my[8] lip because. . .

Lennie: Yeah?

Calvin: I . . .

Lennie: Done[9] what?

Calvin: Had done copied[9] off his paper in school.

Scene II

Pierre: Uhh, I told you don't do that no more.[10, 11]

Calvin: Come on, please leave me alone, please, please.

Pierre: Next time I catch you copying off somebody in there, you know what I'll do? I'll strangle you to death! Don't do that no more,[10] hear?

Calvin: I'm sorry.

Scene III

Lennie: What's that guy[12] name?

Calvin: Pierre.

Lennie: Where[4] he live at?

Calvin: Around our block.

Lennie: How old is he?

Calvin: Fifteen.

Lennie: How big is he?

Calvin: About the size of the other guy named[3] Pierre around our block.

Lennie: Well, tonight it's[13] gonna be a party at 118th Street where I live at. You bring him around there, hear?

Calvin: I surely will.

Lennie: O.K.

Scene IV

Calvin: So when I walked in there, everything was silent.

Lennie: Is that the guy over there?

Calvin: Yeah.

Lennie: Hey you, what[4] you hit my little brother for?

Pierre: Did he tell you what happened,[3] man?

Lennie: Yeah, he told me what happened.[3]

Pierre: But you . . . but you should tell your people to teach him to go to school, man. I know I didn't have a right to hit him. But he was copying off me and the teacher said . . . I forgot to tell the teacher.

Lennie: What[4] you mean you forgot to tell the teacher? What[4] you mean tell my parents to make him go to school to learn? What[4] you mean by that? What[4] you mean?

Pierre: Just like I said, man, he can't be dumb, man. I don't be[14] with him all his life.

Lennie: You basing or you sounding?[15]
Pierre: I ain't doing neither[10] one.
Lennie: That's more like it. But we[7] gonna deal tonight.
Pierre: If you can't face it, don't waste[16] it. If you can't fact it, don't waste[16] it.

SEE A GIRL[9]
Standard English Version

"Look down here," said Suzy.
"I can see a girl in here.
That girl looks like me.
Come here and look, David.
Can you see that girl?"

"Here I come," said David.
"I want to see the girl."
David said, "I do not see a girl.
A girl is not here, Suzy.
I see me and my ball."

Suzy said, "Look in here, Mother.
David can not see a girl.
And I can.
Can you see a girl in here?"

"Look down, Suzy," said Mother.
"Look down here, David.
That little girl is my Suzy.
And here is David."

"Mother! Mother! said Suzy.
"We can see David and me.
We can see Wiggles and a big girl.
That big girl is you."

SEE A GIRL
Black English Version

Susan[17] say,[1,2] "Hey you-all,[18] look down here.
I can see a girl in here.
The girl, she[19] look[2] like me.
Come here and look, David.
Could[20] you see the girl?"

David, he[19] say,[1,2] "Here I come.
Let me see the girl."
David say,[1,2] "I don't see no girl.[10]

---

[9] The setting of this story involves a little girl who looks at her reflection in a puddle. Wiggles is a dog.

Ain't no girl$_{2\ 1}$ in there.
I see me and my ball."

Susan, she$_{1\ 9}$ say $_{1,\ 2}$ "Momma,$_{22}$ look in here.
David don't$_{1}$ see no girl,$_{1\ 0}$ and I do.
You see a girl in there?"

Momma$_{22}$ say$_{1,\ 2}$ "Look down there, David.
That little girl$_{7}$ Susan.
And there go$_{2\ 3}$ David."

Susan$_{1\ 7}$ say, $_{1,\ 2}$ "Momma!$_{22}$ Momma!$_{22}$
We can see David and me.
We can see Wiggles and a big girl.
You$_{7}$ that big girl."

JOHN 3:1-17
Revised Standard Version

Now there was a man of the Pharisees, named Nicodemus, a ruler of the Jews. This man came to Jesus by night and said to him, "Rabbi, we know that you are a teacher come from God; for no one can do these signs that you do, unless God is with him." Jesus answered him, "Truly, truly, I say to you, unless one is born anew, he cannot see the kingdom of God." Nicodemus said to him, "How can a man be born when he is old? Can he enter a second time into his mother's womb and be born?" Jesus answered, "Truly, truly, I say to you, unless one is born of water and the Spirit, he cannot enter the kingdom of God. That which is born of the flesh is flesh, and that which is born of the Spirit is spirit. Do not marvel that I said to you, 'You must be born anew.' The wind blows where it wills, and you hear the sound of it, but you do not know whence it comes or whither it goes; so it is with every one who is born of the Spirit." Nicodemus said to him, "How can this be?" Jesus answered him," "Are you a teacher of Israel, and yet you do not understand this? Truly, truly, I say to you, we speak of what we know, and bear witness to what we have seen; but you do not receive our testimony. If I have told you earthly things and you do not believe, how can you believe if I tell you heavenly things? No one has ascended into heaven but he who descended from heaven, the Son of man. And as Moses lifted up the serpent in the wilderness, so must the Son of man be lifted up, that whoever believes in him may have eternal life." For God so loved the world that he gave his only Son, that whoever believes in him should not perish but have eternal life. For God sent the Son into the world, not to condemn the world, but that the world might be saved through him.

JOHN 3:1-17
Black English Version

It$_{1\ 3}$ was a man named$_{3}$ Nicodemus. He was a leader of the Jews. This man, he$_{19}$ come$_{1,\ 2}$ to Jesus in the night and say, $_{1,\ 2}$ "Rabbi, we know you$_{7}$ a teacher that come$_{2}$ from God, cause can't nobody$_{3,\ 4}$ do the things you be$_{14}$ doing 'cept he got God with him."

Jesus, he[19] tell[2] him say,[2,25] "This ain't[10] no jive,[10] if a man ain't born over again, ain't no way[21] he[7] gonna get to know God."

Then Nicodemus, he[19] ask him, "How[4,7] a man gonna be born when he[7] already old? Can't nobody[24] go back inside his mother and get[27] born."

So Jesus tell him, say,[2,25] "This ain't[10] no jive,[26] this[7] the truth. The onliest way a man[7] gonna get to know God,[7] he got to get born regular and he got to get[27] born from the Holy Spirit. The body can only make a body get[27] born, but the Spirit, he[19] make[2] a man so he can know God. Don't be suprised[3] just cause I tell you that you got to get born over again. The wind blow[2] where it want[2] to blow and you can't hardly[10] tell where it's[28] coming from and where it's[28] going to. That's[28] how it go[2] when somebody get[2,27] born over again by the Spirit."

So Nicodemus say,[1,2] "How[4] you know that?"

Jesus say, "You call yourself[29] a teacher that teach Israel and you don't know these kind of things? I'm gonna tell you, we[7] talking about something we know about cause we already seen it. We[7] telling it like it is[30] and you-all[18] think we[7] jiving. If I tell you about things you can see and you-all think we[7] jiving[26] and don't believe me, what's[28] gonna happen when I tell about things you can't see? Ain't nobody[21] gone up to Heaven 'cept Jesus, who come[1,2] down from Heaven. Just like Moses done[9] hung up the snake in the wilderness, Jesus got to be hung up. So that the peoples[31] that believe in him, he can give them[19] real life that ain't never[10] gonna end. God really did love everybody in the world. In fact, he loved[3] the people so much that he done[9] gave up the onliest Son he had. Any man that believe[2] in him, he[7] gonna have a life that ain't never[10] gonna end. He ain't never[10] gonna die. God, he[19] didn't send his Son to the world to act like a judge, but he sent him to rescue the peoples[31] in the world."

ANNOTATIONS

[1]   Some verbs, like "come" and "say," are not marked for past tense in Black English narratives, even when the context is past time.

[2]   Black English lacks the *-s* suffix which marks the present tense with third singular subjects in standard English.

[3]   When the suffix *-ed* is realized by a stop following a base form which ends in a consonant, the stop is not pronounced (thus, the pronunciation /neym/, for standard English /neymd/). This reflects a Black English phonological pattern in which syllable final consonant clusters in standard English correspond to simple consonants in Black English (see note 16). The pattern illustrates how phonological constraints in Black English affect the presence of certain grammatical categories.

[4]   Sentences which would have a pre-posed verbal auxiliary in standard English due to the formation of a content question generally have no auxiliary at all in the corresponding Black English sentence. For example, the "do" which would appear in the standard English equivalent of questions like "what you mean by nothing?" is absent for this reason.

5   In coordinate noun phrases, the distinction between objective and subjective forms of the pronoun is often neutralized, so that the "objective" form may function as a grammatical subject.

6   Occasionally (and particularly with coordinate constructions), the singular conjugated forms of "be" ("is," "was") occur with the plural subject in Black English.

7   The present tense form of the copula frequently is not realized in a number of different syntactic environments in Black English. Generally, where the contracted form of the copula may occur in standard English the stative condition is indicated simply by word order in Black English.

8   In standard English, sentences like "kiss her on the cheek" and "punch Jack in the stomach" involving a verb of physical contact, a personal nominal reference and a body part, the definite article "the" is used with the body part although it belongs to the same person referred to by the personal noun or pronoun. In Black English, the possessive pronoun is used in these constructions instead of the article.

9   The use of "done" plus the past tense of a verb is a construction indicating completed action. Some speakers occasionally include a form of "have" as in "had done copied . . ."

10   In Black English, negation is typically marked not only in the main verb phrase, but also in each indefinite determiner or indefinite pronoun in the sentence, as well as in certain adverbs like "hardly" and "never."

11   An embedded imperative may be retained in its original quoted form instead of being realized in an infinitive construction (e.g., "I told you don't do that no more" instead of "I told you not to do that no more").

12   Black English lacks possessive -s so that possession is indicated only by the order of items.

13   "It," in Black English, can be used as an "expletive" or "presentative" in addition to its function as a pronoun referring to a specific object or participant. In this usage it is equivalent to standard English "there."

14   The form "be" can be used in Black English as a verb in the same constructions in which "is, am, are, was, were" are used in standard English, but with a different meaning. The use of "be" as a main verb denotes iteration or habituation.

15   The expressions "basing" and "sounding" refer to types of aggressive verbal behavior. "Basing" is a kind of backtalk and "sounding" refers to a special type of ritual insult.

16   The items "face" and "waste" have rhyming endings in Black English be-

cause the final stop member of a syllable final consonant cluster is frequently absent.

17   The use of nicknames like "Jim" for "James" or "Dick" for "Richard" is rare in ghetto communities. Therefore, "Susan" is more natural in Black English reading materials than "Suzy."

18   Unlike most standard English dialects, Black English distinguishes the singular and plural of the second person pronoun ("you" versus "you-all," pronounced /y l/).

19   A pronoun is often used following the noun subject of a sentence in Black English. "Pronominal apposition" functions to focus on the "topic" of the sentence and to indicate the re-entry of a participant in a discourse.

20   In a number of contexts, Black English speakers use "could" where standard English has "can."

21   This construction is a very common stylistic variation of "it ain't no girl in here" or "it ain't nobody who has gone up to Heaven" (cf. note 13).

22   Black children generally call their mothers "Momma." "Mother" is likely to be taken as an abbreviation for a taboo term.

23   The idiomatic expression "there go" is equivalent to the standard English construction "there is" when it refers to the existential location of something. Generally, this construction is limited to the speech of adolescents and pre-adolescents.

24   There are two types of emphatic negative sentences in Black English involving the pre-position of a negativized auxiliary. Black English, unlike most white nonstandard dialects, permits both an indefinite subject and the main verb to carry negative markers. Thus ". . . nobody can't do the things you be doing . . ." is a grammatical sentence in the dialect, meaning that nobody can do these things. To emphasize such a negative statement Black English speakers may pre-pose the negativized verbal auxiliary to the front of the sentence, much as the ordinary English yes-no question formation. Two kinds of stress pattern are associated with this structure. If the stress pattern is "càn't nóbody (do something)," it expresses general emphasis. If the stress pattern is "cán't nobòdy (do something)," it carries the overtone of disbelief.

25   Quotations can be introduced by the form "say" in addition to any other quotative words such as "tell" and "ask."

26   The concept "jive" in the Negro ghetto refers to a particular form of language behavior in which the speaker assumes a guise in order to persuade someone of a particular fact. It is often used to refer to the deception of someone with flattery or false promises.

²⁷ "Get" (or "got") often functions as a passive marker in Black English.

²⁸ When a pronoun ending in /t/ like "it" or "that" precedes the contracted form of "is," the contraction /s/ is pronounced and the /t/ is not (cf. note 7).

²⁹ The expression "you call yourself X" or "you call yourself doing X" implies mild doubt that the hearer really is X or is doing X.

³⁰ The expression "telling it like it is" refers to making an accurate and trust-worthy assessment of a situation, without any attempt to exaggerate.

³¹ -s plural can be suffixed to forms which in standard English form their plural in some irregular way (suppletive forms, internal change, etc.).

Wayne O'Neil

THE POLITICS OF BIDIALECTALISM

Bidialectalism or biloquilism (Jim Sledd has suggested that the expression "doublespeak" is more in keeping with the genius of the language) refers to a movement in education systematically to render lower-class students able to speak both their native dialect and standard English. It is a less vague and haphazard continuation of earlier attempts, as old as popular education, to eradicate dialect. And it offers the lower class a traditional choice: convert so that the on-going social game will be fairer to you. There is no offer to change the rules of the game or its name. Bidialectalism also differs in that it is meant mostly for lower-class blacks and not for the lower class in general. It comes, fortunately, at a time when many blacks are piecing together their identity, saving it from powerful attempts to fragment and destroy it. It is therefore controversial and widely discussed (see, for example, Olivia Mellan, "Black English. Why Try to Eradicate It," *The New Republic*, 28 November 1970, pp. 15-17). But it has not been discussed in a wide enough context, so it is my purpose to do that in the following pages, thus to indicate why this ill-advised attempt to change people should be rejected.

Let me begin with what I understand to be some facts and some pretty good hunches about language and language learning. It is, for example, an empirical assumption that language differences intuitively understood as dialect differences are relatively superficial, that is that they amount to rule differences (in the terminology of the linguistic theory of Chomsky) which fall quite low in the ordered set of rules that constitutes the grammar of a language, the internalized knowledge of a language that speakers possess. We do not expect dialects of a language to differ in any important ways: neither in their underlying constituents nor in their order, not in their major transformations, not in their underlying phonological segments, etc. And in fact work on transformational dialectology has borne this working assumption out. When we look at different languages we do expect rule differences to be more radical, which is also in fact true. Yet in no sense is there any empirical evidence to support such notions as language A is "impoverished" vis-à-vis language B, or that dialect x of language C is impoverished with respect to dialect y of language C, i.e., that the grammar and vocabulary of x is some diminished subset of the grammar and vocabulary of y. Such notions are meaningless, for the grammars of x and y are simply equal sets that intersect in vast and important ways.

Now it is because of this intersection that there is general mutual intelligibility among speakers of the several dialects of any language. Presumably understanding what someone has said to you entails your being able to employ perceptual strategies that get you from the surface noises through to deep structure clues and on to the underlying relationships of words and meaning. Unless there is significant overlap of grammar and vocabulary between speaker (writer) and hearer (reader) the process of understanding will break down immediately. There are, however, dialect relationships cited that involve patience and time on both sides for mutual intelligibility to follow. Hockett somewhere discusses natives in a village talking about the dialects in nearby villages being two-day languages, seven-day languages, etc.: you have to sit around with the folks over there for a couple of days before the noises clear up enough for you to get on with your business. There are also instances of one-way intelligibility: objective ones, between Faroe Islanders and Icelanders, for example; subjective ones, mostly between teachers and lower-class students.

Finally, some hunches. It is reasonable to assume that where general mutual intelligibility exists among the speakers of the several dialects of a language, it will be extremely difficult (because it serves no purpose) for the speakers of one dialect to learn to produce rather than simply understand the other dialect. The dialect differences may of course be quite obvious and plain and even interesting, but if no real problem of understanding hangs on them, to learn to mimic one of the other dialects is to work away at some artifact of a task that has nothing to do with language and communication. Indeed if we were to set up an experiment whose goal was to get speakers of one dialect to learn to speak another dialect, the subjects would be bewildered by any arguments that counterfactually claimed there to be a problem of intelligibility.

There are, however, ways of attacking and breaking down and displacing bewilderment. Let us imagine the following experiment: Say that there was a dialect of English that employed forms of the verb *be* in a number of vacuous ways. For example, instead of expressing predicate adjectives, predicate locatives, and the progressive aspect of a verb by a simple, direct, and economical Subject/Predicate-word structure, i.e., instead of saying "He big," "He here," "He eating supper" this dialect would in its uneconomical way say "He is big," "He is eating supper." Say also that it had a high-front/mid-front vowel distinction before nasals such that rather than having homonymous *pin* for the thing that a tailor hems up a garment with and for the enclosure one keeps animals in, this dialect distinguishes phonologically (what any but the most impoverished context—say a minimal-pair drill—would normally distinguish) *pin* for the tailor's tool and *pen* for the animal enclosure. Say also that speakers of this dialect use imprecise, counter-factual, and confusing words and expressions like *Vietnamization, protective reaction, unarmed reconnaissance flights*, etc. We could of course imagine a whole set of such differences at various points in the language. But these will suffice for purposes of illustration.

How could we then persuade the speaker of this dialect to cease speaking his way and start speaking ours? There are several tacks to follow. First off we could simply tell him that his way of doing it is wrong. The problem with this method is that the subject will probably suffer severe depression and loss of identity, the more so if his family and friends (who do not have the benefit of this particular experiment) turn up on this score to be wrong too. Secondly, we might tell him that it's not exactly wrong, but for him to persist in saying "He is eating supper," "He is out by the pigpen," etc., is a grave social error, at least in the context of the experiment and any similar and vaguely-defined situations. And since those situations aren't about to change, he had better—if he wants to be a good subject and succeed. The consequences of this method (especially if the subject is young) would be very little different from those of the first method discussed. Finally, we could modify the experiment slightly by telling the subject that if he could learn this new way of speaking he would then be richer than people who know only one way—like being told that there are two ways to get from here to the Americana: you can walk or you can hop and you're the richer for that, but you'd best hop if anyone you don't know is watching. Again the consequences of this method, which by the way defines bidialectalism, would seem to be very little different from those of the other two. For hopping is a tough, self-conscious way of going through life and would have to be justified to oneself.

There are certainly several other methods that an alert experimenter could devise but all would be extremely time-consuming and none could avoid the severe psychological consequences to the subject mentioned above—not to speak of frustration, since the chances of the experiment's succeeding are quite low.

Ludicrous as it may seem, such experiments, badly and casually formulated ones as well as neatly and tightly designed ones, are a regular and extensive part of American school curriculums and of school curriculums in general. From the very beginning of popular education in America—from the time that New England school teachers began to move west with their three Marys, there has been a sustained attempt to eradicate dialect, to replace it with preferred, standard speech. For various reasons these attempts have not succeeded, to the same extent and for the same reasons that very little of what goes on at the surface in schools has taken hold, which failure—as I shall indicate later—is not without its purpose. Systematized attempts to eradicate dialect are of very recent vintage and follow from the rapid, post-war development of the social pseudo-sciences. It is also these pseudo-scientists who have changed the name of the game from "eradication" to "duplication," i.e., to "bidialectalism" or "doublespeak."

At this point we can well ask why all the bother, given that the task is unnecessary and difficult (if not impossible), that it consumes an inordinate amount of time out of the formal educational life of a child to no success, and that it successfully entails severe psychological disorientation. The reasons, complex, mixed, and confusing, need to be sorted out.

But first it is best to point out what should be common knowledge: though dialects are from the point of view of their grammars partially separate but equal, they do exist in social, cultural, political, and economic settings that wash away their linguistic equality, replacing it with value judgments that follow from the power and control that speakers of one dialect have over speakers of other dialects and from the low regard in which speakers of one dialect will hold speakers of others. Furthermore in this connection we must distinguish why individuals want to change or "enrich" the language of lower-class children from what motivates institutions. I will not argue that individuals necessarily have well-thought-out, formulated positions—though this may in some instances be the case. But it is certainly the case that institutional, governmental motivation is well-formulated and quite exactly intentioned.

There are, then, a variety of reasons or arguments that individuals will give and that can be ascribed to them in justification of their persisting with the business of dialect eradication or duplication. Let me list some of them:

(1) Cultural Elitism: "The permissive linguists urge speaking and writing the dialectic [sic] language of the region and the racial and economic group; some unschooled areas have considerable raciness of diction. It is not intellectually precise, however, and its jargon takes on strong emotional and constantly warped meanings. It deserves observation, but not inclusion in standard English until its floating (and possibly ephemeral) meanings have settled. 'I gottcha' and 'Yeah, sure, man,' are slurring our speech and 'Do like I say,' 'Tell it like it is' are at a dangerous work of erosion. Respect for, and decent craftsmanship in the use of, language may seem secondary in a world of struggle for survival or for social justice, but if we relax the rear-guard defense of these dignities, whatever survives the assaults of ruthlessness and blind idealism that resorts to anarchic violence will be debased and rudderless" ("A Teacher's Plea for Certain Values," *Boston Globe* [26 November 1970]). Or read any issue of Mortimore Smith's *Bulletin, Council for Basic Education.*

(2) Pragmatism: holders of this position argue that given the social and economic class structure of American society, bidialectalism is the only way out or part of a way out of lower class-ness, or more narrowly, lower-class blackness. For if you hold to the standards of those in power all the good things of life will follow: a college education, a good job, the respect of those in power, etc.

(3) Racism: these people are simply somewhere in their heads bent on putting down blacks. (Bidialectalism or dialect eradication is in this case reserved for a particular segment of the lower class and not meant as in (2) for the lower class in general, or as in (1) for everyone who hasn't graduated from an Ivy League school.) They may of course resort to (2) in their own justifications of what they do, but in fact (3) can be fairly clearly seen in their work. See James Sledd, "Bi-Dialectalism: The Linguistics of White Supremacy," *English Journal* 58.1307-1315, 1329 (December 1969).

Now certainly there are other motivations (e.g., government and foundation dollars) that guide individuals in their pursuit of bidialectalism; yet let's not hang on them. For I think it more important to look at institutional motivations, governmental motivations; i.e., political forces guiding educational systems that are far more important for our understanding of educational problems. I believe that we can dismiss right off the motivations that I have argued guide individuals, except the dollars. They are important, certainly, for the proper functioning of individuals in the schools, but they are not the forces guiding educational systems.

A related digression can clarify this point: When a few short years ago there was rioting and confrontation at Columbia University, one of the charges leveled against the university was that it was pursuing an expansion policy that was racist. On the other hand M.I.T. has successfully (and without confrontation) pursued exactly the same policies in its constructing the Tech Square complex and enticing NASA to Cambridge, but this at the expense of the small industry of Cambridge and the white working class. (All of this is well-documented in S. Shalom and B. Shapiro, *Two, Three, Many Tech Squares: MIT's Role in the Transformation of Cambridge*, Boston: New England Free Press, 1969.) Now either we must argue that Columbia and M.I.T. were (and are) pursuing fundamentally different expansion policies—an argument that is quite difficult to sustain, or that the racist charge against Columbia is superficial and that Columbia and M.I.T. were, in fact, simply expanding their power the way (nonprofit) corporations like government are wont to do and the only difference between the two universities was the color of the skin of lower-class people living at their perimeters. This latter interpretation seems the correct one. By a related argument I would then dismiss the racist charge (insofar as he means this to apply to government and educational systems) in Jim Sledd's essay previously cited. So also would I dismiss (1) and (2), above.

For educational systems serve a quite clear and well-understood political-economic purpose, and serve it quite well. Note carefully what I am saying: American education is effective in a way that the government and the ruling class want it to be—not all in a way that I or most of you want it to be. It ensures the status quo; it ensures that workers will be alienated from their labor, that the managers' sons will be managers, the laborers' sons laborers, etc. It puts people in their place. This quite correct analysis is best presented at length in an admirable book by eight Italian school children, *Letter to a Teacher* (Random House, 1970)—see *The New Republic*, 18 July 1970, pp. 25-26 and *Harvard Educational Review* 40.657-674 (November 1970).

How then does language education—without, remember, worrying about the motivations of individual teachers, school administrators, or textbook makers—fit into this analysis? On this analysis it follows that the enterprise of making lower-class speakers over into middle-class speakers is simply a piece of the educational emptiness that helps maintain the present distribution of power in society. For wasting time there, on a thing that is bound to fail, serves to render school children skilled enough to be exploited but finally uneducated, used to failure, and alienated enough not to oppose exploitation; thus for them to continue to agree that they had their chances to succeed in a free and open society but that they had failed. No one's fault but their own. As the Italian school children say in their *Letter*, "The thing is so clear-cut that we can only smile."

So much for the past, which of course continues into the present—except that the present concern to render blacks bidialectal is an attempt at the most obvious kind of political cooptation and a cruel joke to boot. For what it means is that education is offering a particularly vocal and angry segment of the lower class a special but fore-doomed chance to succeed inside the system. It is a crumb, a symbol that finally something of moment is being done for them. But, in fact, it remains a symbolic gesture only, nothing more—no matter how well it is gotten up in scientistic garb. For the rules of the game are unchanged: there is no new social, political, or economic justice. To their credit, many blacks reject the gesture and insist on the primacy of their own cultural identity and dialect, on their right to change American society in fundamental ways: properly so, for decisions about education belong to the people they affect.

Educational and social reform is ever such gesture. For it is the nature of reform to tinker with the surface in order to secure the underpinnings. At M.I.T., for example—related digression number two—we have just finished spending who knows how many tens of thousands of dollars on a study of M.I.T. education (*Creative Renewal in a Time of Crisis*) which seeks to answer, not how can science and technology serve the people, but rather how can M.I.T. engage its freshman so that they come out the way they are supposed to: good technical servants to the American corporate interests. Indeed all of the educational reform currently about is in response to signals that human alienation is not deep enough, to a desire to better control people, their heads, and their lives. Thomas Szasz's work on the role of psychiatry in defending the social and political status quo simply underscores the point. See, e.g., his "The Psychiatrist: A Policeman in the Schools" (*This Book Is about Schools*, Pantheon, 1970).

It is in this general context that we should understand bidialectalism: it is a modern, fancy, but false promise to put black people up, while in fact putting them on and keeping them down. It does not move one bit towards facing the injustices of American political and economic life. Nor it is intended for that. For this reason *it* should be put down—and for this reason alone. It is uninteresting to me to (because these are not *basic* counter-arguments) that it can't work, that the knowledge for making it work doesn't exist, that the money for making it work if the knowledge existed isn't available. It is enough to understand that double-speak is a response meant to keep things as they are.

Educators ought to do better. For their real job is in direct opposition to efforts to maintain the status quo. Education should
move people to an exultation in and understanding of human differences, to the realization that they can control their own destinies, to
a realization that stupid, pointless, destructive work is not what life
or society is about, to organizing and fighting for a life of peace,
health, and meaning. Bidialectalism is nowhere near any of these
things: it is part of the social and political machinery meant to control.

James Sledd

DOUBLESPEAK: DIALECTOLOGY IN THE
SERVICE OF BIG BROTHER

A SHORT HISTORY OF DOUBLESPEAK

It was only a few years ago that Prof. Dr. Roger W. Shuy, then
of Michigan State University, discovered American dialects.[1] In a little book which James R. Squire, Executive Secretary of the National
Council of Teachers of English, described as "a valuable resource" for
teachers increasingly concerned with "the study of the English language in our schools" (Shuy, "Foreword"), Dr. Shuy informed the
profession that in Illinois "a male sheep was known as a *buck* only to
farmers who had at some time raised sheep" (p. 15) and that "the
Minneapolis term *rubber-binder* (for rubber band)" was spreading
into Wisconsin (pp. 36-37). He also declared that Southerners pronounce *marry* as if it were spelled *merry*; that they pronounce *fog*
and *hog* like *fawg* and *hawg;* that they have a final /r/ in *humor;* that
they make *which* identical with *witch* and rhyme *Miss* with *his;* etc.
(pp. 12-13).

[1] Roger W. Shuy, *Discovering American Dialects.* (Champaign, Illinois: National
Council of Teachers of English, 1967.)

But one does not expect high scholarship from a popularizing textbook, and though Dr. Shuy's discoveries made no great noise in the world of dialectology, the fault was not his alone. As he himself pointed out, American dialect studies were becoming "both more complex and more interesting," and new questions were being asked.

Twenty or thirty years ago dialect geographers were mainly concerned with re-lating current pronunciations, vocabulary, and grammar to settlement history and geography. In the sixties, the problems of urban living have attracted atten-tion, including social dialects and styles which need to be learned and used to meet different situations. We need more precise information about the dialects which set one social group apart from another. (Shuy, p. 63)

One might say metaphorically that the dialectologists, like millions of their compatriots, had left the farm for the big city. There they had discovered the blacks—and were making the best of it. In Sep-tember, 1967, Dr. Roger W. Shuy was no longer a teacher in East Lansing, Michigan, but a Director of Urban Language Study in Wash-ington, D.C.

The trouble with the blacks, as it seemed to the nabobs of the National Council, was that they didn't talk right and weren't doing very well in school. But they were also raising considerable hell with the police; and since the traditional self-righteous pontification against the South showed little promise of quelling riots in Chicago, Detroit, or New York, the greater Powers of the North had assumed a beneficent air and (as one stratagem) had employed a band of lin-guists and quasi-linguists who would pretend to help black folks talk like white folks on all occasions which the Northern Powers thought it worth their while to regulate. This was the origin of bidialectalism, biloquialism, or—in "good plain Anglo-Saxon"—doublespeak. No missionary enterprise of recent times has been more profitable—for the evangelists.

Readers in search of a longer and more reverential history may find it in many sources, including at least six volumes in the Urban Language Series, under the general editorship of Dr. Roger W. Shuy, now Director of the Sociolinguistics Program of the Center for Ap-plied Linguistics. They are particularly directed to the volume en-titled *Teaching Standard English in the Inner City*, which Dr. Shuy has edited with his colleague Ralph W. Fasold (Washington, D.C.: Center for Applied Linguistics, 1970). Further light is shed by other collections of essays, notably the special anthology issue of *The Florida FL Reporter* which appeared in 1969 under the title *Linguistic-Cultural Differences and American Education;* the report of the twentieth annual Round Table Meeting at Georgetown,

Linguistics and the Teaching of Standard English to Speakers of Other Languages or Dialects; and Frederick Williams' anthology *Language and Poverty: Perspectives on a Theme.* Professor Williams includes a recent essay by the British sociologist Basil Bernstein, who in his own way is also somewhat critical of doublespeak; and readers interested in Bernstein's earlier work will find it reviewed by Denis Lawton in *Social Class, Language and Education.* By all odds the best of the bidialectalists is the genuinely distinguished linguist William Labov of Columbia University, whose little book *The Study of Nonstandard English* includes a selected bibliography. Recently, the apostles of doublespeak have been vexed by more numerous and more vocal objectors, and perhaps there is just a hint of admitted failure in the shifting of attention by some biloquialists from doublespeak to the teaching of reading. Linguists, educationists, and others have addressed themselves to reading problems in memorial volumes like *Reading for the Disadvantaged,* edited by Thomas D. Horn, and *Language & Reading,* compiled by Doris V. Gunderson.[2]

THE MONEYED BANKRUPT

It is sad to report that the results of such vast activity have been disproportionately small. The biloquialists themselves do not claim to have produced substantial numbers of psychologically undamaged doublespeakers, whose mastery of whitey's talk has won them jobs which otherwise would have been denied them. In fact, the complete bidialectal, with undiminished control of his vernacular and a good mastery of the standard language, is apparently as mythical as the

---

[2] To list the cited works more formally: Alfred C. Aarons, Barbara Y. Gordon, and William A. Stewart, eds., *Linguistic-Cultural Differences and American Education.* Special anthology issue of *The Florida FL Reporter,* Vol. 7, No. 1 (Spring /Summer, 1969).

James E. Alatis, ed., *Linguistics and the Teaching of Standard English to Speakers of Other Languages or Dialects.* Report of the Twentieth Annual Round Table Meeting on Linguistics and Language Studies. (Washington, D.C.: Georgetown University Press, 1970.)

Frederick Williams, ed., *Language and Poverty: Perspectives on a Theme.* (Chicago: Markham Publishing Company, 1970.)

Denis Lawton, *Social Class, Language and Education.* (New York: Schocken Books, 1968.)

William Labov, *The Study of Nonstandard English.* (Champaign, Illinois: National Council of Teachers of English, 1970.)

Thomas D. Horn, ed., *Reading for the Disadvantaged: Problems of Linguistically Different Learners.* (New York: Harcourt Brace Jovanovich, Inc., 1970.)

Doris V. Gunderson, compiler, *Language & Reading: An Interdisciplinary Approach.* (Washington, D.C.: Center for Applied Linguistics, 1970.)

unicorn: no authenticated specimens have been reported.[3] Even the means to approximate the ideal of doublespeaking are admittedly lacking, for "the need for teaching materials preceded any strongly felt need for theoretical bases or empirical research upon which such materials could be based" (Fasold and Shuy, *op. cit.*, p.126). Consequently, there are relatively few teaching materials available (*ibid.*, p. 128), and those that do exist differ in theory, method, content, and arrangement (Walt Wolfram, in Fasold and Shuy, p. 105). In the words of Director Dr. Shuy,

> A majority of the materials currently available for teaching standard English to nonstandard speakers rest on the uneasy assumption that TESOL techniques [for teaching English as a second language] are valid for learning a second dialect. They do this without any solid proof. We do not have a viable evaluation tool at this time nor are we likely to get one until the linguists complete their analysis of the language system of nonstandard speakers. Most current materials deal with pronunciations although it has long been accepted that grammatical differences count more heavily toward social judgments than phonological or lexical differences.[4]

Taken literally, that confession would mean that the biloquialists will never be able to tell their patrons whether or not their costly teaching materials are any good, because a complete analysis of any language, standard or nonstandard, is another unattainable ideal. The best of existing descriptions of what is called Black English are only fragments, sketches of bits and pieces which have caught the eye of Northern linguists unfamiliar with Southern speech.[5] Advocates of

---

[3] Labov has repeatedly said as much, most recently in "The Study of Language in its Social Context," *Studium Generale*, 23 (1970), p. 52. "We have not encountered any nonstandard speakers who gained good control of a standard language, and still retained control of the nonstandard vernacular." The goodness of the acquired control of the standard language will not easily be assumed by students of hypercorrection, readers of H. C. Wyld on "Modified Standard," or teachers of Freshman English in state universities.

[4] Roger W. Shuy, "Bonnie and Clyde Tactics in English Teaching." In Aarons, Gordon, and Stewart, *Linguistic-Cultural Differences and American Education*, p. 83.

[5] Readers may satisfy themselves of the truth of this proposition by examining the table of contents in Walter A. Wolfram's *Sociolinguistic Description of Detroit Negro Speech* (Washington, D.C.: Center for Applied Linguistics, 1969) or by reading Wolfram and Fasold, "Some Linguistic Features of Negro Dialect," in Fasold and Shuy, *Teaching Standard English*, pp. 41ff. A much more extensive work is the *Study of the Non-Standard English of Negro and Puerto Rican Speakers in New York City* by Labov, Paul Cohen, Clarence Robins, and John Lewis (2 vols.; Columbia University, 1968); but Chapter III of their first volume, "Structural Differences between Non-Standard Negro English and Standard English," is very far from a "complete" grammar of either dialect.

doublespeak must therefore admit that they have still not produced the "absolutely necessary prerequisite to English teaching in such situations, . . . the linguistic analysis and description of the nonstandard dialect."[6]

CAUSES OF FAILURE

At this juncture the irreverent might be tempted to ask a question. If happy, accomplished, and fully employed doublespeakers are not swarming in Northern cities, if tried and tested materials for teaching more of them remain scarce, and if complete descriptions of the relevant dialects are not going to exist while we do, then one might ask just what the biloquialists have been doing with the money and manpower which the Establishment has provided them or whether (more suspiciously) the Establishment really want them to do anything or just to give the impression of a great society on the march toward new frontiers.

One naughty answer would be that the biloquialists have been so busy convening, conferring, organizing, advertising, and asking for more that their intellectual activities have suffered. There is even some expert testimony to this effect:

A recent national conference on educating the disadvantaged devoted less than five percent of its attention during the two days of meetings to the content of such education. Practically all of the papers and discussion centered on funding such programs, administrating them and evaluating them. (Shuy, in Fasold and Shuy, p. 127)

But so elementary a naughtiness is only a partial answer, and in part unfair. It is unfair specifically to William Labov and his associates, who have taught us a great deal, not just about current American English, but about the theory and practice of descriptive and historical grammar; and it does not sufficiently emphasize the extenuating circumstance that well-meaning sloganeers may be trapped by their own slogans as they try to do in a few years a job that would take a generation.

Since the Powers prefer the appearance of social change to the reality, it was not hard to hook governments and foundations on the

[6]William A. Stewart, "Urban Negro Speech: Sociolinguistic Factors Affecting English Teaching." In Aarons, Gordon, and Stewart, *Linguistic-Cultural Differences*, p. 53.

alleged potentialities of doublespeak as if those potentialities had
been realized already or would be on a bright tomorrow; but when
the advertisements had brought the customers, the delivery of the
actual goods turned out impossible. Nobody knows what the biloquialists admit they would have to know about dialects of English to
make doublespeak succeed; and besides this general ignorance (which
some of them have manfully attacked), the biloquialists are working
under some special disadvantages. It is always hard for people who
have not taught much to talk about teaching (though ingenious
youths like Dr. Peter S. Rosenbaum can sometimes manage it),[7] and
it is hard for linguists who have not heard much Southern speech to
talk about speech which is basically Southern: they are constantly
discovering distinctive characteristics of "the Negro vernacular," like
"dummy *it* for *there*," which the most benighted caucasian Christian
spinster in Milledgeville, Georgia, could assure them are commonplace
among poor whites.[8]

There are other difficulties, too, which hamper not only the
biloquialists but all practitioners of large-scale linguistic engineering
(the jargon is contagious). Linguistics in the '60s and early '70s has
been unsettled by new theories, whose advocates are openly skeptical of oversold "applications"; and even in favorable circumstances
"interdisciplinary" efforts like biloquialism are always slow to take
effect, often hampered by disagreements among the congregation of
prima donnas, and sometimes disappointingly unproductive.

Quite as loud as the general lamentation over the failure of
"interventionist" programs for the disadvantaged are the debates
among the interveners. Thus, to the devotees of applied linguistics,
both the Englishman Bernstein and the American partners Engelmann

---

[7] Dr. Rosenbaum's oration on the twentieth Round Table report deserves special
attention, but lack of space forbids an attractive excursus. A couple of quotations will suggest the orientation of this already eminent "linguistic engineer."
(1) "*Learning* means acquiring new or improved control over one's environment.
Teaching means structuring or manipulating an environment so that a learner
through experience in this environment can with facility acquire the desired control" (p. 112). Just how this statement applies to a class in *Beowulf* may be left
to Dr. Rosenbaum to explain. (2) "In experimental computerized versions of
such an environment being developed by IBM Research, the tutor is a computer
itself, communicating with a student by means of a terminal station equipped
with a typewriter, tape recorder, and image projector" (p. 116). It would be un-
kind to blame the tutor computer for Dr. Rosenbaum's prose, since it is well
known that he received conventional humanistic instruction at MIT; but even
acknowledged masters of inanity might envy the following sentence: "As is
understood by all, some students are weaker than others" (p. 114). An antiquat-
ed antiquarian (perhaps unduly vexed by the "structuring or manipulating" of
the now well-oiled Gulf beaches) must ask forgiveness for doubting that a man
who can write like that is likely "to devise a new classroom regime capable of
satisfying all major language learning environment criteria" (p. 117).

[8] William Labov, *The Study of Nonstandard English*, p. 27; Flannery O'Connor,
"A Good Man Is Hard To Find," in *Three by Flannery O'Connor* (New York:
New American Library, n.d.), pp. 133, 139, 142, 143.

and Bereiter are sinners against the light,[9] but neither Bernstein nor Engelmann has rushed headlong to confession. On the contrary, both are recalcitrant.

For all his talk about restricted and elaborated codes (talk which has won him a retinue of American disciples), Bernstein still sees no reason to interfere with nonstandard dialects:

That the culture or subculture through its forms of social integration generates a restricted code, does not mean that the resultant speech and meaning system is linguistically or culturally deprived, that its children have nothing to offer the school, that their imaginings are not significant. It does not mean that we have to teach these children formal grammar, nor does it mean that we have to interfere with their dialect. There is nothing, but nothing, in dialect as such, which prevents a child from internalizing and learning to use universalistic meanings.[10]

Obviously, Bernstein has little in common with the biloquialists except the tendency to talk smugly about *we* and *they* and what *we* have to do to *them*. Engelmann, equally godlike, ranks "The Linguistic and Psycholinguistic Approaches" under "Abuses in Program Construction" and dismisses both:

It is not possible to imply statements about teaching from the premises upon which the linguist and the psycholinguist operate. Attempts to use linguistic analysis as the basis for teaching reading have produced the full range of programs, from paragraph reading to single-sound variations. The linguist's entire theoretical preamble, in other words, is nothing more than an appeal used to sanction an approach that derives from personal preferences, not from linguistic principles.[11]

Unless the Powers are willing to subsidize all interveners equally, such disagreement indicates that at least some seekers of funds should get no more funding for the evaluating of their administrating; and the unfunded (to close this selective catalogue of disagreements) are likely to include some linguists, for linguist can differ with linguist as vigorously as with psychologist or sociologist. Marvin D. Loflin, for example, transmogrifies all Southern whites to pluriglots when he finds "Nonstandard Negro English" so unlike the standard speech of whites "that a fuller description . . . will show a grammatical system which must be treated as a foreign language."[12] Similarly, William A.

[9] See Labov's "Logic of Nonstandard English," reprinted by Williams in *Language and Poverty* from the twentieth Round Table report.

[10] Basil Bernstein, "A Sociolinguistic Approach to Socialization: With Some Reference to Educability," in *Language and Poverty*, p. 57.

[11] Siegfried Engelmann, "How to Construct Effective Language Programs for the Poverty Child," in *Language and Poverty*, p. 118.

[12] "A Teaching Problem in Nonstandard Negro English," *English Journal*, 56.1312-1314, quoted by Wolfram, *A Sociolinguistic Description of Detroit Negro Speech*, p. 13.

Stewart finds enough "unique . . . structural characteristics" in "American Negro dialects" to justify the bold historical speculation that the Negro dialects "probably derived from a creolized form of English, once spoken on American plantations by Negro slaves and seemingly related to creolized forms of English which are still spoken by Negroes in Jamaica and other parts of the Caribbean."[13]

Perhaps it may be so. At any rate, when Stewart's theory is questioned he is quick to denounce what he calls "the blatant intrusion of sociopolitical issues into the scientific study of Negro speech";[14] and his sociopolitical rhetoric, if not his linguistic evidence, has been so convincing that his conclusions are sometimes confidently repeated by persons whose linguistic sophistication is considerably less than his.[15]

Yet Loflin and Stewart have not had everything their own way among linguists. Raven McDavid is presumably one of Stewart's blatant intruders of sociopolitical issues into virginal science:

Even where a particular feature is popularly assigned to one racial group, like the uninflected third-singular present (*he do, she have, it make*)—a shibboleth for Negro nonstandard speech in urban areas—it often turns out to be old in the British dialects, and to be widely distributed in the eastern United States among speakers of all races. It is only the accidents of cultural, economic, and educational history that have made such older linguistic features more common in the South than in the Midland and the North, and more common among Negro speakers than among whites.[16]

William Labov is equally firm in rejecting Loflin's theory of nonstandard Negro English as a foreign language:

In dealing with the structure of NNE, we do not find a foreign language with syntax and semantics radically different from SE [Standard English]: instead, we find a dialect of English, with certain extensions and modifications of rules to be found in other dialects. . . . Striking differences in surface structure were frequently the result of late phonological and transformational rules.[17]

---

[13] "Toward a History of American Negro Dialect," in Williams, *Language and Poverty*, p. 351.

[14] "Sociopolitical Issues in the Linguistic Treatment of Negro Dialect," in Alatis, *Linguistics and the Teaching of Standard English*, p. 215.

[15] For example, Muriel R. Saville, "Language and the Disadvantaged," in Horn, *Reading for the Disadvantaged*, p. 124.

[16] Raven I. McDavid, Jr., "Language Characteristics of Specific Groups: Native Whites," in *Reading for the Disadvantaged*, p. 136.

[17] Labov, *et al.*, *A Study of the Non-Standard English of Negro and Puerto Rican Speakers in New York City*, II. 339, 343.

No amoung of funding can conceal the fact that somebody, in arguments like these, has got to be wrong.

THE SHIFT TO READING

If the shift from doublespeak to interdisciplinary assaults on reading does hint at some sense of failure among the disunited sloganeers of overambitious biloquialism, their choice of a second front will not redeem their reputation as skillful strategists. The familiar tactic of concealing the failure to keep one promise by making another is unlikely to succeed if the second promise is less plausible than the first; and promises to give everyone "the right to read" are notoriously hard to make good on, even for the linguist in his favorite role of universal expert.

The perusal of books on reading like those edited by Horn and Gunderson leaves one considerably sadder, therefore, but little wiser, than when he began. The inquisitive amateur soon accepts the experts' repeated assertion that little is known—and gets tired of their plea for more research and full employment:

After decades of debate and expenditures of millions of research dollars, the teaching of reading remains on questionable psychological and linguistic grounds. When one looks at the research on reading over the past half century, the sheer volume of the literature and the welter of topics and findings (and lack of findings) is incredible. Yet, we are sore put to name even a few trustworthy generalizations or research based guides to educational practice.

Eleven widely different methods, represented by a variety of materials, were tested in some five hundred classrooms of first grade children during 1964-1965. Summary reports . . . revealed that by and large methods and materials were not the crucial elements in teaching first grade children to read.

At the present time we need research into every aspect of the education of the disadvantaged.[18]

If the amateur educationist is already an amateur linguist, he probably already knows Labov's opinion that "the major problem responsible for reading failure" in the ghettos "is a cultural conflict," not dialect interference.[19] He is thus surprised only by the source of

---

[18] Richard L. Venezky, *et al.*, Harry Levin, and William D. Sheldon, in Gunderson, *Language & Reading*, pp. 37, 123, 266, 271.

[19] William Labov and Clarence Robins, "A Note on the Relation of Reading Failure to Peer-Group Status in Urban Ghettos," in *Language & Reading*, p. 214.

Dr. Roger W. Shuy's quite unsurprising statement "that learning to read has little or nothing to do with a child's ability to handle Standard English phonology."[20] A Southern amateur who has consorted with Australians, for example, or vacationed among Lake Country farmers, hardly needs linguistic enlightenment to know that the oddest speech is perfectly compatible with the reading of internationally acceptable English. And the mere happy innocent who cares nothing for either linguistics or pedagogy, if he has reflected at all on what he does when he reads, will know that reading is not just a "language art." The essential processes, even in reading parrot-like without understanding, are inference and judgment in what Kenneth S. Goodman has called "a psycholinguistic guessing game";[21] and most of the linguistic entrepreneurs can claim no special competence in such matters.

SOMNIGRAPHY AND EUPHEMISM

To anyone with a normal dislike for solemn inanity, the contribution of linguistics to the teaching of reading is thus a less promising subject than the sleep-writing and professional euphemism which mark the work of the biloquialists and the inhabitants of schools of education. The name *biloquialism* is itself as fine an instance of verbal magic as one could want. Because nobody likes to admit that his speech makes other people laugh at him or despise him, *dialect* has become a dirty word. Hence its compounds and derivatives, like the older *bidialectalism*, must go too—the hope being, one imagines, that if the name goes the thing will vanish with it. For such wizardry, *doublespeak* is the perfect label.

Educationists make as much fuss over the euphemism *the disadvantaged* as the linguists do over *biloquialism*. They have not contented themselves with the one weasel-word, but have matched it with a number of others: *the culturally different, the linguistically different, the culturally deprived, the intellectually deprived, the culturally antagonized* (Horn, *Reading for the Disadvantaged*, pp. v, 11). It is a touch of genius that after choosing a word to obscure his meaning, a writer can then debate what he means by it. Thomas D. Horn concludes that anybody can be disadvantaged, even when he thinks he is in the catbird seat:

[20] "Some Language and Cultural Differences in a Theory of Reading," *Language & Reading*, p. 80.

[21] "Reading: A Psycholinguistic Guessing Game," *Language & Reading*, pp. 107-119.

Any individual may be disadvantaged socially, economically, psychologically, and/or linguistically, depending upon the particular social milieu in which he is attempting to function at a given time. Indeed, he may be completely oblivious to his disadvantaged condition and perceive others in the group as being disadvantaged rather than himself.[22]

Horn's readers will not deny their intellectual deprivation.

Somnigraphy, the art of writing as if one were asleep, is as zealously cultivated by biloquialists and educationists as euphemism. Sleep-writing must be distinguished from New High Bureaucratian (NHB), which is grammatical and has a meaning but obscures it by jargon. At its best, somnigraphy is neither grammatical nor meaningful; but no sentence can qualify as somnigraphic unless either its meaning or its grammar is somehow deviant. The following statement approaches the degree of vacuity necessary to somnigraphy; but since its distinctive feature is pompous scientism, it is probably to be treated as NHB:

Commands or requests for action are essentially instructions from a person A to a person B to carry out some action X at a time T.

$$A \rightarrow B: X!/T$$

Somnigraphy in the pure state is more easily recognizable:

Illogical comparison: "The selection of informants in this study is more rigid than the original study."

Tautology rampant: "Before a nonconsonantal environment the presence of the cluster-final stop, for all practical purposes, is categorically present in SE."

Failure of agreement: "The difference between the Negro classes appear to be largely quantitative for monomorphemic clusters."

The dying fall: "That we see linguists, psychologists, sociologists, educators, and others exercising varying definitions of language and language behavior, is important to know."

Chaos and Old Night: "Much of the attention given to the sociocultural aspects of poverty can be seen in the kinds of causes and cures for poverty which are often linked as parts of an overall *poverty cycle* (Figure 1)." [But neither the attention to poverty, nor the cures for it, can be found in the cycle itself.]

The *like/as* syndrome: "English, as most languages, has a variety of dialects."

[22] *Reading for the Disadvantaged*, p. 2. Observe the opening for the educationist to decide who gets the works in school because he's disadvantaged without knowing it.

Self-contradiction: "The nativist position carries with it the concept of a distinction between a child's linguistic knowledge and all of the varied facets and factors of his actual speaking and listening behaviors, one factor of which is the aforementioned knowledge." [That is, the child's knowledge both is and is not a part of his behavior.]

Scrambled metaphor: "In brief the strategy is to prepare the child for candidacy into the economic mainstream." [Sooner or later, we will read about the aridity of the mainstream culture—probably sooner.]

Fractured idiom: "Goodman (1965) and Bailey (1965), along with Stewart (esp. 1969), have all discussed the possibility of interference from the dialect on acquiring the ability to read." [And let no man interfere on their discussion.]

The unconscious absurd: ". . . both the linguists and sociologists . . . were relatively free from . . . cross-fertilization. . . ."

Lexical indiscretion: "As long as one operates in terms of languages and cultures conceived as isolates, internally discreet, . . ."

Flatus: "Middle-class children emitted a larger number of . . . self-corrections than the lower-class children did."

The cancerous modifier: "Mrs. Golden's program, as with most of the teaching English as a second language to Negro nonstandard English speakers programs, relies on pattern practice. . . ." [Sounds like somebody needs it.]

Confusion of map with territory: "The rule for the absence of d occurs more frequently when d is followed by a consonant than when followed by a vowel."

The genteel thing: "To improve one's social acceptability to a middle class society, working class people should focus primarily on vocabulary development."

The intense inane: "Reading is a process of recognizing that printed words represent spoken words and is a part of the total language spectrum."

The shipwrecked question: "How do the separate and disparate experiences of individuals lead to a common acceptance of general meaning but which also permit differences of interpretation?" [God only knows.]

Circumblundering a meaning: "The educational world has generally thought of language as lexicon and it is not surprising that they would equate cultural adjustment to the words of the city. . . ."

The undefining definition: "By underlying structure here I mean that ability which even beginning readers have which enables them to avoid misreading via any other manner than by the phonological, and grammatical rules of their native language."

The arresting title: "Economic, Geographic, and Ethnic Breakdown of Disadvantaged Children."

Opposites reconciled: "One obstacle, lack of skill in the use of standard American English, has increasingly been recognized as a major contributing factor to the success of a child beginning his formal education."

WHY THE POWERS PAY

That exhibit, which could be enlarged at will, is neither cruel nor insolent nor joking. The insolence is that the perpetrators of such writing should set themselves up as linguists and teachers of standard English. The cruelty is that people who think and write so badly should be turned loose upon children. The level of simple competence in the use of words is simply low among biloquialists, and to the old-fashioned English professor who still believes that a man's sentences (not his dialect) are a good index to his intelligence, that fact demands an explanation.

The obvious answer is that governments and foundations have put up so much money for doublespeak that they have not been able to find good people to spend it; but that answer simply shifts the question to another level. Why do our rulers act like that? Why should they employ verbicides in the impossible and immoral pursuit of biloquialism? Well-meaning incompetence may characterize many biloquialists; but incompetence has no direction, follows no party line unless some other force is guiding—and the drift of biloquialism is too plain to be accidental. There must be, somewhere, an inhumanity that shapes its ends.

The explanation does not require that inhumanity should be reified in a body of conspirators or that the making of educational policy, at any level, should be viewed as the conscious, intelligent adaptation of public means to private ends. In their dealings with black people, most middle-class white linguists in the United States may be expected to act like most other middle-class whites. Their probable motivations include a real desire to do good, some hidden dislike, some fear, and the love of money and status. Foundation men, bureaucrats, and politicians may be expected to share those foibles; and precisely because the whole conglomerate is shaped and moved by the same forces, it cannot move beyond its limits.

The appeal of doublespeak is that it promises beneficent change without threat to existing power or privilege. If doublespeak were to succeed, the restive communities of the poor and ignorant would be tamed; for potential revolutionaries would be transformed into the subservient, scrambling, anxious underlings who constitute the lower middle class in a technological society. Their children, if there should be a next generation, would rise to be its linguists, its English teachers, and its petty bureaucrats; and doublespeak would be justified by Progress. If doublespeak should fail, as it must, large numbers of young blacks can still be assured that it was they who failed, and not their white superiors; and the blacks' presumed failure in not doing what they could not and should not do can be used against them as a psychological and political weapon.[23] In either event, the white Powers have nothing to lose by their exercise in cosmetology. Both their conscience and their supremacy will be clear.

THE FORM OF THE ARGUMENT

The essential argument for such an explanation should be stated formally enough to keep the issues plain. As a hypothetical syllogism, the argument would look like this:

Unless the biloquialists and their sponsors were misled by their presumed self-interest, they would not pursue the impossible and immoral end of doublespeak so vigorously—or defend themselves for doing it.

But they do pursue, etc.
Therefore they are misled. . . .

Less pedantically, nobody insists on trying to do what he can't and shouldn't do unless there's something in it for him somewhere.

It is the consequent of the major premise that needs attention.

THE IMPOSSIBILITY OF DOUBLESPEAK

The impossibility of establishing doublespeak in the real world has already been argued: the necessary descriptions of standard and nonstandard dialects are nonexistent, and materials and methods of teaching are dubious at best. It may be added here that competent teachers of doublespeak are a contradiction in terms. For tough young blacks, the worst possible teacher is a middle-class white female; and a middle-class black female may not be much better, since she is nearly as likely as her white counterpart to look down on her lower-class students. Such condescending culture-vendors have no chance whatever of neutralizing the influence of the world outside the classroom, a world whre ghetto youngsters have few occasions to use such standard English as they may have learned and where, if they did use it, they might find the effort unrewarding. Their peers

[23] See Wayne O'Neil, "The Politics of Bidialecticalism" [pp. 184-191 in this book], from which I have borrowed the ingenious idea that educational failure might still be political success for the backers of doublespeak.

would blame them for trying to talk like white people, and they would hardly be compensated for such isolation by any real increase in "upward mobility." The black college graduate who makes less money than a white dropout is a sad familiar figure.

Teachers of standard English may be sure, then, of resistance from teen-age students in the ghettos, and unless they are more tactful than the biloquialists, they may be sure of resistance from black adults as well. On the issue of doublespeak the black community is undoubtedly divided. Blacks who have made it into the middle and upper classes, and many black parents, want to see young people make it too. They consider the ability to use "good English" a part of making it (though in reality good English is far less important to success on the job than a great many other qualifications). At the other extreme are the tough teen-agers, the adults who secretly or openly share their values, and some of the more militant community leaders; while in between there are probably a good many blacks of various ages for whom the white world's insistence on its standard English sets off an internal conflict between pride and self-hate.

But the black community is not at all divided in its opposition to doctrines of white supremacy, whether politely veiled or publicly announced. No black of any age is likely to be much pleased by condescension and the calm assumption of superiority:

First, there has been the general attitude, common even among some linguists, that nonstandard speech is less worthy of interest and study than varieties of speech with high prestige. . . . As this relates to the speech of Negroes, it has been reinforced by a commendable desire to emphasize the potential of the Negro to be identical to white Americans. . . .[24]

Even if it were possible to "stamp out" nonstandard English, changing the students' language behavior completely might be detrimental to their social well-being. They may need the nonstandard for social situations in which it is appropriate.[25]

More than the foreign-language student, more than the native speaker of standard English, the second-dialect student needs to know his teacher considers him truly "worth revising."[26]

[24] William A. Stewart, "Urban Negro Speech," in Aarons, Gordon, and Stewart, *Linguistic-Cultural Differences*, p. 51.

[25] Irwin Feigenbaum, "The Use of Nonstandard English in Teaching Standard," in Fasold and Shuy, *Teaching Standard English*, p. 89.

[26] Virginia F. Allen, "A Second Dialect Is Not a Foreign Language," in Alatis, *Linguistics and the Teaching of Standard English*, p. 194.

The neighbor-loving speech which ended with the last quotation was soon followed, understandably, by an angry outburst from a black auditor:

I am outraged and insulted by this meeting. . . . I would like to know why white people can determine for black people what is standard and what is nonstandard.

But two of the linguists present did not get the message—the plain message that it must no longer be whites only who "conduct the important affairs of the community." The first of them rebuked the young lady rudely, once in the meeting and once in a "subsequent written comment": he rapped about "rapping" on sociolinguists and using phony ploys "in political confrontations." The second, in a display of caucasian tact, congratulated her on expressing herself "in perfectly standard grammar."

If those who set themselves up as teachers of teachers behave like that, they may succeed in uniting the divided black community— uniting it against the advocates of doublespeak. Whatever the black community does want, it does not want to be led by the nose.

THE IMMORALITY OF DOUBLESPEAK

The biloquialist, of course, makes a great fuss about giving the child of the poor and ignorant, whether black or white, the choice of using or not using standard English. "He should be allowed to make that decision as he shapes his decisions in life."[27] But the biloquialist obviously sees himself as the determiner of the decisions which other people may decide, and the choice he deigns to give is really not much choice after all. In the name of social realism, he begins by imposing a false scheme of values, of which "upward mobility" is the highest; and he then sets out to make the child "upwardly mobile" by requiring hours of stultifying drill on arbitrary matters of usage, so that in situations where standard English is deemed appropriate the child may choose between "Ain't nobody gon' love you" and "Nobody is going to love you." *Appropriate* will be defined by the white world, which will also fix the punishment if the liberated doublespeaker prefers his own definition. Ain't nobody gon' love him if he does that.

The immorality of biloquialism is amply illustrated by such hypocrisy. Assuring the child that his speech is as good as anybody else's, publicly forswearing all attempts to eradicate it, and vigorously

[27] John C. Maxwell in "Riposte," *English Journal,* 59 (November, 1970), p. 1159.

defending the individual's free choice, the biloquialist would actually
force the speech and values of the middle-class white world on children of every class and color. By *upward mobility* he means getting
and spending more money, wasting more of the world's irreplaceable
resources in unnecessary display, and turning one's back on family
and friends who are unable or unwilling to join in that high enterprise. Every day, by his loud-voiced actions, the biloquialist would
tell the child to build his life on that rotten foundation.

But *tell* is too mild a word: *force* is more accurate. *Force* is
more accurate because the schoolchild would not have a choice between wasting his precious days (with the biloquialists) in the study
of socially graded synonyms and (with intelligent teachers) learning
somethings serious about himself and the world he lives in; and besides, when schooldays were over, the young doublespeaker could not
really choose between his vernacular and his imperfectly mastered
standard English. In every serious transaction of an upwardly mobile
life, the use of standard English would be enforced by the giving or
withholding of the social and economic goodies which define upward
mobility. The upwardly mobile doublespeaker would be expected to
eradicate his vernacular except in some darkly secret areas of his
private life, of which eventually he would learn to be ashamed; and
his likely reward for such self-mutilation would be just enough mobility to get him stranded between the worlds of white and black. There
he could happily reflect on the humanitarianism of the Great White
Expert who saves the oppressed from militancy and sends them in
pursuit of money and status, which literature, philosophy, religion,
and the millennial experience of mankind have exposed as unfit ends
for human life. "That doesn't seem very humane from where I sit."[28]

ON NOT LOVING BIG BROTHER

But the present argument against biloqualism is not a militant
argument (though biloquialists have called it one in the attempt to
discredit it with a label they think is frightening), and it is not primarily a humanitarian argument (though biloquialists have called it in-
humane). Our new teachers of reading cannot read well enough to
tell Mill from a militant. The argument here is the argument of an
unashamed conservative individualist. With his own eyes the arguer
has seen British working people, and chicanos, and black Americans
humiliated by contempt for their language and twisted by their own
unhappy efforts to talk like their exploiters. An expert is no more

[28] *Loc. cit.* But I bet you guessed.

needed to prove that such humiliation is damaging or such efforts an expense of spirit than a meteorologist is needed to warn of the dangers of urinating against the wind; but the weight of the argument rests mainly on the fact that if any man can be so shamed and bullied for so intimate a part of his own being as his language, then every man is fully subject to the unhampered tyrants of the materialist majority. To resist the biloquialist is to resist Big Brother, and to resist him for oneself as well as others. Big Brother is not always white.

In all the variety of his disguises, Big Brother is very near at hand today. In one form he is Basil Bernstein, whose notions about restricted and elaborated codes (as they are interpreted or misinterpreted by Bernstein's American disciples) might vulgarly be taken as supporting an injunction to get the pickaninnies away from their black mammies; in another form he is the arrogant dogmatist Siegfried Engelmann, the amoral educational technologist with a big stick.

The biloquialist follows neither Engelmann nor Bernstein, but his own high-sounding talk should not be taken at face value, either. Doublespeak is not necessary to communication between users of different dialects, since speakers of nonstandard English generally have passive control of standard, if only through their exposure to television; the biloquialist himself assures us that no dialect is intrinsically better than any other; and his announced devotion to freedom of choice has already been exposed as phony, like his promise of social mobility through unnatural speech. When the biloquialist's guard is down, he too can talk the language of dialect-eradication, which he officially abhors:

. . . attempting to eliminate this kind of auxiliary deletion from the speech of inner-city Negro children would be a low-priority task.[29]

Behind the mandarin's jargon and self-praise lies the quiet assumption that it is his right and duty to run other people's lives.

The mandarin will go a long way to make other people see that his good is theirs, so that his values may prevail among the faceless multitude. As educator, his aims are not always educational, but may be as simple as keeping young people off the labor market by keeping them in school, though he tacitly admits that he has planned nothing to teach them there:

The problems of finding suitable programs will be complicated if, as educators anticipate, education is made compulsory for students until they reach the age

---

[29] Fasold and Wolfram, "Some Linguistic Features of Negro Dialect," in Fasold and Shuy, *Teaching Standard English*, p. 80.

of eighteen. Educators will be forced to adapt programs for the group of young people from sixteen to eighteen who under the present system have dropped out of school.[30]

Yet the mandarin's ends, he thinks, justify almost any means.

Intelligence and verbal skills within the culture of the street is prized just as highly as it is within the school:—but the use of such skills is more often to manipulate and control other people than to convey information to them. Of course it is the school's task to emphasize the value of language in cognitive purposes. But in order to motivate adolescent and preadolescent children to learn standard English, it would be wise to emphasize its value for handling social situations, avoiding conflict (or provoking conflict when desired), for influencing and controlling other people.[31]

Between 5 and 10 percent of the 62,000 school children in this city in the American midlands are taking "behavior modification" drugs prescribed by local doctors to improve classroom deportment and increase learning potential. The children being given the drugs have been identified by their teachers as "hyperactive" and unmanageable to the point of disrupting regular classroom activity.[32]

Bettye M. Caldwell . . . has proposed "educationally oriented day care for culturally deprived children between six months and three years of age." The children are returned home each evening to "maintain primary emotional relationships with their own families," but during the day they are removed to "hopefully prevent the deceleration in rate of development which seems to occur in many deprived children around the age of two to three years."[33]

The Defense Department has been quietly effective in educating some of the casualties of our present public schools. It is hereby suggested that they now go into the business of repairing hundreds of thousands of these human casualties with affirmation rather than apology. Schools for adolescent dropouts or educational rejects could be set up by the Defense Department adjacent to camps—but not necessarily as an integral part of the military. If this is necessary,

[30] Robert J. Havighurst, "Social Backgrounds: Their Impact on Schoolchildren," in Horn, *Reading for the Disadvantaged*, p. 12.

[31] William Labov, "The Non-Standard Vernacular of the Negro Community: Some Practical Suggestions," ED 016 947, p. 10.

[32] Robert M. Maynard, "Children Controlled by Drugs," despatch from Omaha to *The Washington Post*. In *The Austin American*, June 29, 1970, p. 1. Yet they jail the kids for smoking pot.

[33] Labov, "The Logic of Nonstandard English," in Alatis, *Linguistics and the Teaching of Standard English*, pp. 28-29. Labov, who here as usual is much above his fellow biloquialists, is criticizing Bettye M. Caldwell's article "What Is the Optimal Learning Environment for the Young Child?" in the *American Journal of Orthopsychiatry*, 37 (1967), pp. 8-21. *Ortho* is a bit optimistic when the proposal is to disrupt the families of mothers whom Bettye M. Caldwell has judged inadequate.

it should not block the attainment of the goal of rescuing as many of these young people as possible.[34]

In June the Camden (N.J.) Board of Education hired *Radio Corporation of America* to reorganize its entire school system. According to *Education Summary* (July 17, 1970), the management contract for the first year of the USOE pilot project requires that RCA "be responsible for identifying Camden's educational needs; specifying priorities organizing demonstration projects; training school personnel for functions they can't perform adequately now; organizing the system on a cost-effectiveness basis; and arranging for objective valuation of results."[35]

There is not much doubt that the use of such means will corrupt whatever end is said to justify them. It is not, for example, a super-abundance of new teachers which now keeps them from finding jobs, but the government's decision to pay for war in Viet Nam and not for education. To solve this financial problem, school boards are encouraged to choose education on the cheap. When they make their bargains with the big corporations, the corporations get direct control both of education and of whatever money the school boards do spend. The corporations can thus keep up their profits; teachers are made subservient automatons; and the country is delivered from the danger that either teachers or students might occasionally think. Disrupted families, drugged students, schools run by business or the military—these are the typical products of Big Brother's machinations.

The role of the biloquialist in our educational skin-flick is not outstanding: he is not a madam, just a working girl. His commitment, however, to the corrupt values of a corrupt society makes him quite at house with the other manipulators, and his particular manipulations have their special dangers because a standard language can be made a dangerous weapon in class warfare.

Standard English in the United States is a principal means of preserving the existing power structure, for it builds the system of class distinctions into the most inward reaches of each child's human-

---

[34] Kenneth B. Clark, quoted by George H. Henry in reviewing Alvin C. Eurich's *High School 1980* in the *English Journal*, 59 (1970), p. 1165. Henry's review is a splendid denunciation of manipulators inside and outside the NCTE.

[35] Edmund J. Farrell, "Industry and the Schools," NCTE *Council-Grams*, 31 (Special Issue for November, 1970), pp. 1-3. Farrell takes a strong stand against the takeover by industry—with the natural consequence that Robert F. Hogan, Executive Secretary of the Council, warns readers to "keep in mind that the point of view is Mr. Farrell's, not a reflection of Council policy or position." When George Henry called it likely "that English will find itself taken over by the USO—Foundation—Big Business—Pentagon Axis," he also said that the appeasing executives of the Council complain only mildly of such barbarian invasions, "because by virtue of being high in the Council one is eligible for a place in the Axis" (Henry, *op. cit.*, pp. 1168-69). But unlike RCA, Henry is not an objective evaluator.

ity: the language whose mastery makes the child human makes him also a member of a social class. Even rebellion demands a kind of allegiance to the class system, because effective rebellion, as the world goes now, requires the use of the standard language, and the rebel is not likely to master the standard language without absorbing some of the prejudice that it embodies. In the United States, the child "knows his place" before he knows he knows it, and the rebellious adult is either coöpted into the ruling class or has to fight to get a hearing. Biloquialism makes capital of this situation.

Big Brother and his flunkies are in control now; there is no doubt of that. But they have not won the last battle as long as resistance is possible, and resistance is possible until Big Brother makes us love him—if he can. If resistance saves nothing else, it saves the manhood of the unbrainwashed resister. The conservative individualist opposes biloquialism just because he does believe in individuality, to which liberty is prerequisite. "Tell the English," a bad poem says, "that man is a spirit." He is; and he does not live by beer alone; and the *radix malorum* is the businessman's morality of "getting ahead," which the biloquialist espouses when he argues that "right now, tomorrow, the youngster needs tools to 'make it' in the larger world."[36]

Both physically and spiritually, *that* "larger world" is unfit for human habitation.

WHAT TO DO

The biloquialist's favorite counterpunch, when he is backed into a corner, is the question "If not biloquialism, what?" and he pretends, if his critic does not spin out a detailed scheme for curing all the ills of education, that in the absence of such a scheme doublespeak remains the best available policy for English teachers. The pretense is foolish, like doublespeak itself. Whatever English teachers ought to do, they ought not to follow the biloquialist, and the mere establishment of that fact is a positive contribution. To know what's not good is part of knowing what is.

The cornered biloquialist will often make his question more specific. It's all very well, he will concede, to expose linguistic prejudice as an instrument of repression and to work for social justice, though he himself may not be notably active in either cause; but in the meantime, he asks, what will become of students who don't learn standard English?

[36] Right again: John C. Maxwell, *English Journal*, 59 (1970), p. 1159.

The beginning of a sufficient reply is that the advocate of doublespeak must answer the question too, since there are probably more biloquialists than doublespeakers whom they have trained. In the foreseeable future there will always be distinctions in speech between leaders and followers, between workers at different jobs, residents of different areas. And in a healthy society there would be no great harm in that. Millions of people in this country today do not speak standard English, and millions of them, if they are white, have very good incomes. But in job-hunting in America, pigmentation is more important than pronunciation.

There is not, moreover, and there never has been, a serious proposal that standard English should not be taught at all, if for no other reason than because its teaching is inevitable. Most teachers of English speak it (or try to speak it); most books are written in it (somnigraphy being sadly typical); and since every child, if it is possible, should learn to read, schoolchildren will see and hear standard English in the schools as they also see and hear it on TV. Inevitably their own linguistic competence will be affected.

The effect will be best if teachers consciously recognize the frustrations and contradictions which life in a sick world imposes on them. Because our ruling class is unfit to rule, our standard language lacks authority; and because our society has been corrupted by the profit-seeking of technology run wild, an honest teacher cannot exercise his normal function of transmitting to the young the knowledge and values of their elders. In fact, the time may come, and soon come, when an honest teacher can't keep his honesty and keep teaching. At that point, he must make his choice—and take the consequences. So long, however, as he stays in the classroom, he must do his imperfect best while recognizing its imperfection, and must find in that effort itself his escape from alienation.

Specifically, and without pretense:

1. We English teachers must have—and teach—some higher ambition than to "get ahead." We have the whole body of the world's best thought to draw on. The daringly old-fashioned amongst us might even recommend the Ten Commandments.

2. We should do all we can to decentralize power, to demand for ourselves and for other common men some voice in shaping our own lives. Reason enough to say so is the truism that men are not men unless they are free; but if the practical must have practical reasons, we all can see that in education as in everything else, conditions vary so much from state to state, from city to city, from city to country, from neighborhood to neighborhood, that no one policy for the whole nation can possibly work. Decisions about our teaching must *not* be passed down, as they now are, from a tired little mediocre in-group, who in the best of circumstances are so involved in the

operation of the professional machinery that they can't see beyond its operation. A useful rule of thumb might be to never trust a "leader in the profession."

3. As politically active citizens, we must do whatever we can to end the social isolation of "substandard speakers," so that differences in speech, if they do not disappear of themselves, will lose their stigmatizing quality.[37]

4. As English teachers we should teach our students (and if necessary, our colleagues) how society uses languages as its most insidious means of control, how we are led to judge others—and ourselves—by criteria which have no real bearing on actual worth. We must stigmatize people who use dialects as stigmatizing; and if that means that we as correctness-mongers get blasted too, then we deserve it.[38]

5. We should teach ourselves and our white students something about the lives and language of black people. For communication between dialects, receptive control is what matters. In the United States, most black children are already likely to understand most kinds of English that they hear from whites. Presumably white people have the intelligence to learn to understand the blacks. The Center for Applied Linguistics may even be capable of learning that white ignorance is a bigger obstacle to social justice than black English is.

6. In teaching our students to read and write, our aim should be to educate them, to open and enrich their minds, not to make them into usefully interchangeable parts in the materialists' insane machine. We should know and respect our children's language as we

[37] For such suggestions I have been told both that I believe that English teachers can change the world by political action, perhaps by revolution, and at the same time (because I oppose biloquialism) that I advocate "do-nothingness." Though I hope I have more awareness of human tragedy than to believe that the NCTE, or RCA, or even an Educational Laboratory can abolish pain, I would certainly not teach English if I did not believe that to some small extent English teachers indeed can change the world. If I did not believe that English teachers can act politically for good, by parity of reasoning I would not bother to attack the evil politics of doublespeak. On the subject of revolution, I wrote in the essay which has been criticized as perhaps inciting to revolt that "the only revolution we are likely to see is the continued subversion, by the dominant white businessman, of the political and religious principles on which the nation was founded" (*English Journal* 58, p. 1312). I leave it to the objecting and objectionable biloquialist to reconcile the conflicting charges of do-nothingism and political activism, but I do resent the suggestion that I consider English teachers brave enough to start a revolution. I have never entertained such a false and subversive idea in my life.

[38] This suggestion has nothing to do with the self-seeking proposal by foolish linguists that the English language should be made the center of the English curriculum. I would indeed teach prospective teachers of English in the schools a good deal more about their language than they are usually taught now; but only a biloquialist would believe—or pretend to believe—that to suggest a college curriculum in English for prospective English teachers is to suggest the same curriculum for every schoolchild. A "language-centered curriculum" for the schools would be a disaster.

demand that they know and respect our own. And we should make no harsh, head-on attempt to *change* their language, to make them speak and write like us. If they value our world and what it offers, then they will take the initiative in change, and we can cautiously help them. But we must stop acting as the watch-dogs of middle-class correctness and start barking at somnigraphy.

7. As teachers and as citizens, we must defend the freedom of inquiry and the freedom of expression. Neither is absolute, and it is often hard to strike a balance between the demands of the society that pays us and the intellectual duties of our calling. It is clear, however, that subservience to government and indifference to social need will alike corrupt inquirer and inquiry and thus endanger the freedoms that no one else will cherish if we don't. When we allow our choice of studies to be governed by government subsidy, we have committed ourselves to the ends of the subsidizers. When pure curiosity guides us, we tacitly assert that the satisfaction of curiosity is more important than any other purpose that our research might serve. Along both roads we are likely to meet the amoral intellectual, whether for hire or self-employed. The prime contention of this indirect review is that the biloquialist, by his acquiescence in the abuse of standard English as a weapon, forfeits some part of the respect which otherwise would be inspired by achievements which are sometimes brilliant, like Labov's. For despite the politician's scholar who says that scholarship is politicized when scholars question his privy politics, scholars *are* teachers, and scholar-teachers citizens.

PART SIX

AND THE "OTHERS"

Murray Wax

CULTURAL DEPRIVATION AS AN
EDUCATIONAL IDEOLOGY

Indian education is a cross-cultural transaction, bringing together within the school the youthful members of the local Indian community and the educators who represent the national U.S. society.[1] To understand the processes and problems of Indian education, the researcher must study both parties to the situation—the educators and the pupils—as well as the nature of their interaction.[2] Many previous studies have been deficient in this regard because they have narrowed their gaze to the Indian children alone, as if their peculiar characteristics were sufficient to account for their scholastic successes and failures.

On Pine Ridge and many other reservations the educators are employees of the Bureau of Indian Affairs and participate in its unique society and culture. While many scholars have criticized Bu-

[1] Murray Wax, "American Indian Education as a Cross-Cultural Transaction" *Teachers College Record*, LXIV, 8 (May 1963) 693-704

[2] Everett C. Hughes and Helen M. Hughes, *Where Peoples Meet: Racial and Cultural Frontiers* (Free Press of Glencoe, 1952). See especially the chapter, "North America: Indians and Immigrants," pp. 18-31.

reau policies and personnel and some social scientists have worked for the Bureau—indeed, an anthropologist is now its Commissioner—those who have known it from the inside have not chosen to describe its membership, social dynamics, or ideology. Yet, if we are to understand the dynamics of modern reservation communities, we must study not only the Indians but also those who are trying to educate, guide, manipulate, and otherwise deal with them.

At the upper levels of administration of the Pine Ridge Agency, Bureau ideology is now phrased as if it were a local variant of the national educational ideology of *cultural deprivation.*[3] The Indian home and the mind of the Indian child are described as if they were empty or lacking in pattern. A leading Agency official expressed the view—and the problem as he saw it—in the following words:

The school gets this child from a conservative home, brought up speaking the Indian language, and all he knows is Grandma. His home has no books, no magazines, radio, television, newspapers—it's empty! He comes into school and we have to teach him everything! All right. We bring him to the point where he's beginning to know something in high school, and he drops out. . . . Because at this time he has to choose between Grandma and being an educated member of the community.

Another official put the matter to us this way:

The Indian child has such a *meager* experience. When he encounters words like "elevator" or "escalator" in his reading, he has no idea what they mean.
But it's not just strange concepts like those. Take even the idea of *water.* When you or I think of it, well, I think of a shining stainless steel faucet in a sink, running clean and pure, and of the plumbing that brings it, and chlorination and water purification, or of the half-million dollar project for the Pine Ridge water supply. But the Indian child doesn't think of water as something flowing into a bathtub.

As this person spoke, our minds were flooded with visions of the creek which ran a few hundred yards from the Sioux homestead where we had camped during the summer, and we recalled its coolness and vegetation, the humans and animals that had come there to bathe, the flights of mosquitoes at dusk, not to mention the ancient cars and the yelping of their enthusiastic escort of dogs. So, one of us gambited, "I guess the Indian child would think of a creek." But the administrator insisted on the universally miserable quality of Sioux experience, "Or of a pump, broken down and hardly working."

[3] Frank Reissman, *The Culturally Deprived Child* (New York: Harper & Row, 1962).

Carried far enough, this Ideology of Cultural Deprivation leads to characterizations of Sioux life which are deplorably fallacious. One person who had worked on the Pine Ridge Reservation for many years asserted in a public meeting that "Indian children have no home experiences in art or music" and that Indian children are not told stories by their parents. (Even a music teacher in secondary school stated that Indians had no musical experience.) Another person, also of many years' experience, remarked, "We must go back to the (Indian) home to find the lack of patterns that should have been learned."

In the face of this repetitive and rigid usage of such terms as empty, meager, and lacking in pattern, we at length began to feel that these administrations were perceiving the Indian mind as the land-hungry settlers had perceived the continent:

The White people speak of the country at this period as "a wilderness," as though it was an empty tract without human interest, or history. To us Indians it was as clearly defined then as it is today; we knew the boundaries of tribal lands, those of our friends and those of our foes; we were familiar with every stream, the contour of every hill, and each peculiar feature of the landscape had its tradition. It was our home, the scene of our history, and we loved it as our country.[4]

So far as we could see, this reservation Ideology of Cultural Deprivation serves the following functions: First, it places the responsibility for scholastic defeat on the Indian home and the Indian child; since the child is seen as entering school with an empty head, then surely it is a great achievement if he is taught anything whatsoever. Second, the Ideology is a *carte blanche* that justifies almost any activity within the school as being somehow "educational"; for, if the child is presumed deficient in every realm of experience, then the task of the school can properly be defined as furnishing him with vicarious experiences to compensate in every aspect of his life. Finally, the Ideology justifies the educators in their isolation from and ignorance of the Indian community; for, if the child actually had a culture including knowledge and values, then they ought properly to learn about these so as to build on his present status, but if he is conceived of as a vacuum on entering school, then the educators may properly ignore his home and community.

Before continuing with a description of the Pine Ridge scene, we should like to add that we believe that a similar constellation of

---

[4] Francis LaFlesche, *The Middle Five: Indian School Boys of the Omaha Tribe* (Madison: University of Wisconsin Press, 1963), p. xx. LaFlesche was born about 1857 and wrote this passage about 1900.

attitudes and relationships currently plagues schools in urban settings.[5] Children who come from lower-class and impoverished ethnic
groups are regarded as empty and cultureless rather than as having a
culture and social life of their own which educators must learn about
in order to be competent in their jobs. Children from lower-class Negro homes are especially subject to this mishandling, since many
"liberals" refuse on political grounds to recognize that their families
have a distinct subculture.

On the Pine Ridge Reservation—and perhaps in other reservations and urban lower-class settings—the Ideology of Cultural Deprivation seems closely associated with the secularized version of the
Protestant ethos. On the one hand, the Indian mind is seen as empty,
and on the other hand the Indian will is seen as lacking. In citing materials to document and illustrate the one view, we must inevitably do
the same for the other. Besides, the person who is regarded by Bureau
personnel, both in Pine Ridge and often elsewhere, as the intellectual
authority for their educational philosophy was himself a dedicated
exponent of that ethos, who seems to have exhorted the Sioux and
regulated his official life according to its maxims.

As principal of the Little Wound Day School in Pine Ridge
during the school year 1936-1937, Pedro T. Orata kept elaborate
records and produced a four-volume report for the Bureau. Later,
he condensed this into a book, *Fundamental Education in an Amerindian Community*, which was still being quoted on Pine Ridge during
the 1960s. From the pages of this book there emerges so extreme a
contrast between his own ethos and that of the traditional Sioux
community in which he worked that the effect is at first sometimes
comic and then later pathetic and tragic. For example, he does not
merely complain (as one might expect) that the farmer paid by the
government was working hard daily while any number of able-bodied
Sioux were sitting about the local store, but he assesses as "the most
difficult problem: the fact that 'They (the Indians) sat there all day
and seemed to enjoy doing so'"![6]

How extreme his views were can be understood from the tale of
his pages about a winter crisis: South Dakota, twenty degrees below
zero, knee-deep in snow on poor roads; an epidemic of flu in the
community that had disabled four of six teachers and two of his
bus drivers; two radiators frozen in the school and below-freezing

---

[5] Compare the criticism of the concept of "cultural deprivation" to be found in
Dr. Eleanor Leacock's "Comment" in *Human Organization Monograph*, II
(1960), pp. 30-32.

[6] Pedro T. Orata, *Fundamental Education in an Amerindian Community*
(Lawrence, Kans.: Haskell Press, U.S. Bureau of Indian Affairs, 1953), p. 51.

temperatures in the classroom. Of the 140 pupils, twenty had made it to school. Undaunted, Orata exhorts his staff:

Could we have done better today? When the boys (Indian pupils) stood around the furnace room and loafed, don't think they were not getting educated. They were. They were learning to loaf. There is no such thing as absence of education, at any time . . . . If those boys were not learning to work, they were learning to loaf . . . . If those boys repeated what they did ten times, what would happen?

And the dutiful "straight man" on his staff answers, "They'd be sitting in the furnace room all the time."[7]

From the perspective of Orata or of his contemporary disciples on Pine Ridge or in the BIA, Indians must adopt the Protestant ethos if they are to be morally acceptable or socially employable. Insofar as Indians do not have this ethos, it is not that they share some other value system, but that they have none.

So far we have been concentrating on the form of this Ideology that seems to have become established among Bureau employees. However, we should mention a recent discussion which we fear may help to contribute to a new variant of it. Under sponsorship of the Association on American Indian Affairs, Drs. E. E. Hagen and Louis C. Schaw, a social psychologist and economist, have written a report on the Rosebud and Pine Ridge Reservations in which they characterized the Sioux as being passive, apathetic, and hostilely dependent.[8] In opposition to these terms, we must state that our own observations are that Bureau personnel are as hotile toward the Indians as the latter are toward them (and on both sides there are individuals who are not hostile); also, that Bureau personnel are utterly dependent upon the continued existence of the "backward" Indians, because if Indians managed their own affairs then the local Indian Agency would provide no employment (this dependency is therefore especially marked among the lower and less skilled echelons of the Bureau). Our own observations again are that "apathy" is a convenient label to apply to people who don't happen to agree with the program that a government official or other reformer happens to be pushing. Frankly, when we went to Pine Ridge, we did expect to see apathetic people. Instead we saw people whose lust for life reminded us of the descriptions of Restoration England, and today we are inclined to feel that it is the urban lower middle class who are culturally deprived and whose children have such meager experiences.

[7] Ibid., p. 135-137.

[8] "The Sioux on the Reservations: The American Colonial Problem" (preliminary edition; Cambridge: M.I.T. Center for International Studies, May 1960), p. VI-8 *passim.*

Armando Rodriguez

THE MEXICAN-AMERICAN—DISADVANTAGED?
YA BASTA!

The treaty of Guadalupe Hidalgo, concluding the Mexican-American War of 1848, automatically provided American citizenship to all those living in what is now our five southwestern states of Arizona, California, Colorado, New Mexico and Texas. The majority cultural groups living there at the time were Spanish-speaking and Indian. The diversity among these groups in customs, attitudes and aspirations was tremendous. As a result, with the absence of any program of acculturation by the United States, Spanish-speaking peoples remained Spanish-speaking and culturally isolated—unassimilated citizens subject to the dominance of a foreign American culture.

By 1870 the West became a prime target for economic exploitation with the coming of the railroads. The need for labor was great, and the West turned to Mexico and the Far East for manpower. The increased population gave little help to a growing country whose eyes were not on creating institutions to meet the rising problems. George Sanchez in his paper "Spanish in the Southwest" says, "Virtually no thought was given to the educational, health, economic, or political rehabilitation of these Spanish-speaking peoples. And after 1910 the opportunity passed."

Only in the past decade, over ninety years after the West became a target for rapid economic development, has the United States focused its attention and some of its resources on the more than five and one-half million Spanish-speaking citizens in the Southwest. Add to this group another half million Spanish-speaking citizens who have left the Southwest, one and a half million Spanish-speaking Puerto Ricans and a half million Cubans—and the United States is faced with a cultural and linguistic human resource bank from which little has been taken and to which even less has been given.

What the United States found when it took a look at this potentially rich resource of cultural diversity was shocking. They found that more than 80 percent of the Mexican-Americans live in urban communities. That California and Texas account for more than 80 percent of the population. That 50 percent of the Mexicanos are under 20 years of age. That 87 percent of the Mexican-Americans live in urban poverty pockets in the Southwest. That East Los Angeles has an estimated population of over 700,000 ranking only behind Mexico City and Guadalajara. That the unemployment rate as late as 1966 was 7.7 percent for Mexican-Americans in urban areas. That an estimated 150,000 Mexican-Americans were still a part of the migrant agricultural labor force of the Southwest.

In education, the median school years completed was 7.7, and the median level of education among Mexicanos was 8.6 years of school as compared with 10.5 for the Negro, and 12.1 for the Anglo and "others." As late as 1964, 18 percent of the Mexican men and 22 percent of the Mexican women were classified as "functionally illiterate." This compares with 9 percent for Negro men and 4 percent for Negro women. The real tragedy in the education of the Mexican-American is revealed in the astounding dropout rate. More than 50 percent of the Mexican-American students in two of the predominantly Mexican-American high schools in Los Angeles leave school before graduation. Approximately the same is true in the predominant high school in San Antonio. Texas has found that along the Mexican border more than 90 percent of the Mexican-American students drop two grade levels behind by the 4th grade. Dr. Tom Carter of the University of Texas at El Paso estimates that more than 80 percent of the Mexican-American youngsters starting school in Texas do not finish. The number of Mexican-Americans enrolled in college, obviously, presents an even more distressing picture. Less than 1 percent of the student enrollment on the seven university campuses in California is Spanish-surnamed. And yet the Spanish-surnamed public school enrollment in California is more than 14 percent of the total school enrollment.

With this sort of picture there was little hesitancy on the part of government officials concerned with the status and welfare of many citizens to label the Mexican-American "disadvantaged." Such a labeling immediately suggested that some means must be developed to lift the Chicano from the depth of his economic, social, educational and political deprivation. Unfortunately some of the earliest efforts in this "rehabilitation" involved applying the same processes to the Mexicano as were being applied to other "disadvantaged." Both the economic and the educational community was guilty of this destructive approach. These efforts were another in a long line of activities basically designed to assimilate a people into the dominant culture. Consciously or otherwise the general pattern of treatment of the Mexican-American since 1848 has been one of the conqueror and vanquished rather than one of equal treatment in civil rights and language as promised in the Treaty of 1848. The result has been, with some notable exceptions, almost a century of cultural isolation and rejection by the minority group of the language of the majority people in the Southwest. The notable exceptions have occurred when

Mexican-Americans have organized and demonstrated to obtain some relief from their oppressive treatment.

The Mexican-American of today rejects the label of "disadvantaged." Dr. Jorge Lara-Braud, Director, Hispanic-American Institute of Austin, Texas puts it sharply when he says, "Hispanic-Americans, however, have repudiated the idea of rehabilitation as a condition for their share of the American Dream." This single statement clearly states the position of the Chicano. Cultural and language diversities are no shackles that must be stripped off before a full partnership in the American Society can be attained. Mexican-Americans are "advantaged" peoples because they possess the richness of differences that will bring to the United States what the whole American Dream is all about—a free, democratic, and pluralistic United States of America. Whether it be the poorest, most illiterate "barrio" dweller or the most sophisticated Mexicano, the determination is equally deep to retain and strengthen his identity as an American in the true sense of the word. This means a retention and a practicing respect for his cultural heritage and its role in creating in the United States a dominating attitude that difference is strength and not destruction, that difference is what life is all about.

Harold Howe II, immediate past U.S. Commissioner of Education in his speech, "Cowboys, Indians, and American Education," points vigorously at the problem ". . . Other cultures are not merely different; they are *inferior*. They must be wiped out . . . In a hundred subtle ways, we have told people of all origins other than English that their backgrounds are somewhat cheap or humorous. And the tragic thing is that this process has succeeded. Of the incredible diversity of languages and traditions that the people of a hundred nations brought to this country, virtually nothing remains except in scattered enclaves . . . more often viewed as objects of curiosity rather than respect."

The determination of the Mexican-American to preserve and strengthen his cultural heritage and make it a workable substance in the total society of the United States places a premium on his leadership in developing a working hypothesis on bilingual, bicultural education. The very core of such a hypothesis can be found in a statement by Dr. Jack D. Forbes in his *Handbook for Educators* when he says, "The Mexican heritage of the United States is very great indeed. For at least 6,000 years Mexico has been a center for the dissemination of cultural influences in all directions, and this process continues today. Although the modern United States has outstripped Mexico in technological innovation, the Mexican people's marked ability in the visual arts, music, architecture, and political affairs makes them a constant contributor to the heritage of all North Americans. The Mexican-American people of the United States serve as a bridge for the diffusion northward of valuable Mexican traits, serve as a reservoir for the preservation of the ancient Hispano-Mexican heritage of the Southwest, and participate directly in the daily life of the modern culture of the U.S."

The cry, Viva La Raza and Viva La Causa, resounds through hundreds of communities, rural and urban, in the the Southwest and Midwest today. To many school people the cry brings fear. It signals a demonstration, a "blowout," a confrontation. Such action does take place frequently. But much more often the cry conveys a message that we are a people with much to offer our country—let us give —we are the advantaged speaking, let us lead the way to a multi-lingual, multi-cultural nation. A country where its resources in humanities matches its resources in technological accomplishments.

The direction to be taken in this movement forward to a pluralistic society is already outlined. The National Advisory Committee on Mexican-American Education in its report to the Commissioner of Education—*The Mexican-American: Quest for Equality*—makes the following recommendations:

1. We must immediately begin to train at least 100,000 bilingual-bicultural teachers and educational administrators.

2. We must make use of current knowledge and encourage further research to assist in creating educational programs that promise learning success for the Mexican-American.

3. We must agitate for priority funding by the U.S. Office of Education to develop educational programs immediately.

4. We must see that testing instruments are developed that will accurately measure the intelligence and achievement potential of the Mexican-American child.

5. We must promote programs to assist state legislatures in taking necessary action to permit instruction in languages other than English.

6. We must help the various states to recognize the need for state-wide programs in bilingual education.

7. We must provide assistance, through Federal funds, to Mexican-American students in pursuit of a college education.

8. With the leadership of the Federal Government, we must increase the number of adult basic education and vocational programs to equip the Mexican-American adult with skills and knowledge necessary to become a partner in our economic society.

9. We must encourage parental involvement programs at the state and local levels.

10. We must encourage state and local education agencies to use more effectively the Mexican-American personnel on their staffs.

11. We must foster a joint effort of the Federal Government and private enterprise to produce instructional materials that are designed expressly for Mexican-American students.

The Chicano Youth Movement, through its many organizations such as United Mexican-American Students (UMAS), Mexican-American Youth Association (MAYA)—to identify a couple—is placing before the schools specific items that in their opinion are imperative in making the school a viable factor in the stimulation of the bilingual, bicultural society. These requests include such basic items as:

1. Textbooks and curriculum revised to show Mexican-American contributions to the development of the United States and to include Mexican-American folklore.

2. Qualified bilingual Mexican-American counselors.

3. Special TESL classes for the non-English speaking students.

4. One elective year of Latin American culture and history taught by a qualified bilingual instructor.

5. Students not grouped into slow, average, superior classes and grouping not based on current tests which often mistake language problems for lack of intelligence.

What is not spelled out in any of these recommendations, however, is the imperative need for drastic attitudinal change both within the dominant cultural group and within the Mexican-American Community. And this attitudinal change must be the primary concern of the public school. Every person in the school dealing with a student must become culturally cognizant of the significance of recognizing the enriching values of cultural heritage. It must permeate their very being that the person with a bilingual, bicultural asset is "advantaged" and from that position can be a vital factor in the enrichment of the school, the community, all of society. Language teachers, especially, must assume a leading role in the promotion of this belief. Bilingual, bicultural curriculum and education will require an intense effort by all teachers—but such a movement will never gain broad and popular support without a vigorous acceptance and promotion by the language teacher.

There are two areas for immediate action in creating the attitude that bilingualism and biculturalism is an advantage to all. The first is a revision of the traditional Anglo-oriented-middle-class curriculum which has far too often destroyed a desirable concept of self for the Chicano. An acceptance of oneself as a "good" person—as a person with dignity of personality—a person accepted as OK by others, especially non-Mexican-Americans. This will require exactly what the Chicano youth are saying in their requests—curriculum that includes a study of Mexican-American heroes and the cultural contributions of the Hispanic culture to American culture.

The second part is equally important—it is the neglect in the Anglo-oriented curriculum of the Anglo himself in relation to the Mexican-American. Attitudinal change is, at the very best, a difficult path—but the first step must be taken by the majority group in becoming sensitive and compassionate for the non-Anglo. One of the best books for getting into these subtle psychological areas is the Association for Supervision and Curriculum Development publication *Perceiving, Behaving, Becoming.*

The introduction in *The Mexican-American: Quest for Equality* briefly states the problem and poses the challenge, "Failure to provide education to hundreds of thousands of people whose cultural heritage is 'different' has resulted in shameful waste of human resources. The melting pot ideology that we speak of so proudly has not produced a moral climate in which all citizens are accepted on the basis of individual worth. Educators, especially, must search their consciences for an answer to the question: Is only a monolingual, monocultural society acceptable in America? Never before has the need for equal opportunity for all Americans been so sharply put into focus. And no group is in greater need of equal educational opportunity than the Mexican-American."

And there is no better time than now to move boldly toward the creation of a national environment in which bilingual, bicultural assets are respected as an "advantage."

Terry Link

22,000 "RETARDED CHILDREN" FACE
SECOND CHANCE

Soledad, California—Nine children in this rural town 160 miles south of San Francisco were recently "graduated" from a public school class for the mentally retarded.

They were in it on the strength of their first intelligence tests, in which they had attained dismal scores ranging from thirty to seventy-two. Incapable of absorbing more, they had been kept busy cutting out paper figures.

But when they were retested recently they had made dramatic gains, an average of fifteen points each. They averaged seventy-five in the verbal section of the IQ test and eighty-four in the performance section.

Unfortunately, their lawyers charge, the difference in scores wasn't a miracle of pedagogy but a horrible instance of injustice. The children—all youngsters from largely Spanish-speaking families—had been classified as mentally retarded on the strength of English-language IQ tests.

Worse, it was no isolated slip-up, say lawyers for the California Rural Legal Assistance foundation.

They have begun legal action which promises to bring retesting in Spanish for the 22,000 California Chicano kids who were classified as retarded after they flunked English IQ tests.

The class in which the Soledad children were placed had one teacher and thirteen pupils, twelve of them Mexican-American. According to eleven-year-old Maria, one of the plaintiffs, most of the pupils' time was spent doing "baby stuff"—coloring and cutting pictures out of magazines.

School districts receive about $550 extra in state aid for each pupil enrolled in such classes.

The children were retested when the California Rural Legal Assistance foundation sent Victor Ramirez, a certified school psychologist from San Diego, to retest them in Spanish.

The day he arrived in Soledad, he found only nine of the fourteen children available for retesting. Of the nine, seven now scored above the seventy points which the state of California uses to classify retarded children. One scored on the dividing line and the ninth scored three points below.

The most dramatic—or pathetic—case was eight-year-old Diane, who had scored thirty in her first IQ test. (This score should indicate that Diane was so retarded that she couldn't even take care of herself physically—which she obviously could.) In Spanish, Diane's score jumped from thirty to seventy-nine.

The children, whose names were withheld, range in age from eight to thirteen. They are mostly the children of farmworkers and live in a labor camp maintained by the city of Soledad. They also share a Mexican heritage and an imperfect grasp of middle-class English.

The parents of one had already protested to school authorities the placement of their child in a class for retarded children, without success.

A suit was filed against the state board of education in behalf of the nine retested children and five other Soledad children who were threatened with placement in the retarded class. It asked that they be placed in normal classes and be given special tutoring to make up for what they had missed.

It also asked the retesting in Spanish of all California's 22,000 Chicano children placed in classes for the retarded.

The fourteen children got both the transfer and tutoring they asked.

The state board of education has also agreed to retest in Spanish those children who scored between 50 and 70 ("educables"), but not those who scored between 30 and 50 ("trainables"), arguing that the 30-50s are "probably bona fide mentally retarded," in the words of one school official.

The state also promised in the future to test bi-lingual children with a bi-lingual psychologist, or at least with an interpreter if a bi-lingual psychologist is unavailable. Lawyers for the California Rural Legal Assistance foundation are reluctant to discuss the state of their negotiations, saying they are also trying to get the agreement strengthened with a court order.

The change won't necessarily happen soon. Even in Soledad, the five children who missed the retesting are still in the class for the retarded, according to the Soledad superintendent of schools, Wendell Broom.

"The parents of these children were all sent letters stating that they could request different placement for their children, but we haven't heard from them," he said. "So we assume they are satisfied."

As well as the nine retested Soledad children did, even their new IQ scores may be assumed to be too low because of the cultural bias of a test which concludes that a labor-camp child is dull indeed if he doesn't know who wrote *Romeo and Juliet*, the color of rubies, why it is "better to pay bills by check than by cash," and the meaning of such words as umbrella, microscope and chattel and to identify C.O.D., Genghis Khan and hieroglyphics.

Also, some of the retested children may have missed those bits of information by virtue of having spent several years in a cut-and-paste class for retarded children.

In the "performance" section of the IQ test—which requires the completion of pictures, arranging blocks and the use of codes—none of the retested children had scored in the retarded range and only three had scored as low as in the 70s.

Diane—who had never been taught the alphabet because she supposedly wasn't smart enough to take care of herself—scored ninety-six on performance.

Although Soledad school authorities declined to transfer the nine children until a suit was finally filed on January 12, they then quickly provided the transfer and special remedial training.

For instance, one thirteen-year-old girl left the "baby stuff" for a seventh-grade class which covers geography, mathematics, home economics and physical education.

She also attends special, smaller classes for reading, speaking, writing and vocabulary. In addition, there is tutoring in math.

The Soledad children were not unique.

In Monterey county, which encompasses Soledad, 18.5 percent of the pupils have a Spanish surname, but almost 33 percent of the pupils in mentally-retarded classes have such a name.

Statewide, a study of racial distribution in the public schools cited in the suit showed 13 percent of all pupils have Spanish surnames. Yet 26 percent of the 85,000 in mentally retarded classes have such names.

"It is statistically impossible that this maldistribution occurred by random chance (odds in excess of one in 100 billion)," the plaintiffs' suit charges.

If California's Chicano children were in retarded classes at the same ratio as California's Anglo children, there would be only 9,750 instead of 22,000.

Nor were state school officials ignorant of this situation. Last June, forty-seven Mexican-American children were selected at random from classes for the mentally retarded, approximately half were from rural areas and half from urban. When tested in Spanish, forty-two of them scored above the seventy IQ ceiling for mentally retarded, and more than half of them over eighty.

And San Francisco public school officials recently admitted that thirty-five of the eighty Spanish-speaking pupils in elementary classes for mentally retarded did not belong there. The children were retested in Spanish last September at the request of David Sanchez, a member of the city board of education. It was he who first announced the results of those tests on January 23 and charged that only two of the thirty-five pupils had so far been transferred to regular classes.

One child cited by Sanchez scored 67 on the English test but her IQ was put at 128.

While the children of Soledad have obviously won an important victory and the legal basis for a more fair educational system has been laid down, the problem is far from being uprooted.

Martin Dean, assistant superintendent for special services in San Francisco, probably enunciated the new code word when he said, "I admit we don't have the proper tools to test bilingual youngsters, but on the other hand, I don't think it was as much the fault of the test as it was the cultural deprivation of the child . . ."

If "cultural deprivation" is the villain, the fault is thrown back on the minority group—not on racism or on culturally biased tests.

It means America the melting pot can't cope in its schools with children whose background differs from the 3,184 white, native-born Americans, mostly from cities, whose scores in 1937 were used as the scale for the Stanford-Binet IQ test, or the 2,200 Anglo-Americans used in 1950 to set up the Weschler test.

A court order does not insure compliance by individual school districts and even where compliance follows, at what pace? Some say it will take until June just to retest 175 junior and senior high school students with Spanish surnames in mentally retarded classes in San Francisco.

Nor will second-language testing affect the black pupils in San Francisco's mentally retarded classes.

Although blacks represent twenty-five percent of the total pupil population, they account for fifty-three percent of the children in mentally retarded classes—the same ratio which the CRLA suit found statewide for Spanish surnamed students and called "statistically impossible."

EIGHTEEN MONTHS LATER

Eighteen months after the federal court ruling in the case of the nine Soledad children, advocates of reform in the system of placing pupils in classes for the mentally retarded were frustrated and disappointed; professional educators responsible for placing reforms in practice were more content. Overall, some change had been achieved and there was the promise of more to come; but, at the moment, still a promise.

"We thought we could make these changes and bingo! 20,000 kids would come out," said Martin Glick, one of the California Rural Legal Assistance attorneys who had handled the complaint of the Soledad children. "But it just didn't work that way. Some of the kids came out but the ratio of minority kids enrolled in the classes has not changed drastically."

Initial retesting throughout the state resulted in the transfer of 3,158 Spanish-surnamed pupils. Significant numbers of other ethnic groups—1,630 blacks, 1,978 whites, 36 Orientals, and 34 Indians—were also transferred.

"Our feeling was that this showed some improvement but not nearly enough," Glick said. "One reason, I think, is because in some of these cases, the kids have just been in there too long."

Two of the Soledad pupils, who were returned to regular classes and also given supplementary tutoring, smiled shyly but responded enthusiastically when asked how they were getting along in school.

"The other kids were glad for me to be out," said thirteen-year-old Maria. "They didn't call me 'mentally retarded' and 'dum-dum' no more. The teacher, she didn't want me to go. She got mad when they took me out. She started crying."

Twelve-year-old Arturo said he enjoyed the change from the special class where he had been limited to "coloring, then reading some times and play and a little math and P.E." for three years. "Last year we were doing science and multiplying in math. We were learning about rocks, birds, all kinds of animals in science," he said.

But the pessimistic expectations which children like Maria and Arturo meet every day in school were voiced by Wendell Broom, superintendent of schools in Soledad. "I would say that, basically, the youngsters have not made any fantastic achievements, of course. But there is no question that they've made some social adjustment since they've been with their peers on an all-day basis. I think here is the one area where I've seen some change. It's been attitude and as far as the social aspect of school; but achievementwise, there just hasn't been any great change."

Maria's mother doesn't agree that her daughter has not made any advances since leaving the special class. After being placed in the special class, Maria had "rapidly" begun losing her ability to write and to do anything with letters because there was nobody to urge her to write or read. She spent most of her time dancing. That's what they taught her. Now, says her mother, Maria "gets good grades on her report cards. She writes well. She reads and writes very well. Certainly much better than she ever did in the special class."

Broom also said that although 80 percent of the district's 1,350 pupils are of Mexican descent, little progress had been made in hiring bilingual psychologists. There are none in the Soledad district, he said, and "I'm not sure what the county has. (In California, all the school districts in a county are grouped for administrative purposes.) I think they have now a couple of bilingual people that are employed, maybe even more than that, I don't know. But I know they've turned their attention to this too."

In San Francisco, where the issue of pupil placement in the classes for the mentally retarded was raised at about the same time as the Soledad case, "there's been no major breakthroughs," according to David Sanchez, a member of the board of education.

Sanchez said that within the past year he had visited a class for Filipino children conducted in Tagalog with English being taught as a second language. "There was a second-generation Mexican-American in there. It just so happened the teacher thought he looked like a Filipino. Here's a kid who should have been in a bilingual class in Spanish and it took me three weeks to get him reassigned.

"When you have kids who have had eight and nine years of education in Latin America in an urban area and they come here and are given the English version of the Stanford-Binet by a person who does not speak Spanish, why you're going to have some injustices done," Sanchez said.

Although the California Board of Education and the legislature had approved the idea of developing new tests, Sanchez said, "as usual there was no money allocated to do this. As a result, most of the districts still use the same type of test. Even with a Spanish version, you're talking about content items that may not be applicable to the child's experience."

A new test of mental retardation is being developed by Jane R. Mercer, a University of California at Riverside sociologist who has spent eight years studying the problem. She found that in one district, "Although teacher-principal teams referred Mexican-American and Negro children at about the same rate as their percentage in the population and proportionately fewer were given intelligence tests by school psychologists, about three times as many Mexican-American and Negro children appeared among those failing the intelligence test as we would expect from their proportion in the population of the school district.

"Subsequently, this disproportion increased so that four times more Mexican-American and three times more Negro children were placed in special education classes than would be expected from their percentage in the district because proportionately more Mexican-American and Negro children with low IQs were recommended and were ultimately placed. It was at the point in the referral process when the intelligence test was administered that the sharp ethnic disparities first appeared," she wrote in an article entitled "Institutionalized Anglocentrism: Labeling Mental Retardates in the Public

Schools." This research and other work done by Dr. Mercer indicates that the prime source of misplacement of pupils is the IQ test as it is now administered, rather than overt prejudice on the part of teachers and principals.

Here efforts are now directed to refining a test which will allow for a pupil's sociocultural background and recognize performance in areas of life outside the school. From tests already done, she concludes that seventy-four percent of the pupils in classes for the mentally retarded are misplaced.

Her approach, called pluralistic evaluation, "modifies the normative framework by which the meaning of a particular score is interpreted rather than making changes in the form and content of the text itself. In a pluralistic evaluation procedure, a person is evaluated as intellectually subnormal only when he scores in the lowest 3.0% of his own sociocultural group on a standardized test," she wrote.

"If the person scores more than one standard deviation (15 IQ points) above the mean for his group, then he probably has high normal ability, even if his actual IQ is 100—average by the standard norms of the test. Conversely, a Mexican-American child who manages to achieve a score of 75 on an IQ test when he comes from an overcrowded, Spanish-speaking home in which the father has less than an eighth grade education and was reared in a rural area, and his mother does not expect him to go beyond high school, is well within the normal range for persons, like himself, who have had little exposure to cultural materials needed to pass an Anglo intelligence test."

Les Brinegar, chief of the Division of Special Education in the State Department of Education, says he is convinced the present placement process "really isn't that bad but there is a problem with lack of appropriate instrumentation." The department, he said, has "done everything we could short of actually advancing money we don't have to advance" to support Dr. Mercer's efforts to develop a better test. (Earlier portions of her research were subsidized by Department of Education grants, but Governor Ronald Reagan has drastically curtailed such spending in recent years.)

Brinegar said it is "very likely" that introduction of the Mercer test or one developed elsewhere in the country is two to five years away. In the meantime, he said, "we're attempting to glean everything we possibly can to improve the test items which are in use throughout the state" and disseminating this information to school districts in seminars and memoranda.

He firmly rejected any moratorium on testing minority children for placement in the classes. "We don't think that would be very wise," he said. "On one hand you have the problem, which is a current issue, the placement of children who may not be mentally retarded. But you also have an equally important, maybe even more important problem on the other side of the scale; that is, there is such a thing as mental retardation and there is a need on the part of mentally retarded children to have specially designed programs.

"If you totally stopped placing children in special programs, you would begin to make some decisions which could very tragically affect a lot of lives. We've had many unfortunate incidents reported to us concerning children placed back in regular classes," he said. Part of the difficulty arose from the transfer of pupils from classes for the mentally retarded which followed in the wake of the Soledad decision.

"The great majority of the students who were transferred out of the special classes are not getting any assistance in making the transition," Brinegar said. Such assistance was permitted but not made mandatory in the guidelines for re-evaluation adopted by the state Board of Education, he said, "and not all school districts have such a program."

"I don't have a personal feeling that a lot of lives have been harmed by the special classes," Brinegar said. "The contention of some people is that it has been very bad for all those children. The fact of the matter is probably it's been very good for the majority of them to have individual attention and individually developed curriculum."

Brinegar's assumption that the special classes have a positive effect was successfully challenged in the Soledad case. Had that class been all that Brinegar feels the special classes are, it seems unlikely that a court-ordered rescue of the nine children would have been necessary. Brinegar's viewpoint is also challenged by Harold Dent, chief of pupil personnel services in the Berkeley Unified School District and co-chairman of the Bay Area Association of Black Psychologists.

Dent said that in his experience there are "few programs which really deal with the needs of individual students: but that this is more a problem of inept teachers than of school district policies, I would fathom a guess that the great majority—and I would even go to eighty or ninety percent of the classes—don't meet the needs of the minority kids particularly and, I would suspect, the nonminority students who are there."

Dent and several colleagues recently tested eight black pupils in San Francisco classes for the mentally retarded. "Seven of them were functioning at a level higher than what would be necessary to place them in a special education class according to law," he said. "Two of us saw the one child whom we felt needed this kind of program without the other's knowledge and came to that conclusion without completing the testing situation. There are some who need this special education and we're willing to recognize this. We're not trying to eliminate the whole program; we're trying to help the program focus on those that need it and help those who don't need it but who are already inappropriately placed."

The Bay Area Association of Black Psychologists, assisted by the Urban League and the National Association for the Advancement of Colored People went through four months of negotiation in the spring of 1970, trying to get a moratorium on IQ testing in the placement of minority pupils in the classes for the mentally retarded. These negotiations were fruitless, Dent said, and he accused the State Department of Education of not conducting them in good faith. Now the group's efforts are directed toward a lawsuit to end the testing.

Since those negotiations halted, Wilson Riles has been elected state superintendent of public instruction, becoming the first Negro to head the Department of Education. However, it was Riles who appointed Brinegar to his post and backs the demand for continued testing despite imperfections in the method.

In an interview, Riles acknowledged the problem. "In some cases, I know it's plain prejudice," he said, citing a black girl who was placed in a class for the mentally retarded upon entering junior high school. The girl's mother, noticing a change in her daughter's attitude, went to school to find out what was wrong, Riles said. When she was finally told that her daughter was in a class for the retarded, she pointed out to the counselor that the previous year the girl had been in an accelerated class. This was verified by the girl's records, Riles said.

"Now you can say that that was a mistake, that they got the record mixed up, but I would think that it was just a little bit of prejudice on someone's part. I would say that the chances of it happening to an Anglo child would be minimal," Riles said.

Such obvious cases of prejudice aside, Riles said, "It's not a problem simply of placing youngsters in classes for the mentally retarded simply because of language. This happens in some cases and where it happens, there is no way to justify it. But there are other complicating problems involved in this. For example, youngsters who are poor tend to do less well in school regardless of the language pattern or type. Youngsters coming from less advantaged backgrounds do less well in school than children from middle-class backgrounds who have every advantage."

Riles also said "no one has raised the question of what do you do about the child who comes from a Spanish home and is illiterate in both English and Spanish. The assumption is that a child coming from a Spanish home is literate in Spanish and therefore if you tested him in Spanish rather than in English with a Spanish-speaking teacher that he would pass. It's not so simple."

The thrust of his administration will be "to have a method by which you diagnose the need of youngsters, their problems, their aptitudes and then if you find they are deficient, you gear your program to take care of these specific problems," Riles said.

"I don't believe in group placement. I think children should be taught as individuals regardless of who they are. I know that individuals do not all move at the same rate, do not all learn the same thing at the same time and I think the job of the school is to see that whoever the child is, he is taught in the way his individual needs are met and that he moves as rapidly as it's possible for him to move.

"I'm against grouping in the regular class program which assumes that there are some children who are fast learners and some children who are slow learners. The fact of the matter is that sometimes children are fast learners and there are other periods in their lives when they are not fast learners. And with every child, you are dealing with a situation where in some kinds of skill subjects, the child moves rapidly because of his interest and in something else he's not moving at all," Riles said.

"I know for example that to function in this society you have to know basic English. I further know that any normal child can learn and I feel that the instructional program should be geared to do that and not make excuses. Here's where your grouping children is a copout. I feel that if a child is not learning, then immediately someone has to determine why he's not learning and then give him the kind of assistance and help so that he will learn," Riles said.

At this point in time, none of the above may be read as a final answer. The mechanisms to implement Riles' strategy of educational diagnosis and delivery for every pupil have not yet been instituted. Moreover, the process he outlined is remarkably similar in some ways to the much more limited process now applied to children suspected of mental retardation. Those children already undergo analysis of their problem followed by placement in a special program which educators believe will help them. Riles stressed his rejection of any form of ability grouping, however, which seems to rule out what many consider the worst facet of the present program.

The advocates of reform have not yet mounted their best attack. When they do, the educational establishment may not prove unyielding. State Department of Education refusal to suspend IQ tests would probably vanish in the face of a court ruling that the tests be dropped. The department's support of Mercer's work and a slow but steady decline in the number of pupils classed as mentally retarded—there were 57,148 in 1968, 54,078 the next year, and 47,864 last year—does not indicate antipathy toward the reformist point of view.

In a slightly different context, but nonetheless applicable here,

Riles said: "There's no grand conspiracy by people not wanting to improve themselves. There is a certain natural inertia that is built in, where people don't want to change. But most of them do want to improve. So you have to have something that can demonstrate that it can be done better."

Maria and Arturo know there is a better way; their classmates, parents, attorneys, and the courts know there is a better way. Dr. Mercer knows a better way and so does Dr. Dent. I hope they are able to help thousands of other youngsters and their parents find a better way.

Chief Joseph

AN INDIAN APPEAL

At last I was granted *permission* to come to Washington and bring my friend Yellow Bull and our interpreter with me. I am glad I came. I have shaken hands with a good many friends, but there are some things I want to know which no one seems able to explain. I cannot understand how the government sends a man out to fight us, as it did General Miles, and then breaks his word. Such a government has something wrong about it . . .

I have heard talk and talk, but nothing is done. Good words do not last long unless they *amount* to something. Words do not pay for my dead people. They do not pay for my country, now overrun by white men. They do not protect my father's grave. They do not pay for my horses and cattle.

Good words do not give me back my children. Good words will not make good the *promise* of your war chief, General Miles. Good words will not give my people good health and stop them from dying. Good words will not get my people a home where they can live in peace and take care of themselves.

I am tired of talk that comes to nothing. It makes my heart sick when I remember all the good words and all the broken promises. There has been too much talking by men who had no right to talk. Too many *misinterpretations* have been made; too many misunderstandings have come up between the white men and the Indians.

If the white man wants to live in peace with the Indian, he can live in peace. There need be no trouble. *Treat* all men alike. Give them the same laws. Give them all an even chance to live and grow.

All men are made by the same Great Spirit Chief. They are all brothers. The earth is the mother of all people, and all people should have equal rights upon it. You might as well expect all rivers to run backward as that any man who was born a free man should be contented penned up and denied liberty to go where he *pleases.* If you tie a horse to a stake, do you expect he will grow fat? If you pen an Indian up on a small *spot* of earth and compel him to stay there, he will not be contented nor will he grow and prosper.

I have asked some of the Great White *Chiefs* where they get their authority to say to the Indian that he shall stay in one place, while he sees white men going where they please. They cannot tell me.

I only ask of the government to be treated as all other men are treated. If I cannot go to my own home, let me have a home in a country where my people will not die so fast. I would like to go to Bitter Root Valley [western Montana]. There my people would be *healthy;* where they are now, they are dying. Three have died since I left my camp to come to Washington. When I think of our *condition*, my heart is heavy. I see men of my own race treated as outlaws and driven from country to country, or shot down like animals.

I know that my race must change. We cannot hold our own with the white men as we are. We only ask an even chance to live as other men live. We ask to be *recognized* as men. We ask that the same law shall work alike on all men. If an Indian breaks the law, punish him by the law. If a white man breaks the law, punish him also.

Let me be a free man—free to travel, free to stop, free to work, free to *trade* where I choose, free to choose my own teachers, free to follow the religion of my fathers, free to think and talk and act for myself—and I will obey every law or submit to the penalty.

Whenever the white man treats the Indian as they treat each other, then we shall have no more wars. We shall all be alike—brothers of one father and mother, with one sky above us and one country around us and one government for all. Then the Great Spirit Chief who *rules* above will smile upon this land and send rain to wash out the bloody spots made by brothers' hands upon the face of the earth. For this time the Indian *race* are waiting and praying. I hope no more *groans* of wounded men and women will ever go to the ear of the Great Spirit Chief above, and that all people may be one people.

PART SEVEN
THE END

But don't stop reading now!

    The poem in this last section invites the reader to consider the feelings of a student in an inner-city classroom, and the cartoon following it reminds us that a sense of humor doesn't hurt at all.

Janice Gilmore

WHITE TEACHER

WHITE TEACHER:

I am the new black young male. I am different from my father before me, my children after me will be different from me. But listen, White Teacher, I am here now, today, and I must be reckoned with. See me? Here I am.

I come from different places, White Teacher,
1) I come from the black ghettos
2) I come from the integrated neighborhoods
3) I come from the predominantly white suburbia, but most important, I come from a Black Heritage of which I am very proud.

I may not always meet your middle class expectations, White Teacher, but I will meet all your humane requirements. Will you meet mine?

I do not like to be called "boy", White Teacher, if you must refer to me other than by my name, call me man-child. Call me black man-child, but do not call me boy.

Contrary to common belief, White Teacher, I want to learn— I do not want to learn white idealism—but black realities. I am no longer interested in your so-called white "heroes", your heroes who held my people as slaves in chains. Tell me what my black brothers have done to help make this Country. Tell me about my black sisters, the mothers of this world— Don't lie to me, White Teacher, let me be proud of my Heritage. You learn about it, so you can teach it to me.

Teach me also plenty math and science, as one day I will be a leader of this old Country. You may not want to believe this, White Teacher, but I will lead *your* people as well as mine. Prepare me, White Teacher, prepare me.

It's true, my environment may have put me behind my white-middle class brother academically. But Teacher, I got the capacity. I can be stepped on without flinching, spit on without moving, discriminated against without batting an eye. I can do all this and still learn. Can you teach me?

My hair is a great source of pride to me, do not belittle me by rubbing my head when you talk to me. If you must touch me, rest your hand upon my shoulder as you would a man.

I've got soul, White Teacher, I enjoy singing and dancing. I can do both well. I do not come to school to perform for you and your peers. I am not your personal spectacle. Never make that mistake. I will no longer dance to your beat.

Discipline is a way of life for me, when I need it, I expect to be disciplined. But did you hear me White Teacher? Disciplined, not persecuted. Discipline me as you would my white brother. No more harsh— No more severe.

I am not a natural born thief, White Teacher. If something is missing, don't come to me first. Remember your white brothers have been stealing you blind for centuries. Check them out sometimes too. Who knows, you may find what is missing.

My home is not a gambling joint, bookie hangout, or drug warehouse. My home may not always be the best by your standards, but it's my home, White Teacher, and I love it.

Hate me if you must, White Teacher, but do not just tolerate me. For mere tolerance is harder to accept than outright hate. But while you're hating, White Teacher, remember that hate usually kills the hater.

Please, White Teacher, judge me as an individual—my brother before me may have been a genius, my sister after me may be a genius, but I am me. I want to be judged as me.

I do not want your pity. Men children do not grow into men by being nutured on pity. We grow into men by being nutured on love, trust and understanding. Either way we grow into adults—what kind of an adult will you help me to grow into?

And by the way, White Teacher, if my name is Joe, don't call me Sam or Pete. We are all black, but if you just look, and you don't have to look too closely, you can see we are different. If my name means nothing to you, can I truly be an individual in your eyes?

Have I gotten through to you White Teacher? Do you know I am here? I'm here now. I'm alive, vibrant, and black. See me White Teacher, see me as I really am. Meet your new, black, man-child pupil. Meet your new challenge.

See me White Teacher, and you know something? I will see you. I may not love you, I may not love you, but I will respect you. I will grow into someone you can be proud of. You know, White Teacher, it may really be worth your time and effort to keep me from being a bitter, hatefilled individual. Because you know, it just might be that someday I will be teaching your child!!! It's something to think about White Teacher. Do you hear me White Teacher? You'd better LISTEN!!!!!!!

Doonesbury
by GB Trudeau.